MUSINGS
AN URBAN DESIGN ANTHOLOGY
EDITED BY VICTOR ANDRADE, SHELLEY SMITH & DITTE BENDIX LANNG

DEPARTMENT OF ARCHITECTURE,
DESIGN & MEDIA TECHNOLOGY
AALBORG UNIVERSITET

AALBORG UNIVERSITY PRESS

Musings - an urban design anthology
Edited by Victor Andrade, Shelley Smith & Ditte Bendix Lanng

1. edition

© Aalborg University Press, 2012

Layout: Martin Frank Petersen & Senad Gvozden
Printed by Toptryk Grafisk ApS, 2012
ISBN: 978-87-7112-062-2

Published by:
Aalborg University Press
Skjernvej 4A, 2nd floor
9220 Aalborg
Denmark
Phone: (+45) 99 40 71 40
Fax: (+45) 96 35 00 76
aauf@forlag.aau.dk
forlag.aau.dk

All rights reserved. No part of this book may be reprinted or reproduced or utilized in any form or by any electronic, mechanical, or other means, now known or hereafter invented, including photocopying and recording, or in any information storage or retrieval system, without permission in writing from the publishers, except for reviews and short excerpts in scholarly publications.

List of Contents

5   Preface

6   Introduction
       Victor Andrade, Shelley Smith & Ditte Bendix Lanng

Performativity

Articles

18   Deturned City Design - tools for experiential urban living
       Hans Kiib

30   Experiencing Perfomative Urban Spaces
       Gitte Marling

36   A Case Study of Mediated Urban Architecture: Red Pavilion 2010
       Esben Skouboe Poulsen, Hans Jørgen Andersen, Ole B. Jensen & Mads Brath Jensen

Student studio projects

46   Kulturator 27 - a time based design
       Mikkel Stensgaard & Simon Wind

48   Encountering Chernobyl - design interventions in the city of Pripyat
       Daniel Bejtrup & Dina Brændstrup

50   The Sensuous Stories of Urban Space
       Helena Kaae

52   Lindholm Strandpark - a cultural hub of Aalborg
       Nicolai Hagbarth Hansen

Mobility

Articles

56   Bumps in the Road - mobility and spatial experience through the lens of parkour
       Shelley Smith

66   Critical Points of Contact - between urban networks and flows
       Ole B. Jensen, Simon Wind & Ditte Bendix Lanng

74   Urban Design and the Tracking of Secondary School Students in the Urban Landscape
       Henrik Harder, Peter Bro & Anne-Marie Sanvig Knudsen

Student studio projects

86   The New Nørreport
       Ann Sofie Christensen, Kristian Overby, Sebastian Andersen & Thomas Oxvig Håkonsson

88   A Matter of Planning? - with the light rail towards a new Aarhus
       Line Morsing Nielsen & Maria Vestergaard Jensen

90   Dynamic eastern Jutland - a vision
       Sille Christiane Linnet & Lisa Gedsø

Transformation

Articles

94   Transforming Vestergade vest into a Ludic and Shared-Use Space
Victor Andrade, Ole B. Jensen, Henrik Harder & Jens C. O. Madsen

102   Enhancing the Landscape - architectural installations in the landscape
Lea Louise Holst Laursen

112   A Case Study of Urban Transformation Projects
Anne Juel Andersen

120   Urban Design and Spatial Equity: The Favela-Bairro Programme Experience in Rio de Janeiro, Brazil
Victor Andrade

Student studio projects

128   Haderslev Nature School - landscape and architectural interventions in the Haderslev hospital area
Martin Frank Petersen, Senad Gvozden, Siri Laursen & Sofie Brincker

130   The New Story of Odense - riding on a roof top, playing on a rail track, living in a fairytale
Jacob Bjerre Mikkelsen, Ida Sofie Gøtzsche Lange, Marion Højris Jensen, Rasmus Davidsen & Stine Ellegaard Jakobsen

132   Climate Design - working with vulnerable urbanities in Mozambique
Stine Sonne & Anne Lærke Jørgensen

134   Intensified Concorde Neighborhood
Lucile Hamoignon

136   The New Karolinelund - Aalborg's diverse venue
Jakob Charmoth Nielsen

138   Meadow Patterns with an Edge - urban development in the northern freight rail area in Aarhus
Rikke Schjødt Brink

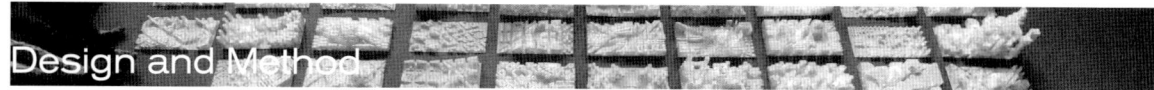

Design and Method

Articles

142   Urban Songlines - the city experienced by ordinary people
Gitte Marling

154   Designing Concepts and Strategies
Hans Kiib

166   Unfolding Architecture - workshop events retold
Shelley Smith

174   WE LOVE THE CITY - a pragmatic approach to urban design
Lasse Andersson

186   Biographies

Preface

Contemporary urbanity highlights a paradigmatic shift in the urban design discipline caused by the emergence of such factors as globalisation, informational flow, and flux. It is from this point of departure, and ensuing schools of thought, that this book has come into being – with contributions from researchers and students in the Urban Design Programme at the Department of Architecture, Design and Media Technology at Aalborg University. The contributions included in this publication focus on some of the issues challenging urban design and urban designers. At the beginning of the 21st century, there is an indispensable and strategic necessity for the current profession of Urban Design in the facing of these issues.

To these ends, the contents of this book explore the relationship between research and education in the field of urban design and identify contemporary themes that urban designers in the professional and academic arenas are dealing with in order to enhance the quality of life in our built environments, especially in the spaces we share. This book aims to fulfill the critical need for a link between research production and teaching in the field of urban design and does so by highlighting four core areas of urban design theory and practice – Performativity, Mobility, Transformation and Design and Method.

In short, the goal of this book is to unfold the multi-layered definition of urban design as seen through the eyes of the students and researchers of the Urban Design Programme at Aalborg University. The research group is comprised of individuals that work in the field of urban design, in both academic and professional capacities, and with experiences from around the world. As the teaching at Aalborg University is research-based, the student projects represent a variety of interpretations of the research group's thematic approaches and are seen as essential inclusions to the discussion of contemporary urbanism that this book intends. A word of caution is in place here. This small contribution by way of sharing articles on urban design and projects dealing urban design is by no means comprehensive or all inclusive. It is a momentary glance at a selection of the present production of urban design research and studio works.

This book is indeed a joint effort, and its coming into being should be ascribed to many people, not least of all the researchers of urban design at Aalborg University, whose collective engagement in stirring urban design through research, teaching, and debate, is the prerequisite of this collection of articles and student projects. We would like to thank all the authors – of both articles and projects – for their contributions which so aptly exemplify some of the key notions of, and approaches to contemporary urban design. We would also like to thank the anonymous peer reviewer who provided insightful comments for each contribution in this book as well as for the book as a whole. Not least of all, Senad Gvozden and Martin Frank Petersen deserve a huge thank you for their role in designing the layout, and laying out the book. Furthermore, we would like to acknowledge and express our gratitude to the Department of Architecture, Design and Media Technology at Aalborg University for their part in financially supporting this publication.

It is hoped that the articles and projects presented in this book provide a source of inspiration to students, professionals, researchers and practitioners alike, and that used as a resource, the book can perhaps contribute to starting discussions, forming networks and furthering innovative thoughts and solutions in this ever changing and constantly current framework for human activity - Urban Design.

Victor Andrade, Shelley Smith and Ditte Bendix Lanng

Aalborg University

December 2012

Introduction
Victor Andrade, Shelley Smith & Ditte Bendix Lanng

It is the ambition of this book to identify and debate critical topics affecting contemporary academic and professional endeavours in the discipline of urban design. The source of the musings that constitute this book stem from the Urban Design programme at Aalborg University. The ensuing collection folds urban design studio works and research into one experimental and reflective perspective.

The book is indicative of the breadth of the field that is the discipline of urban design, and of the amount of comment and discussion related to this discipline. Its scope is broad and the boundaries of its agency are fuzzy and sometimes contested (Carmona et al. 2010). We cannot here do full justice to the inspiring and engaging viewpoints of the professional and scientific debate on the discipline of urban design, but we encourage interested readers to dive into the content of this book, and also to consult the bountiful literature references provided by the contributions in the book. Our attempt here is to briefly illuminate the discipline of urban design in order to position the book in this rich and varied field. Our account is characterised by a fascination with the multiplicity and diversity of methods, processes, and products of urban design, rather than by an urge to fix a frame around the discipline.

The origins of urban design can be located in a postwar concern for the unintended consequences of the functional planning agenda, such as urban sprawl, spatial fragmentation, and lack of sensitivity to the 'human association' (Joseph Lluis Sert, cited by Mumford 2009). This gave rise to the urban design agenda in the 1950s, notably with the first international 'Urban Design' conference at Harvard in 1956, and the subsequent establishment of the first Urban Design programme at Harvard´s Graduate School of Design (Carmona et al. 2010; Krieger 2009). Urban design as a discipline was brought forward to supplement functional urbanism with considerations for urban life: human scale and the collective urban population (Mumford 2009).

Contemporary urban design can be regarded as centering on the relationships between activities and spaces, and as synthesizing visual and aesthetic concerns with public use and the experience of urban environments (Carmona et al. 2010). The contemporary urban environment is characterised by such factors as new technologies, cultural shifts, flux and globalisation, making for a dynamic, and at times overwhelming, complexity. It has provided challenges to traditional ways of thinking and working with the built environment, and to the methods utilised by the discipline of urban design. Joan Busquets, Professor of Urbanism at the Barcelona School of Architecture (ETSAB) has indicated the emergence of a new urbanistic culture in this century that calls for the definition of new concepts, and the development of new strategies (Busquets 2007). Busquets has taken up the challenge presented by this new urbanistic culture, by elaborating a taxonomy of emergent and innovative methods with which to design and deal with contemporary urban areas and their complexities, and with which to intervene in these built environments. Another response to contemporary urbanity can be found in the coining of the term 'stirring' by Raoul Bunschoten and his studio Chora, in the book *Urban Flotsam – Stirring the City* (Bunschoten 2001). 'Stirring the city' refers to moving the city, considering it and affecting it. Bunschoten's concern was for the thinking about and the designing in, what he defined as an unstable urban condition. Through writings and studio works a rich operational methodology was developed to detect emergent urban phenomena, to interlink urban processes, and to unfold and animate urban development scenarios. Bunschoten identified an urban situation different from previous models and set about finding ways of working with it, not least of all by introducing the notion of stirring, an activity that contained aspects of disruption and dissolving, of movement and change. Bunschoten and Chora's way of working accessed theory, developed methodologies and proposed solutions in a changed urban field.

In a complementary perspective, the landscape architect and theoretician James Corner (1999) processed the term of 'mapping', a term that rather than just 'tracing' what exists, comprises a truly creative act invoking the uncovering of potential to be realised in the contemporary urban environment. This was characterised by the merging of disciplines and the identification of sites that challenged definition in traditional terms. And his office, Field Operations, utilises theory and develops methodologies for the proposal of strategies and solutions that help give identity to the unidentified.

Many aspects and ambiguities influence the urban design discipline: working in a broad sense with the built environment, we seek to add qualities to both the process and product of urban design, and we deal with the spatial as well as the technical, social and cultural, shaping visual qualities while also organising and managing urban territories. It is important here to note that the meaning of ´urban´ is broad and inclusive, bringing

DANCERS AT LUNCH IN FRONT OF THE PLAYFUL AND CURVING POLYCARBONATE FACADES OF LABAN DANCE CENTRE BY HERZOG AND DE MEURON 2012

Introduction

to our concern cities, towns, villages, and hamlets (Carmona et al. 2010). This is exemplary of the physical, 'locational' level, and addresses urban form however, as indicated above, the discipline of urban design has an influence as well on the mental, psychological level – one that addresses urban life.

Krieger (2009) refers to urban design as a frame of mind, more than a technical discipline. Those, sharing this frame of mind, are urban-minded, and committed to cities and to improving urban ways of life:

> "To be urban-minded means learning from Las Vegas and Venice and Shanghai but not conflating these into a universal formula for future urbanization. To be urban-minded requires genuine affection for the energy and messy vitality of cities, and seeking inspiration in that vitality rather than distilling it into a few set patterns. To be urban-minded requires an inquiring sensibility and acceptance of multiple inputs – yes, being a generalist, but a synthesizing generalist, not a dilettante." (Krieger 2009: xvi)

Though there is no singular general definition of urban design, one of its preoccupations is public space between buildings (Krieger 2009). The urban spaces, voids between buildings, and streets, are its paramount concern. As such, urban design covers a gap between a number of other disciplines (Carmona et al. 2010), and has a strong interdisciplinary dimension, enjoying a fairly dynamic interaction with disciplines such as traffic planning, urban planning, urban engineering, landscape architecture and architecture. The problems posed and challenges presented when dealing with the qualities of the built environment are often too complex to be handled by one individual or even by one profession alone; urban design can therefore be considered an integrative activity (Carmona et al. 2010) – one which engages in, and develops through interaction with and knowledge coming from such fields as engineering, sociology, economics and political science, to name a few. In that regards, this book indicates and celebrates the plurality of practicing and thinking in urban design.

Against this backdrop, it seems more fruitful, rather than seeking clarity regarding the boundaries of urban design, to concentrate on what is at its core (Carmona et al. 2010). It is by no means the intention of this book to define the borders of urban design as a discipline in one specific theoretical or professional locality. On the contrary, what we hope to do is to contribute with an assortment of research and studio works providing a peephole into the debates of the morphing and rich heart of urban design. We regard it as both necessary and challenging to continue this debate, musing about our discipline and the way we work with it: our methods, the forms and spaces we suggest, the theories we use, the possibilities for intervention that we explore, the relations to other disciplines that we benefit from, and so forth. The continuous searching regarding what we do, and how we do it, in order to gain greater insights, knowledge, and inspiration is of course a challenge. But it is a necessary challenge since we – experienced or green in the field – practitioners and researchers alike – must deal with the urban in all of its complexity, fluidity, diversity. Cities themselves never cease being stirred by societal changes, technological developments, everyday practices, calls for sustainable futures etc. and as such, the matter of our efforts is continuously changing, and calling for us to repeatedly reconsider our urban design agency. This book aims to be a catalyst for that debate.

In this book we present a varied account of the urban design field in four chapters that reveal core themes framing theoretical and practical challenges of an emerging urbanistic culture today: Performativity, Mobility, Transformation, and Design & Method.

1. Performativity

In contemporary urbanity, lifestyles have changed to not only include, but to demand recreation, entertainment and a variety of forms of consumption. In sync with urban densification – both in physical form and cultural content – questions regarding what kind of impact this urban development has on everyday life and whether this densification can also enhance and enrich the experience of everyday urban life have come to the forefront. Precisely experience has become key in this discussion, and here the possibility for experience exceeds that of merely participating in intended activities. Rather experience is seen as being enabled by a programmable framework – a stage - for the unfolding of, and exposure to, urban life with all of its idiosyncrasies.

The chapter on Performativity examines the potential for life and living that design can set the stage for, by creating a backdrop for the senses and by providing a forum for personal narratives.

The chapter leads with Hans Kiib's article 'Deturned City Design – tools for experiential urban living'. Kiib's article is concerned with large art installations in contemporary urban environments. He takes a critical position in relation to what he finds to be an overload of leisure- and funscapes in inner city experience economy transformations. He draws on the 1960s Situationist movement to show examples from a wave of contemporary 'Instant Urbanism' projects. Kiib advocates the development of 'relate architecture' which fosters bodily, emotional, cognitive and reflective, and socially transformative engagement in the city. This architecture is relevant to both permanent and temporary urban interventions, and may provide new perspectives to everyday city spaces.

WATER FOUNTAIN WITH JETS PLAYING FROM THE PAVEMENT, RUSSEL SQUARE, LONDON 2012

SUPERKILEN IN COPENHAGEN BY BIG 2012 © GITTE MARLING

Introduction

Gitte Marling´s article 'Experiencing Performative Urban Spaces' provides a theoretically based description of the sensory aspects of performative urban design, as well as the interaction – active, passive, between people and between site and users - that can encouraged, through the case of Frederiksberg Square in Copenhagen. The case is documented through both observation and interview and is thereby illuminated through a number of angles and from a number of viewpoints.

Esben Skouboe Poulsen, Hans Jørgen Andersen, Ole B. Jensen, and Mads Brath Jensen have contributed with the article, 'A Case Study of Mediated Urban Architecture: Red Pavilion 2010'. This article provides the reader with a unique opportunity to view a design work placed in a theoretical context, and as a real, existing (having existed) 1:1 model on which theory can be 'tested' through experimentation and observation. That the pavilion was a one-time 'offer' and no longer in existence only adds to the interest it generates in the article through the descriptions and the pictures of it. In addition, the interdisciplinarity of the author team and their direct involvement in making the Red Pavilion a physical reality serve to exemplify the broadness and inclusiveness of the urban design discipline.

Four Master and Bachelor student projects end the chapter and span from an architectural infill in Norway by Mikkel Steensgaard and Simon Wind, over design musings on contemporary Chernobyl by Daniel Bejtrup and Dina Brændstrup, and sensuous stories of urban space in the small city of Randers in Denmark by Helena Kaae, to a volume-and-space study of a coastal cultural hub in Aalborg, by Nicolai Hagbarth Hansen. These projects illuminate the topic of Performativity through inspiring and varied proposals for urban design interventions.

The articles and projects presented here bear witness to the potential performativity possesses to manifest spatial and temporal urban situations that, deriving from human behaviour, can stimulate interaction and foster an understanding of the human condition.

2. Mobility

By highlighting urban mobility in a contemporary context, this chapter addresses the need to re-think this area of urban design. Urban mobility and accessibility are inextricably linked to design in our cities today, and mobility covers a range of ideas that, in their essence, have to do with movement pure - but not so simple.

The large scale of contemporary cities raises questions of not only how people get around, but also how they experience on an individual and small scale level in the necessity of movement, how flows, fluxes and networks influence human patterns and contacts and become themselves social constructs, and how the concept and experience of space is changed by movement.

Mobility as a part of everyday life is here to stay and the need to understand this as a viable sensory and connecting capacity, being engaged on many levels in efficient and sustainable cities, is an important area of study and practice. In this chapter the articles and projects presented indicate the variation in this theme and its actuality as a factor that is certainly related to making cities workable, but that is more importantly related to making cities liveable.

Shelley Smith´s article 'Bumps in the Road – mobility and spatial experience through the lens of parkour' takes its point of departure in a debate about how the concept of space and the perception and experience of space have been altered by contemporary urban development. Moreover, the article provides a journey to the parkour universe that functions as a lens through which to view and understand aspects of urban space. Concluding, the author suggests that the traceur experience of space highlights the possibility of viewing contemporary urban spatial surroundings in new ways that could in turn be inspiring and useful for urban designers.

The article 'Critical Points of Contact – between urban networks and flows' by Ole B. Jensen, Simon Wind and Ditte Bendix Lanng takes its point of departure in the concept of 'Critical Points of Contact',. a concept that has been developed to aid analysis and design intervention in contemporary urban societies where multiple networks and systems interact, overlap, exist in parallel, converge, conflict etc. creating unheeded complexity. The article explores the concept's operational significance to spatial design in a number of urban design studios of the master programme.

In an effort to link mapping, planning and design, the article 'Urban Design and the Tracking of Secondary School Students in the Urban Landscape' by Henrik Harder, Peter Bro and Anne Marie Sanvig Knudsen demonstrates a number of ways in which data collected by GPS technology enables statistical analysis of urban activity such as citizens' time spent in plazas, parks, or window-shopping, etc. In addition, the authors indicate how to manage and analyse this data for further planning and design actions.

Dealing in different scales with the complex flows, times and spaces of the contemporary city, three student projects are presented. Firstly, Ann Sofie Christensen, Kristian Overby, Sebastian Andersen and Thomas Oxvig present a design proposal for the redevelopment of a transit hub – The New Nørreport – in the centre of Copenhagen where they had to deal with a complex net of form, flows and functions. With the project titled 'A matter of planning? - with the light rail towards a new Aarhus', Line Morsing and the transit

CYCLISTS, CAR DRIVERS AND BUS DRIVERS CHOREOGRAPHING ON THE ASPHALT, LONDON 2012

MORNING TRAFFIC CONGESTION, RIO DE JANEIRO 2012

Introduction

RESIDENTIAL COMPOUNDS, RIO DE JANEIRO 2012

SÃO PAULO'S SKYLINE 2011

system of Aarhus – second largest Danish city – where they propose a light rail system. Finally, Sille Christiane Linnet and Lisa Gedsø played with sense, speed and flows, and explored creative solutions for enhancing new experiences for the users of the highway linking Randers and Kolding.

3. Transformation

This chapter deals with transformation of urban areas in different contexts around the globe. Changes to urbanisation can be witnessed at the global level, but they are also manifest in the great diversity of the changes affecting regions and landscapes. The articles and student projects presented here reveal social and cultural challenges relating to globalisation, and explore the physical impact of current urban development trends. Today there is a need to look at the built environment as a fluid landscape of different forms, experiences, times, flows, structures, lifestyles, communities and cultures. This complex urban landscape demands new urban design methods and interventions that can realise its potential and deal with its challenges. In this manifold context, the articles and projects in this chapter address innovative design strategies, methods and interventions for urban transformation which endeavour more diverse, tolerant and sustainable cities. In their article 'Transforming Vestergade Vest into a Ludic and Shared-Use Space', Victor Andrade, Ole B. Jensen, Henrik Harder and Jens C. O. Madsen explore and debate shared-use spaces – particularly in a Danish context – via an historical account that draws theoretical perspectives into the discussion, and a case study that registers design parameters and processes in the actual use of Vestergade Vest, Odense. Specifically this article is interested in looking at the interchanges and interrelationships between pedestrian, bike and car traffic occurring in the same space and how strategies for use are developed by decision makers and designers, as well as the actual users of the space negotiating it in daily situations. The article also has the overriding intention of discussing this type of space as a strategy for (re)generating lively public spaces in urban settings, e.g., by introducing the ludic as an aspect of these spaces in daily life.

Lea Holst Laursen's article 'Enhancing the Landscape – architectural installations in the landscape' intends to link landscape, architectural practice and current trends in urban development. By looking at a contemporary situation in which the potential in the landscape itself can become realized as an attractor for urban growth and the creation of identity, the article references landscape (urban) theory, as well as presenting case studies of existing projects. The article creates a bridge between theory and practice, and illustrates a spanning of scales; from large scale landscape contexts to sensory/human experience and materials – a key issue in urban design.

Anne Juel-Andersen's article is based on her research as a business PhD with a collaboration between Aalborg Municipality and Aalborg University. In the article, 'Case Study of Urban Transformation Projects', the study of the transformation of three areas of Aalborg is the scenario for a reflexive debate about urban regeneration strategies in a post-industrial city. This article focuses on how urban transformation interventions in dense city centres are part of shifting discourses and rationales.

The last article of the chapter, 'Urban Design and Spatial Equity: The Favela-Bairro Programme - Experience in Rio de Janeiro, Brazil', authored by Victor Andrade, introduces the dichotomy of the formal/informal city in the megacity of Rio de Janeiro, Brazil. Using a case study, the article examines the success of physical interventions led by the local government in integrating the urban fabric and reducing differences between formal and informal areas. The article explores the social and spatial segregation of Rio de Janeiro and highlights the challenges and limitations of urban design interventions in transforming a segregated city into a democratic and tolerant city.

The six student projects presented in this chapter are examples of urban design intervention as potential catalyst to urban transformation towards a determined vision of urbanity. Retrofitting a decommissioned hospital and redeveloping its surroundings, Martin Frank Petersen, Senad Gvozden, Siri Laursen and Sofie Brincker suggested the transformation and regeneration of the site with the project titled 'Haderslev Nature School - landscape and architectural interventions at the Haderslev hospital area'. Immersed in a 'charming' atmosphere, the project 'The New Story of Odense - riding on a roof top, playing on a rail track, living in a fairytale' – developed by Jacob Bjerre Mikkelsen, Ida Sofie Gøtzsche Lange, Marion Højris, Rasmus Davidsen and Stine Jakobsen – was inspired by Hans C. Andersen and presents a creative reuse of a centrally located, highly trafficked road - a scar - in the urban fabric of Odense. While Maputo – Mozambique`s capital – has faced rapid growth and climate changes, and in this scenario Stine Sonne and Anne Lærke Jørgensen developed the project 'Climate Design – working with vulnerable urbanities in Mozambique' where they design a regional plan in the 'water basin scale', and then present a zoom-in with solutions for public spaces, social housing and infrastructure in the scale of a neighbourhood. Taking as a point of departure of the concept of Intensifying, Lucile Hamoignon presents a design proposal for a neglected social housing area in Lille, France. In her project 'Intensified Concorde neighbourhood', the potentialities of the neighbourhood are intensified by her design in order to revitalize its spaces and empower the community. The project titled 'The New Karolinelund – Aalborg's diverse venue' transforms a decommissioned amusement park in the core of Aalborg into a lively and multifunctional neighbourhood that helps to mend the surrounding urban fabric while reinterpreting the strong image of the closed park. And finally, 'Meadow Patterns with an Edge – urban development in the northern freight rail area in Aarhus', by Rikke Schjødt Brink transforms a derelict area into a viable cultural centre that uses landscape – both past and present - as an organising strategy.

4. Design & Method

The size, complexity and speed of contemporary urbanism poses some extremely interesting challenges to the how and the what of urban design. In this chapter, the unique relationship between what we do and how we do it in the context of urban design is explored. The urban context has undergone radical changes within an extremely short period of time relative to the history of human urban settlement. This has of course had irrefutable effects on both urban form and urban life, and with the creation of new urban contexts, situations, constellations, requirements and agendas, a new set of design parameters has been introduced. Factors such as flux, velocity, temporality, globalisation and dynamic, diverse and constant change are aspects comprising contemporary urbanity and demanding new design and research tools.

So how do we plan for temporality? Can we map experience? How can we identify and ultimately realize potential within this new and complex framework? How do we integrate diverse and enormous factors to create experiential spatialities? This chapter, through articles, workshop tracings and a look at an exhibition in love, attempts to give some insight into what makes it possible for us as designers and researchers to act, react, investigate, create, engage, and hopefully, ultimately, understand and embrace our urban reality.

In her article 'Urban Songlines – The City Experienced by Ordinary People', Gitte Marling provides a unique insider's look at the development of a method 'designed' to uncover the connections of everyday people taking part in their everyday activities in the complexity of the contemporary urban situation. The inspirational sources for the Urban Songlines method are traced and its use is exemplified using Roskilde Festival - itself an example of the urban trend of Instant Cities - as a backdrop.

Hans Kiib focuses on the design-based methods in concept development and its application with the purpose of developing new design concepts. The article, 'Designing Concepts and Strategies', presents the application of a method used in workshops intendes to generate ideas about the Aalborg waterfront redevelopment. In its conclusion, the article aims at developing a critical view regarding adaption of the workshop results by planners.

Shelley Smith´s article 'Unfolding Architecture – workshop events retold' explores the technique of folding as a tool that has the potential to foster spatial understanding a priori scale and content. The article presents a theoretical discussion about space and plays this up against an urban design student workshop. The text highlights a relationship between theory, practice and teaching in a creative academic environment.

Lasse Andersson's article 'WE LOVE THE CITY – a pragmatic approach to urban design' is the finale of the book. It encourages a revision of thinking and practice – both student project/teaching-based, and professional – regarding the making of the built. With a point of departure in a passion for 'the city' – the article focuses on the title slogan 'the city in the building and the building in the city' as a play between scales in the built environment and the practices that have traditionally worked within this sphere. The author discusses this 'new paradigm' through a workshop held with 4th semester bachelor students, and the subsequent exhibition held at the Utzon Centre in Aalborg entitled - WE LOVE THE CITY that showcased this student work alongside the professional work of the Copenhagen based architectural office ADEPT.

Reflections

The musings in this anthology can be seen as snapshots in a continuum rather than being seen as forming a definitive ending in their totality. The names of the categories in this book seem to confirm this by hinting at activities of a processional nature. Performativity, mobility, transformation, describe exchange, movement and change – and when held up to more static methodologies and products, they raise the question of how to tackle the doing, i.e., the design and method, in a framework characterised by flux. The contributions in both article and project form tell a story of a dynamic and fluid process that acts, reacts and interacts – and in that respect it seems more appropriate at this juncture rather than to conclude, to reflect.

Etymologically, reflect stems from reflectere, from the Latin, reflexio, 'a reflection', and is comprised of re – meaning *back* and flectere, meaning *to bend* – literally a bending back. A bending back, seen in a physical sense, certainly requires a good amount of flexibility, but this is also true of the mental activity of reflecting. This flexibility translates to an openness to see, to consider and ultimately to learn from, and this activity is essential in a continuing process. Also of note, is that the bending back takes place from a stationary position that pauses in the flow to take stock of where one has been in order to be informed about where one is going. Moreover, continuing in this linguistic line of thought, an interesting perspective on reflecting, on where we are and what we are doing in this reflecting, can be found in the opposites. Antonyms of to reflect are: to ignore, to refrain, to neglect. This opens for the emergence of a wonderfully positive aspect. In the act of reflecting here, and through the material being reflected upon, what this anthology expresses is an engagement in our field and a willingness to effect change – to pay attention instead of ignoring, to initiate rather than to refrain and to care rather than to accept neglect.

When keys words are plucked from the articles and the projects contained in this publication, the following streams emerge revealing an inspiring multiplicity:
There is experiencing, encountering, exploring, tracking, intensifying, unfolding, transforming, enhancing, riding, playing, loving and living.
Work takes place with flows, stages, diversity, spatial equity, culture, landscape, temporality, networks, vulnerability, songlines, installations, interventions and visions.
The sensuous, and the in-betweens are found, potential and poetry are discovered.

The contributions in this book cover a wide range of theoretical positions and design strategies. They address social issues and physical form, the framework of life and the living of it, the sensory and the cerebral. As evidenced by the biographies, the contributors themselves represent a breadth of cultural, experiential and educational backgrounds.

This publication represents a meeting point of all manner of differences and serves to illuminate not only what we have done, but also a path ahead. It is hoped that this collection of musings evidences a dynamic, fertile, and above all else, a living field, within which the work will continue to move forward - and occasionally bend back.

In summation

The chapters contained in this book highlight issues and interests at the core of the Urban Design department, in research and practice, at Aalborg University. However, all in all, this publication expresses perhaps most simply a fascination with, and a commitment to, working with the urban condition and this can be just as simply stated, to borrow from the final contribution contained in this work: 'WE LOVE THE CITY!'

References

Bunschoten, R. (2001) *Urban Flotsam – Stirring the City*. Rotterdam: 010 Publishers.

Busquets, J. (2007) *A New Lens for the Urbanistic Project. Barcelona*: Harvard University & Nicolodi Editore.

Carmona, M. et al. (2010) Public Places – Urban Spaces. *The Dimensions of Urban Design*. Burlington: Architectural Press.

Corner, J. (1999) ´The Agency of Mapping´. In Cosgrove, D. (Ed.) *Mappings*. London: Reaktion Books Ltd.

Krieger, A. (2009) ´Introduction: An Urban Frame of Mind´. In: Krieger, A. and Saunders, W.S. (Eds.) *Urban Design*. Minneapolis: University of Minnesota Press.

Larice, M. and Macdonald, E. (Eds.) (2007) *The Urban Design Reader*. New York: Routledge.

Mumford (2009) ´The Emergence of Urban Design in the Breakup of CIAM`. In: Krieger, A. and Saunders, W.S. (Eds.) *Urban Design*. Minneapolis: University of Minnesota Press.

Deturned City Design
- Tools for experiential urban living
Hans Kiib

In an urban context there is an increasing need to find adequate architectural responses to urban challenges where tourism and the experience economy are in focus. New architectural concepts are looking away from modernism's strong attachment to 'form and function' towards 'the sensual and the narrative'. You often see that new expressive architecture is coupled with old industrial buildings in order to create strong stories about a future; similarly, art installations and temporary architecture are emerging and providing the audience with spatial experiences questioning the way we use urban spaces and how we interact in everyday city life.

This article presents urban design tools in relation to experiential urban living looking at the artistic methods and tools that are involved in temporary architectural installations in urban environments today.
It draws lines back to the era of architectural avant-garde in the 1960s, when the Situationist Movement criticized the absence of atmosphere in modernistic architecture and suburban cities. In line with this, they promoted mapping tools and artistic 'construction of situations' that could evoke a more comprehensive way of experiencing city life.
The intentions and methods of the Situationist Movement are compared to present art installations and temporary architecture in public spaces. The article analyzes the methods and the architectural tools in these kinds of 'constructed situations', which mirror and reflect the present poverty of our urban environment and give way to other experiences in public spaces. The article puts special emphasis on temporary architecture, which may provide a special freedom to construct spatial situations that promote experimental life. Through symbols, ornaments and decorations it is possible to create recognizable urban sceneries in which people can be involved in aesthetically and bodily challenging situations. It advocates the development of 'relate architecture' in temporary urban installations. The conclusion is that this kind of temporary architectural installation may contribute to a more experiential urban living and become a threshold for new demands to the design of our urban environments in general.

Höhen Rausch – just another funscape?

During a weekend in July 2009 I visited Europe's Capital of Culture, the Austrian city of Linz.
More than one hundred thousand people from the area thronged the streets of Linz to watch a carnival performance. In adjacent squares street artists, jugglers and small groups of opera singers attracted crowds while rain showers tried to spoil the fun.

On a rooftop of the museum adjacent to the pedestrian precinct a big balcony had been constructed. From this balcony people could watch the crowd. The balcony was part of a big art installation called 'Höhen Rausch'. A poster with a man in a flying balloon gondola promised that this installation would provide a surprising experience. An old Ferris wheel had been raised on the roof, making it possible to be lifted up another 20 metres and experience the city from a bird's eye perspective. Furthermore, a 10-metre-long bus had been erected as a tower amongst all the ventilation pipes, thus reinforcing the fact that this installation really would try to make you see the cityscape from a new angle. A series of ramps guided you round, and on your way down again you had to pass a shower adding more water to the wet surface. This time, however, your umbrella would be converted into a primitive loudspeaker as the water hit the plastic surface at different frequencies. Händel's Water Music, The Beatles' Yellow Submarine and other well-known tunes would serenade your ears as you passed through the different showers.

Safely back on the pavement, I had an ambivalent feeling of leaving an art installation similar to a rooftop funfair. Did this art provide a number of new perspectives on the city? Or was this just another 'funscape'?

Critical reflections

I have to admit that my expectations – related to this weekend in Linz – were biased by my readings on the subject of temporary theme parks and festivals. I was afraid that this was just another cultural festival where art installations and theatrical performances were to be located in public spaces without really providing artistic experiences or new knowledge and learning.

In 2002 the Dutch researcher Trazy Metz contributed to the discussion on the increasing transformation of inner cities into zones related to leisure and fun. In her book 'FUN. Leisure and Landscape (2002), Trazy Metz describes how local people in Amsterdam escape from their homes when millions of people invade the streets and canals to participate in gay parades, opera festivals, marathons, etc:

"Entertainment has conquered the Nederland. Leisure is more than the time that you can spend as you like. It has become an omnipresent culture of fun with an enormous economic importance. Our social identity is determined by the way we spend our leisure at least as much as by the work we do or

the possessions we own... We spend an increasing amount of time, money and kilometres on our fun. Never before has the Netherlands had so many events and festivals, so many shopping Sundays, so many parties, second homes, ski slopes, mega-cinemas, kids' paradises and stadiums...the influence of all these activities on our environment is also becoming more visible." (Metz 2002)

On the one hand, events have become an important part of city life. 'Events break up the routine of everyday life', and events 'provide an opportunity to celebrate life' in general. It appears, therefore, that events should be a very important part of cultural planning and in the design of 'a cultural city'. However, there is also a downside to this. As many events are organized by professionals with economic interests or with specific habits, they can be a burden for the inhabitants living close to or in the middle of the event area. For these people, 'the cultural city' is becoming 'a funscape city' (Marling and Zerlang 2007).

There is nothing wrong with a spectacle designed as a carnival where people are challenged with regard to their perception of city life. I really appreciate being involved in sensory landscapes that challenge my senses – my bodily senses, my hearing, my sight and my memory.

However, a quick analysis of the Linz event is that it may not change anything!

As stated by a range of critical researchers (Kunzmann 2004; Madanipour 2008; Landry 2010 and Skot-Hansen 2010), the danger of staging festivals is that they all contribute to a general indifference and commercialization of city life.

"Every city promotes its own carnival atmosphere, but increasingly they look the same everywhere." (Madanipour 2008: 41), *and*

1: HÖHEN RAUSCH, LINZ 2009

"The problem with these spectacles is also that everyday life seems even more dull and gray after the circus wagons and jugglers are gone." (Skot-Hansen 2010: 128)

However, an analysis of the cultural city must also include a more critical perspective acknowledging that these urban interventions run the risk of fuelling social exclusion, cultural homogeneity and a culture of fear of others (Marling & Zerlang 2007: 6-7).

The creation of new urban interventions aimed at satisfying the demand for experience and stimulus thus does not necessarily need to be commercial and instrumental. Instead, the more critical insights of contemporary urban theory point to the potential for creating learning environments and situations where multiple and heterogeneous social groups may create new public domains - understood as 'places where exchange between different social groups is possible and also actually occurs' (Hajer & Reijndorp 2001: 11). Thus cultural projects and performative urban spaces may be thought of as sites of 'learning from the stranger' and places of 'civil society based interaction'. In the words of Hajer and Reijndorp: 'public domain is thus not so much a place as an experience' (Hajer & Reijndorp 2001: 88).

Relate Architecture as Sensual and Experiential Activity

The question is how this relates to the making of urban spaces and architecture? One of the most direct attempts to deal with this question is the work of Anna Klingmann. According to her, designing for experience requires connecting architecture to the user's personal dreams and desires (Klingmann 2007: 19). Accordingly, architecture and urban interventions may contribute to engaging its public on the level of the senses in meaningful connections (Klingmann 2007: 51). The city may be discussed as a site of 'use', 'symbolism' and 'experience'. In other words, we may ask how city designs and urban spaces produce value. This means that urban spaces and interventions herein may have not only an important use value and symbolic value, but also an experience value (Klingmann 2007: 44).

With reference to Bernd Schmitt's analysis of marketing we may want to rephrase our understanding of architecture (and urban intervention) in the experience economy along four distinct dimensions leading to a fifth level of synthesis. In Klingmann's terminology we would be looking at a synthesis of 'sense architecture', 'feel architecture', 'think architecture' and 'act architecture'. Assuming that these four dimensions all merge into a single synthesis, we may start to speak of 'relate architecture' in which sensing (our bodily engagement with spaces), feeling (our emotional engagement with spaces), thinking (our cognitive and reflective engagement with spaces) and acting (our socially transformative engagement with spaces) come together in a strong emotional and cognitive relation between subjects and urban architectures (Klingmann 2007: 50). In the experience economy urban interventions may thus facilitate new deliberation processes and forms of interaction that point towards progressive experiments and hybrid socialisations. What matters is no longer architecture as functions and iconic brandscapes, but architecture as sensual and experiential activity.

Learning from the Situationist Movement

This leads us back to the origins of the concept of 'détournement' and 'instant urbanism' as it was defined by avant-garde artists some fifty years ago. Groups of frontrunners evolved around the Frenchman Guy Debord (Lettrist International) and the Dane Asger Jorn (Cobra), who were challenging the emerging consumer society. In 1957, 'Situationist International', which became a unifying movement of critical artists and architects, was formed. They argued that the task of the visual arts and architecture was not merely to embellish; the artists were supposed to get involved in the public debate – to question and create 'new and alternative images' of important aesthetic, ethical and moral social issues. The role of art should move outside the world of galleries and museums. Art was to be moved into the cityscape, the media, politics, festivals, etc.

The Situationists communicated their ideas through satire, happenings, 'counter manifests' and utopian proposals for new cities and environments. 'Unitary Urbanism' from 1959 was one such counter manifest. It proclaimed that "Unitary Urbanism acknowledges no boundaries; it aims to form a unitary human environment in which separation such as work/leisure and public/private will finally be dissolved" (Debord 1959). At the same time, 'Unitary Urbanism' would seek broader and more experimental challenges in city life and architecture. It would be a manifest for a redefinition of the spaces of the city through participation, games and the construction of situations; architecture was to be infinitely formable and provide flexible, mobile structures with limited life spans. (Ferguson 2007)

'Situationist International' became a broad artistic movement with many different subgroups applying a range of different artistic praxis. In general, the tools activated can be grouped into the following:

- Dérive and psycho-geographic mapping
- Experimental behaviour, happenings and plays
- Situationist architecture

Dérive and Experimental Behaviour

The experiential praxis was related to the original statement on 'constructed situations' that could bring critique of existing living conditions and also draw up normative hypotheses regarding city life, art and architecture. The organization claimed that any given constructed situation would bring about a movement and an atmosphere so forceful that it would stimulate new forms of behaviour and yield glimpses of future improvements of social life based on human interaction and play (Sadler 1998). The mission 'to construct situations' should be a noble alternative to creating traditional works of art. It was considered a 'historical necessity' and an escape from the traditional, alienated artistic practice in which the artist was separated from his/her audience.

In the praxis of dérive it turned out that a main focus could be to map the 'hidden places' of the city. By mapping the 'hidden places' and maybe adding new dimensions – e.g. adding private functions to the public space or turning the freeway into a semi-private space for accommodation – you would add a conflict between the 'normal' and the 'constructed' to the space. The 'atmosphere of disorder' could draw new perspectives to the given perception of the place.

In an urban context, the constructed situations could be comprised of new plays and games, which could turn 'the city on its head' – into 'a deturned city'. Odd and awkward situations would attract attention and provide food for thought and also lead to altered behaviour and other types of social interaction. The constructed situations should be perceived as a kind of performance in which all spaces were treated as performative spaces and all people as actors; artistic success should be measured in relation to a minimization of the avant-garde artist's role in the situation. (Sadler 1998)

Situationist Architecture

Situationist architecture advocated a need for projects that could confront functionalist urban development models. Situationist architecture should display a new way to integrate the many facets of city life in a continuum of hybrid functions whilst advocating *a pleasure-driven and eventful everyday life.*

Situationists even envisioned a reconstruction of the city based on an atmospheric breakdown – carried out on the basis of careful psycho-geographic studies. These should be based on the town's atmosphere-creating elements and on the development of these. The city should be turned into a machine for production of discrete and varied atmospheres (Wigley 1998: 23).

To some extent this work became a very important source of architectural ideas and utopian thinking on urbanism in the 1960s. In particular, groups of young French and British architects pursued its criticism of the uniform architecture of modernism – which ignored the fact that human needs are different, diverse and changeable – both in far-reaching projects but also in urban scenography for exhibitions, events and happenings.

One of the earliest concept projects from Britain was 'Fun Palace' by Cedric Price from 1960. The project was described as 'a place' where everyone may 'choose freely'. Fun Palace did not look like an entertainment complex, but rather an enormous, unfinished structure reminiscent of a scaffold at a construction site or a shipyard. Its structure, which could be assembled from simple, industrially produced components, could be extended and added to horizontally as well as vertically to form a large spatial grid that could harbour many different activities.

Price's ideas influenced an entire generation of architects. He promoted a structural architecture characterized by openness and freedom to change. The Archigram group developed his ideas in several projects on a smaller scale. The industrial capacity should be exploited – not to homogenize, but for an architectural diversity tailored to localized needs.

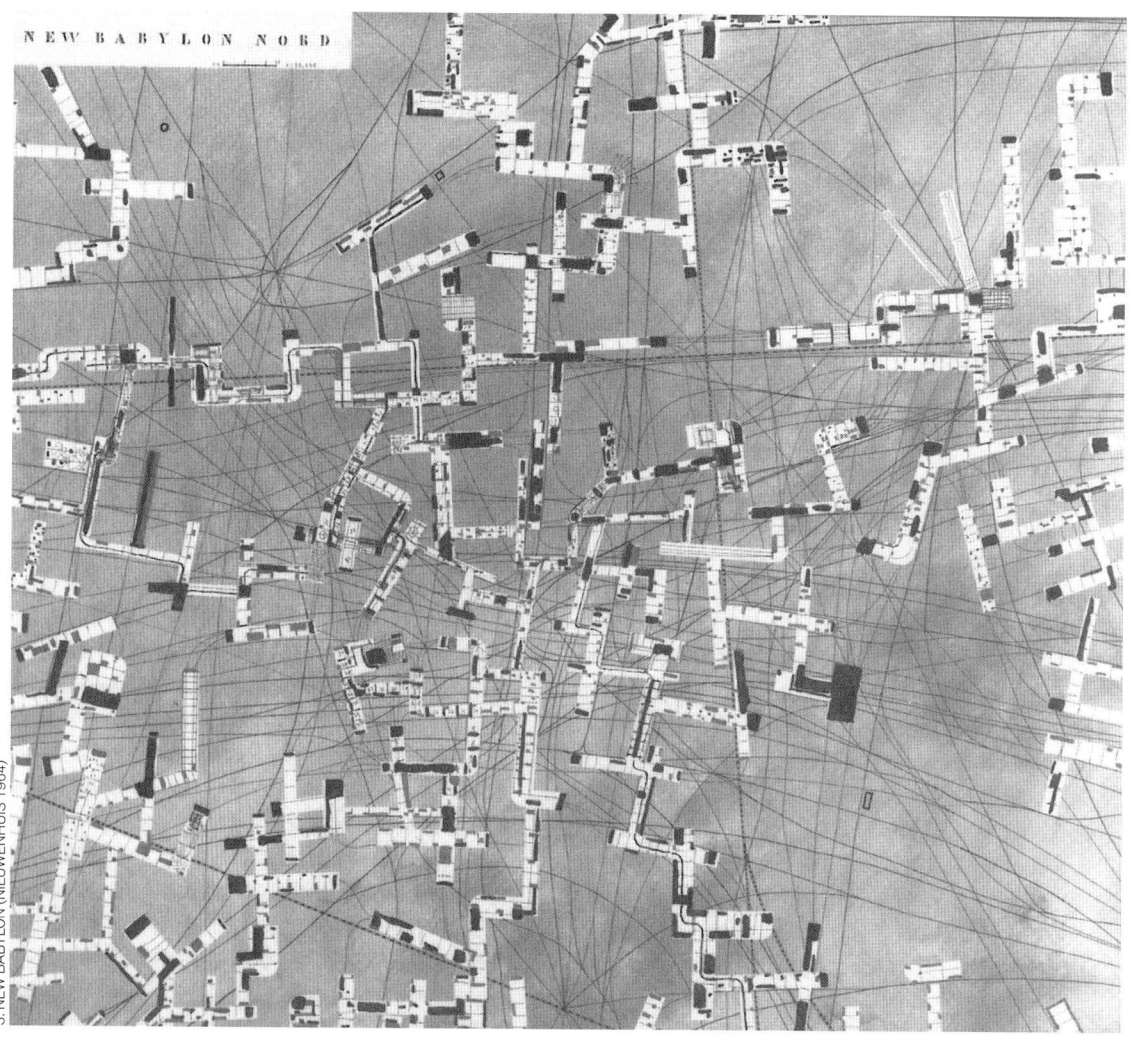

3: NEW BABYLON (NIEUWENHUIS 1964)

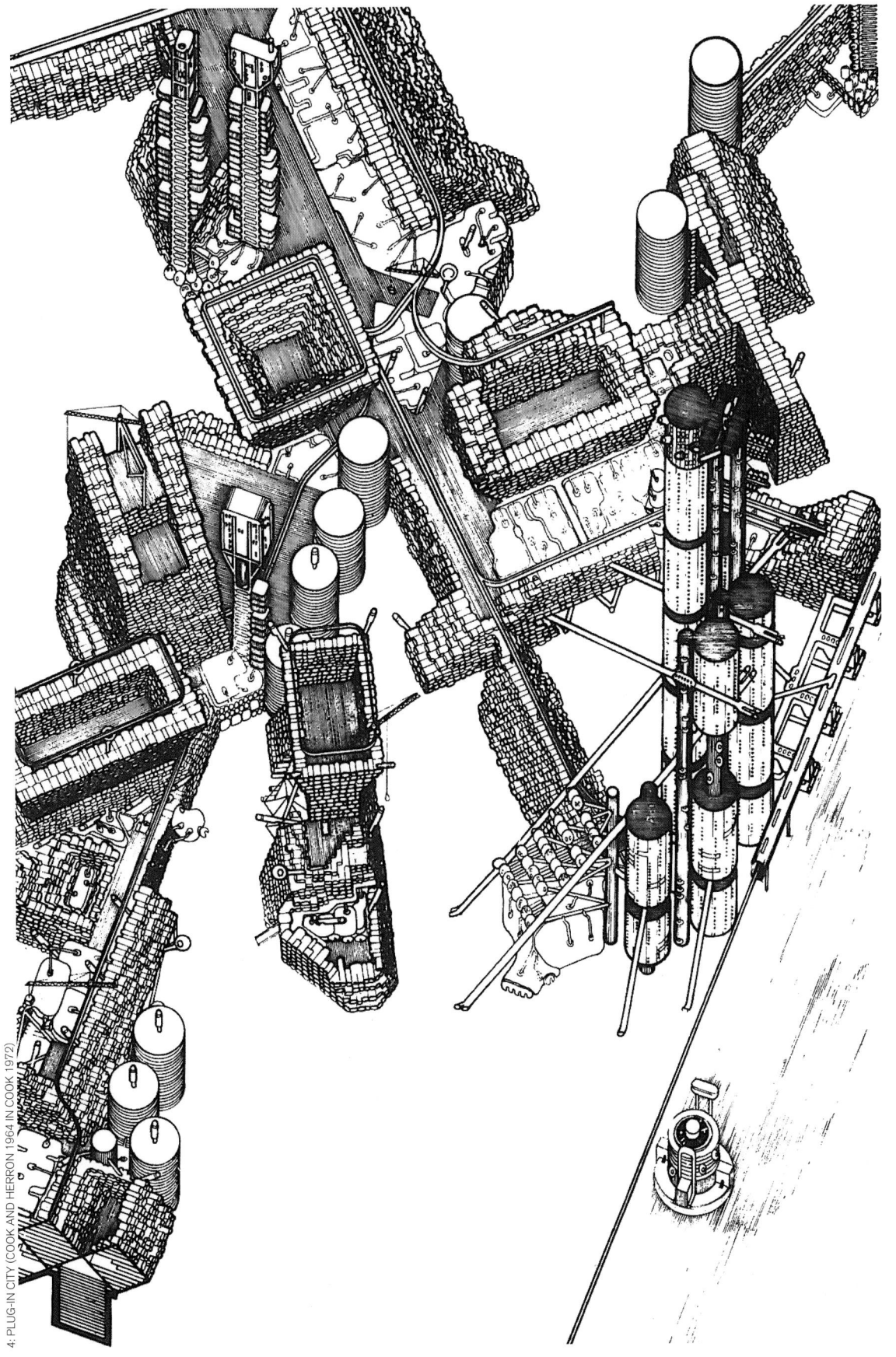

4: PLUG-IN CITY (COOK AND HERRON 1964 IN COOK 1972)

Deturned City Design - Tools for experiential urban living
Performativity

The 'Instant City' project from 1969 looked back to the ideas behind 'the deturned city' and applied them to a mobile, urban structure which is reminiscent in many ways of festival design as we know it today. It consisted of a sophisticated set of mobile units – information pavillions, learning environments, cultural scenes, laboratories, exploratories and sports arenas – which could be integrated into existing urban societies. They could be mounted on rooftops or in open fields and function as additional 'new, innovative layers' to the existing functions of the permanent city. 'Instant City' placed great importance on temporary architecture as a 'learning machine', able to serve as a technological and cultural innovation force in relation to the existing society (Cook 1972). 'Fun city' related to leisure had been replaced by 'experience city' related to learning and aesthetic living enhanced by temporary structures and acupunctural cultural interventions.

Deturned City Today

None of the mega-scale utopian architectural projects were built. However, the ideas behind Situationist thinking related to 'Unitary Urbanism' are very much alive in performance art, temporary architectural installations and public space design today. Through exhibitions and counter-planning projects, a new wave of projects has arisen under some of the same headings used by the Situationists.

A number of current projects are all based on 'situation construite' in the public sphere. They can be categorized according to their artistic ambitions, but also very much in relation to the different focus in the Situationist praxis:

- 'Temporary Architecture', which has references to 'Fun Palace' and 'Instant City',

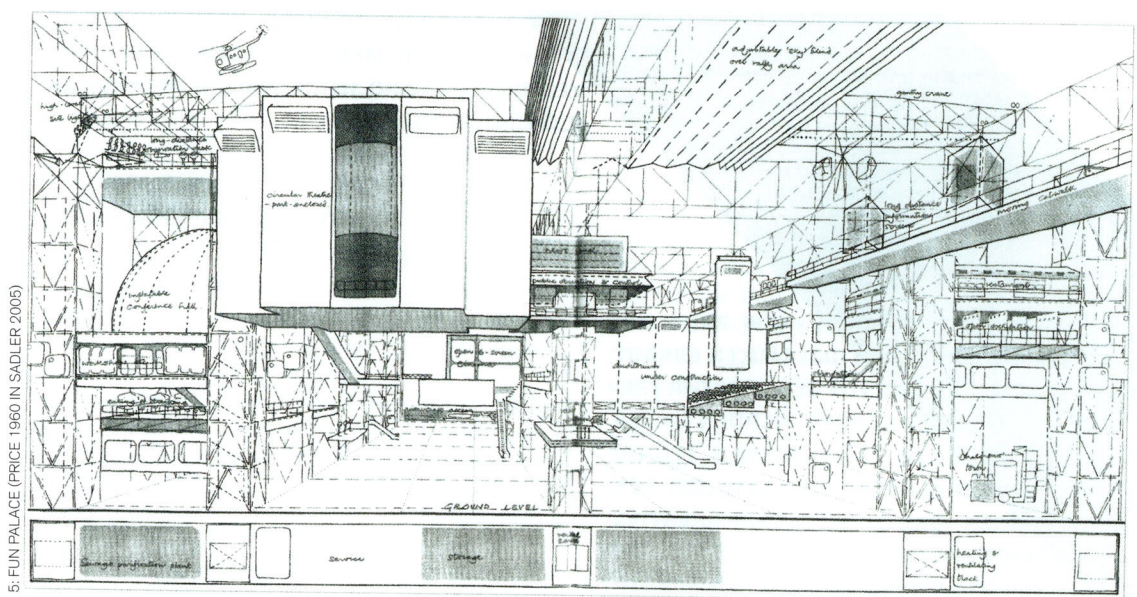

5: FUN PALACE (PRICE 1960 IN SADLER 2005)

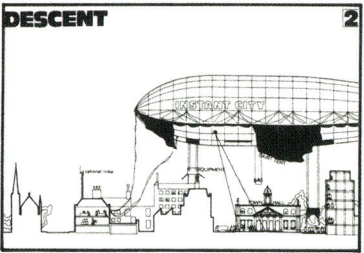
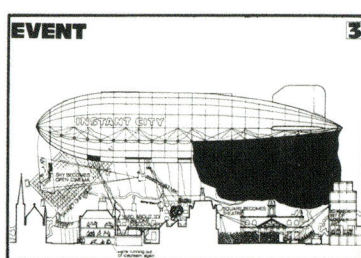

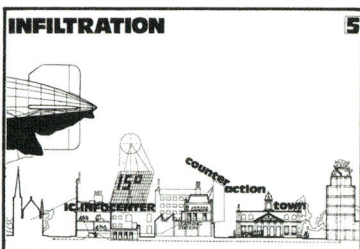
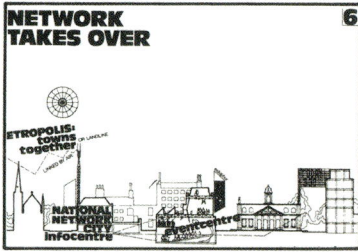

6: INSTANT CITY AIRSHIP (COOK 1972)

- 'Urban Actions', which have much in common with the general ideas behind 'situation constructed' and 'experimental behaviour';
- 'Urban Nomadism', which has a lot of references to floating city dwellers and moving cities;
- 'Movement' (e.g. parkour) focuses on the irrational excavation of hidden places or unexpected aspects of city life.

Present projects insist on adding alternative features to art in public places, and to providing new perspectives on urban conflicts and on poor life conditions through play, artistic interaction and architectural design.

Dérive New Europe

Dérive strategies are being up-scaled and new technologies added. The Metropolis project, Copenhagen 2007-2017, attempts to combine street theatre with a critical review on urban policy, city life and those left over after planning. Through art installations and performance in the city, Metropolis highlights questions on what we want with our cities. By applying dérive strategies with physical performance in different urban contexts it raises critical awareness of 'social behaviour' and of 'urban design policy' in our cities across Europe today.

In Project Cargo Sophia from 2007, two Bulgarian truck drivers invite the audience to take a ride in containers through Copenhagen. On the one hand, it is a simulated long-distance ride from Sofia to Copenhagen, where they have never or have only rarely been; on the other hand, the truck would bring the audience to abandoned or neglected suburban sites of Copenhagen.

Between video clips and stories from life on the road, the truck drivers opened up the window at key points of the stories. The performance mixed the realities of neglected suburban Copenhagen with a lorry driver's experiences of the world through a windshield.

The performance is obviously about Eastern Europe's long-distance drivers and the new European Community. In the enlarged EU a lot of people have become the nomads of cargo transport. They work and live on less than 6 mobile square metres in front of their 40-ton load, fewer than 25% use a safety belt, 350 are injured and 20 die annually in road accidents in Germany alone. Time is money and there must be no empty runs. Paper, meat or steel pipes - customers order what they need and this flow of demand is transforming highways between the many cities of Europe into 'moving cities' related to a growing 'floating population' working end experiencing the New Europe.

With artistic interventions, Metropolis helps participants to raise an architectural counter-discourse and a critical look at the architects' role and power. They make us experience the "residual sites" of the city. The performance wants us to discover, experience, sense, learn and recognize - and perhaps ultimately decide on the architectural qualities of that city's diversity of good and bad.

Re-Act-Architecture

A lot of projects in relation to experimental behaviour combine two or more elements. 'Add-on 20 Höhenmeter' from Vienna, 2005, is a steel pipe scaffold installation with temporary homes, car wash bath, a spa, etc. which has the appearance of a vertical building whose skin has been peeled off. The structure consisted of different platforms that rose 20 metres high. In them,

7: CARGO SOPHIA, COPENHAGEN 2007

custom-made spatial modules interlocked with prefabricated parts that had been imaginatively altered from their original functions. The 'building' was placed on a public square and invited the general public to participate and to explore, offering a wide range of views and vistas from various levels. The transparent structure intentionally put intimate private spaces into a public sphere, making the installation into an invitation to explore new relationships between private and public. It created the illusion of a vertical compact city where you could be accommodated (stay overnight) and live in an unexpected and mixed social environment. This project has clear references to the 'Instant City' project from 1969, but it also has references to Dada and Fluxus, and is founded on interaction between people on the basis of principles of 'react and act!'

Instant Transparent Skin

In relation to the utopian architectural projects from the 1960s the contemporary instant architecture and performative spaces are far more modest in scale. However, conceptually the projects still have strong messages. The architectural office 'Raumlabor Berlin' has carried out a number of projects which point to architecture as a means for social interaction and social emancipation (Maier and Rick 2008).

The Kitchen Monument is temporary architecture and scenography which has been playing a significant role in different community actions, providing an involving and inclusive framework for weak social groups. The architecture is an enormous, inflatable plastic bubble,

which can be placed under a motorway bridge, in a backyard, or in other 'forgotten' or ignored locations in the city. The aim is dialogue, debate and social inclusion.

This instant architecture allows us to test the cohesion of the community and its ability to adapt new social interaction. Raumlabor has provided an interesting tool for the creation of trust in the city: 'the transparent skin'. It is a powerful urban scenography, which can enhance a new layer of social interaction embodied in neglected urban spaces.

Ephemeral Architecture

Another example is the 'Blur Building' at EXPO, Switzerland 2002, by Diller & Scofidio + Renfro. The Blur Building is a fog-mass resulting from natural and man-made forces. Fine mist through 35,000 high-pressure nozzles provides a clean 'architecture of atmosphere'. A smart weather system reads the climatic conditions of temperature, humidity, wind speed and direction and regulates water pressure at a variety of zones. Upon entering Blur Building, visual and acoustic references are erased. There is only an optical 'white-out' and a 'white-noise' of sounds from pulsing nozzles. Contrary to the immersive environments of the lake and the mountains, the Blur Building is weakly defined. Here there is nothing to see, and orientation is dependent

10: KITCHEN MONUMENT, DUISBURG 2005 © RAUMLABOR

11: KITCHEN MONUMENT, DUISBURG 2005

on our senses. This 100-metre-wide and 25-metre-tall performative space intentionally neglects the powerful economic forces running Swiss Expo 2002, refusing to focus on architecture as a branding tool. The building is totally devoted to the memory of great natural forces – an artificial context for a strong experience and thus questioning the economic genius of the exhibition.

Conclusion

If we go back to experiences in Linz in 2009, it is clear that experience architecture cannot build on the 'surprising combinations of elements and set designs' alone. As Klingmann stated, it is important to work with 'relate architecture', where on one hand the urban scenography 'speaks to us' and provokes our senses or our thinking, and on the other hand we as humans interact with the architecture in the process of experiencing the space.

In Klingmann's terminology we would be looking at a synthesis of 'sense architecture', 'feel architecture', 'think architecture' and 'act architecture'. Assuming that these four dimensions all merge into one, we can speak of 'relate architecture' in which sensing (our bodily engagement with spaces), feeling (our emotional engagement with spaces), thinking (our cognitive and reflective engagement with spaces) and acting (our socially transformative engagement with spaces) come together in a strong emotional and cognitive relation between subjects and urban architectures (Klingmann 2007: 50).

In this respect a great deal can be learnt from the current 'Instant Urbanism' projects, which share the following common traits:

- They treat architecture as an urban scenography;
- They stage 'private' or 'neglected' problems and put them on the public agenda;
- They aim at creating either a physically or emotionally aesthetic experience;
- They aim at giving the participant an unexpected visual or physical experience that may provoke or change individual and collective behaviour; give pause for thought and possibly, in extension hereof, initiate a process focusing on the given subject.
- They (often) have a social commitment and an ethical agenda, be it directly or indirectly.

The analyses from the present cases bear clear references to the discussions in the 1960s concerning 'situation construite'. There are many parallels to 'Dérive Strategies', 'Experimental Behaviour', and 'Instant City' projects which focus on a sophisticated set of information pavilions, learning environments, cultural scenes and urban laboratories. The temporary urban scenography is able to promote fun, participation and reflection. All in all, these 'artistic constructions' represent a 'new experiential layer' in the city. 'Situation Construite' in public spaces contributes to highlighting the ability of the city to connect people in open social communities and offers new aesthetic experiences and cultural practice.

"We want to build new worlds where fiction is reality and games are new rules for democracy. We want to encourage creativity, reflection and renew social behaviours. If space is made by dynamics of exchange, then everybody can be architects of our world.
Architecture can expand into trans-disciplinary fields, where new tools can be explored. Our recipe: Marinate construction with video, music, graphic design, photography and gastronomy, without forgetting to leave space for interaction, freedom, informality and unpredictability. Your project can result in spatial video games, architectural buildings, musical environments and/or thematic food feasts."
(Ferguson 2007: 11)

In this quotation from Exyzt it becomes clear that the aesthetics of the urban installations are in opposition to the rational organisation of everyday city spaces and to the 'funscapes' emerging in all city centres. Humour is an important part of the 'situations construite' related to grave, global problems – whether it be man-made environmental disasters, refugees of war and poverty, and last, but not least, social discrimination of minorities. With humour and art as vehicles, these projects enable individual and collective engagement – to act and re-act! In this crossroads, where a sensible architectural scenography is allocated in awkward urban settings, it is able to come closer to the experiential design of our urban environment, and perhaps through this to redefine city life.

References

Cook, P. (Ed.) (1972) *Archigram*. New York: Princeton Architectural Press.

Debord, G-E. (1959) ´Positions situationnistes sur la circulation`. In: *Internationale situationniste*, 3.

Fattinger, P., Orso, V. and Rieper, M. (2007) ´Add On. 20 Höhenmeter`. In: Ferguson, F. (Ed.) *Instant Urbanism, Tracing the Theories of the Situationists in the Contemporary Architecture and Urbanism*. Basel: Christof Merian Verlag.

Ferguson, F. (Ed.) (2007) *Instant Urbanism, Tracing the Theories of the Situationists in the Contemporary Architecture and Urbanism*. Basel: Christof Merian Verlag.

Hajer, M. and Reijndorp, A. (2001) *In Search of New Public Domains*. Rotterdam: NAi Publisher.

Kiib, H. (2010) *Performative Urban Design*. Silkeborg: Aalborg University Press.

Klingmann, A. (2007) *Brandscapes. Architecture in the Experience Economy*. Cambridge: MIT Press.

Kunzmann, K. (2004) ´Culture, creativity and spatial planning`. In: *Town Planning Review*, 75 (4): 383-404.

Landry, C. (2000) *The Creative City. A toolkit for Urban Innovators*. London: Earthscan.

Landry, C. (2010) ´The Sensory Landscapes of Cities`. In: Kiib, H. (Ed.) *Performative Urban Design*. Silkeborg: Aalborg University Press.

Madanipour, A. (2008) ´Urban Life in Public Spaces`. In: Pagh, C. and Vesterdal, I. (Eds.) *Changing Metropolis, Introducing artistic and cultural actions in city making*. Copenhagen: Via Design.

Maier, J. and Rick, M. (2008) *Acting in Public, Raumlabor Berlin*. Berlin: Jovis.

Marling, G and Zerlang, M. (2007) *FUN CITY*. Copenhagen: Arkitektens Forlag

Marling, G., Kiib, H. and Jensen, O. (2009a) ´The Experience City: Planning of Hybrid Cultural Projects`. In: *European Planning Studies*. 17 (6): 863-885.

Marling, G., Kiib, H., and Jensen, O. (2009b) *experience city.dk*. Silkeborg: Aalborg University Press.

Metz, T. (2002) *FUN. Leisure and Landscape*. Rotterdam: NAi Publishers.

Nieuwenhuis, C. (1964) ´Neu Babylon`. In: Conrads, U. (Ed.) *Programme und Manifeste zur Architektur des 20. Jahrhunderts*. Gütersloh: Bertelsmann Fachverlag. pp.170-171.

Pine, B. and Gilmore, J. (1999) *The Experience economy. Work is Theatre & Every Business is a Stage*. Boston: Harvard Business School Press.

Prostel, V. (2003) *The substance of style: How the rise of aesthetic value is remaking commerce, culture, and consciousness*. New York: HarperCollins.

Sadler, S. (1998) *The Situationist City*. Boston: Massachusetts Institute of Technology.

Sadler, S. (2005) *Archigram, Architecture without Architecture*. Boston: Massachusetts Institute of Technology.

Skot-Hansen, D. (2010) ´New Stages, New Experiences`. In: Hans Kiib (Ed.) *Performative Urban Design*. Silkeborg: Aalborg University Press.

Wigley, M. (1998) ´The Architecture of Atmosphere`. In: *Daidalos*. 68: 18-27

Experiencing Performative Urban Spaces
Gitte Marling

Overture

A cloud of mist hovers over the square. Light and airy, it creates a field of tension between itself and the square's heavy materials of concrete and stone. Now and again the wind takes the cloud and throws it around. Whirling across the square in graceful leaps, it dances like a feather-light ballerina.

A couple of 5-7 year old boys arrive on bicycles. The small legs pedal hard, and with a precise aim for the cloud they steer directly into it and disappear for a couple of seconds. Then they reappear. They enjoy themselves loudly and intensify the game. In and out, visible and invisible, round and round they go while building up speed – the cloud of vapour has now two eager partners in the dance.

A little way from there, an elderly man has settled down on a flight of steps. He enjoys the sun and the scene on the square, while he follows the boys' game from his slightly withdrawn position. He is focused and does not take any notice of the many pedestrians and cyclists passing by at the outer edge of the square.

Through a case study of Frederiksberg City Centre, this article will present a new urban design discourse in relation to performative urban spaces. In consequence of this, the question is asked of how these new types of urban spaces can be understood and analysed.

Frederiksberg City Centre

Frederiksberg City Centre consists of five urban spaces, each with their particular function and visual expression. They vary in size from small, intimate green spaces to smaller actual squares, Falkoner Plads, to the large open space, Solbjerg Plads, where it is possible to establish a variation of activities and programmes. The squares have been designed by Stig L. Andersson (SLA) and were finished in the spring of 2007. Together they cover an area of 18,000 sq. metres.

There were many challenges in developing the new city centre on this piece of former wasteland. The land had been out of use since the railway station from 1864 was closed in the middle of 1990s. One was that all the new institutions practically turned their backs on the former railway station and the former railway track. Therefore it was important to transform the backs into fronts. Another challenge was the large difference in ground levels. For this reason a sequence of spaces had to be created in order not only to link different design programmes, but also connect different levels in section. Finally, there was the challenge to create still zones in an area, which is also defined as a transit space with approximately 30,000 pedestrians and cyclists crossing daily. The flow of pedestrians comes from the movement to and from the shopping centre, the new metro station and the different educational institutions. Most of the bikes cross the area on a 'high speed bicycle lane', which goes right through the area.

Use and Behaviour

The article is based on observations and analyses of the urban architecture. Furthermore it involves interviews with central actors of the design process, first of all with architect Stig L. Andersson, who was responsible for the design.

Stig L. Andersson has seen it as his task to stimulate urban life and catch the attention of some of the many people passing through on a daily basis – to make them slow down and sharpen their awareness of the place and each other. It has been a challenge to make them experience as much as possible, so they get a sense of trust and belonging to the space they are moving in. He says that the goal has been to make even transiting citizens feel familiar with the space. They are to feel that they belong:

"The new heart of the city is going to be here …it is here people will come and relax, read the paper and smoke a pipe - and it is here the skaters are going to be. This is the place where you can experience all that which you don't see anywhere else. It is all going to happen in a jumble of pathways and connections, where people in great haste hurry to get from A to B." (Andersson, Interview May 14th 2008)

Locally, people have embraced the spaces, chief gardener Karsten Klintø, declares:

"On a good summer's day life is buzzing here, and on Solbjerg Plads a lot of different arrangements are held by the municipality and others. Then marquees are put up … During the Frederiksberg Days from the 15th - 17th of June there is outdoor serving and all sorts of activities…
The high school pupils move out into Falkoner Plads. They are sitting on the slopes - yes everywhere. They also move into the lower part…
We actually think we have succeeded extremely well in generating the activities, which were called for- and for which there is a need.
In the 'Pinetet' (a kind of plinth) the small green area with different pine trees (outside Copenhagen Business school) there is plenty of activity during the daytime, where perhaps 150 students sit in a very small area…. They lean against the trees, just having a good time or working in groups and whatever else they want."
(Klintø, Interview June 4th 2008)

Apart from the daily users, local citizens go there to take in the special arrangement with light, which have been installed in connection with the spouts of mist and on the water-wall. The water-wall has a series of lights, which flicker behind the waterfall in shades of blue. The town architect also emphasises the spotlights, which partially light up the squares, making spaces appear darker in between. With the effect of a stage design, the so-called 'pinetet' is accentuated, which - with its red trees – gives the whole place an artistic touch.

The area is a transit space and can therefore be used as a 'single-minded' space. That means that you can just pass by, or just sit and work by yourself. But the many possibilities for shorter or longer pauses of activity, programmes and arrangements mean, however, that the spaces have an 'open-minded' quality. 'Open minded' means, that there is a mix of programs, and possibilities for fulfilling more than just one function - including doing something together with others. (Waltzer 1995).

The area invites people to pause and take a break, to spend an hour at a café or a couple of hours as an observer. Actually it is more than just an 'open minded' space. It also seems to have the potential for becoming a public domain, where cultures and life styles seem to merge, and where social coding and cultural learning take place. (Hajer and Reijndorp 2001)

The behaviour of the kids and the students' activities are observed. Older people on the benches observe the kids and the young people, and possibly, the young people observe each other in particular. The users of the library meet 'the fitness- people' and picnics on the pinetet reveal different food cultures.

Architecture and Spatial Character are the Points of Departure

The first step in the design process was to form the space. According to Andersson the spatial character and form in particular is the most important. He chose his point of departure in the architecture and spatial potential of the area. The facades of the buildings were used to create walls in the spaces. Spatial arrangement also arose through working with the large variations in the levels of the area, where Falkoner Plads is situated about one floor higher than Solbjerg Plads. According to Andersson the area had the character of neglect with the outline shape of a dog.

'The dog' became five new urban spaces, which are just as different as the buildings are. The spaces tie the buildings together and the whole appears as a conglomerate of an extremely dense city, in which each square, indoors and outdoors, has different programmes, so that it is in constant change. Andersson explains the concept as follows:

"We consider each space as individual, in the same way as rooms in a building are, with doors between them. When you open a door and enter a new room, you forget what you just left, because now you are in a different world. This is how a building works, and this is also how the urban spaces work here. Because of that the material you walk on changes and the light changes. This is most obvious at night,

where you walk from one experience of light in the middle of the square to another one on Solbjerg Plads, to a third one at the entrance to the square, a fourth one by the metro and a fifth one at the 'pinetet' with a grouping of lit pine trees of different kinds. The planting also changes. In some places it is very dense and vigorous, while in other places it is light and fluffy, when the wind catches it..." (Andersson, Interview May 14th 2008)

Performative Experience of Nature

With its open possibilities for interpretation and sense of place, the understanding differs from a classic, romantic view of nature: the planting is lit in different ways so that the experience changes from day to night. On the pinetet (the plinth) in Solbjerg Plads, as already mentioned the trees are lit up with red light in the evening. At the metro station, the lighting of the crowns of the trees projects fine filigree patterns on the pavement. Particularly beautiful tree trunks are lit and so on.

This effect lighting, inspired by the world of theatre, creates a quite unique atmosphere of nature as stage-set. One may talk of the performative experience of nature – and possibly of a new performative view of nature, which by emphasising the sensory parameters rather than the functional ones, differs from the functionalistic view of nature.

Another way of integrating nature into the city is through sound. Soft music or animal sounds are emitted from 32 sound-wells.

"The whole project is about sensing the place where you are. About sensing yourself. About experiencing this place with your own senses and to have your senses stimulated. Hearing, listening: to hear the frogs jumping from one loudspeaker to another. Then there are no limits to how associations to one's childhood and to all sorts of other experiences related to frogs can emerge. To some extent, these are all linked to nature, and then this becomes an experience of nature. Perhaps a sense of wonder is awakened, because these sounds and the smells of the city are incongruous."
(Andersson, Interview May 14th 2008)

According to Andersson it is a success if it is possible to awaken wonder and reflection, because it indicates the process of getting a new insight.

Andersson uses the specific Scandinavian weather as a point of departure in his designs:

"I think it is fantastic when it has just rained and the sun suddenly appears. This creates a kind of pouring light, penetrating the water-dense sky while reflecting in all the wet areas. I have wanted to create an urban space, which can catch this. I have attempted that with the circles milled into some of the concrete tiles. The circles gather the rainwater. Sometimes it works and other times it does not. It depends on how it rains…
The two clouds of steam out there whizz around the whole square, when the winds comes up. Then they moisten the surface, and the water collects in some of the rings. If you experience that in low sunlight it works in one way. If it is raining, it works in an-

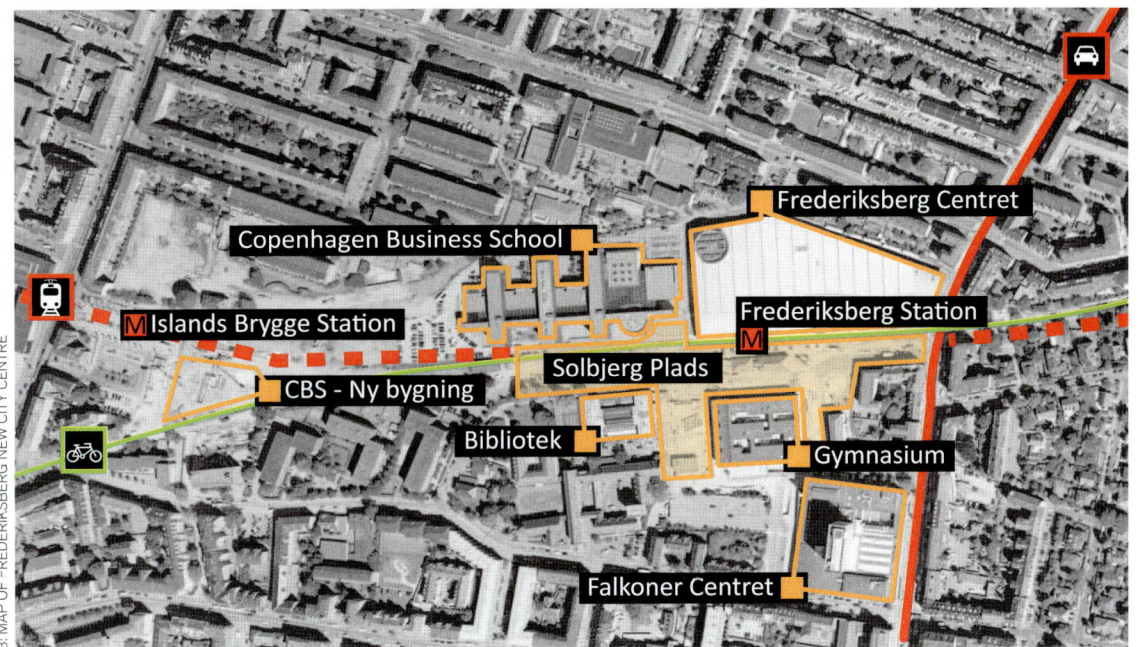

3: MAP OF FREDERIKSBERG NEW CITY CENTRE

4: TREES IN SOLBJERG SQUARE ARE LIT UP WITH RED LIGHTS © SLA

other. Then the square, the trees and everything else merge with the sky. It becomes grey in grey, which actually is a fantastic tone in jazz music" (Andersson, Interview May 14th 2008)

The architectural experience is free. The aim is not to control it, even though much thinking has gone into the ways in which experiences and sensory impressions can be created. We have different preferences, and we experience in different ways. In the spaces we are free to dream our own dreams:

"There is no one answer to what you can experience in these spaces. Whether you are there during the daytime or at night, in winter with snow everywhere or on a sunny day: the value lies in the experience, which takes place in exactly the moment you are there, the period of time you spend in this particular place." (Søberg, art historian, SLA, Interview May 14th 2008)

Søberg emphasises a particular feature of the project: it represents a confrontation with the notion that architecture is something which has been completed by the architect:

"The interesting thing is the break with the understanding that the work is something complete and which sends an explicit message to the receiver who then receives in a passive way, as is often the

case with architecture and urban spaces.
This project represents a break. There is a more complex interplay between the architecture and those who are spending time in the square. There is awareness that the work can be open, the work can be something arising out of the interaction with the user or spectator".
(Søberg. Interview May 14th 2008)

The link to performative installation art is interesting. The narrative of the Frederiksberg City Centre lends itself to a discussion of performative architecture and urban architecture.

Understanding of Urban Spaces / Making Sense

What knowledge about the analysed urban spaces may this small case study provide?
Performative urban spaces cannot be understood with the help of analyses of form and performative installations described as isolated elements. Urban spaces also have to be understood via the identity and significance, which become integrated through use (Augé 1995). Thus, the study of urban spaces is an interdisciplinary pursuit, in which the physical design of space and human behaviour together make up the pieces of the whole puzzle. Yet another important piece is the transformation of place over time and the time related memory linked to this.

If we therefore consider the urban spaces as a synthesis of form, time and social practise (Soja 1996) the case study contains a number of applicable data and descriptions:

The architectural analyses give a picture of the physical context, of the shape, orientation and spatial linkages. Furthermore, they give an image of architectural content regarding materials, colours and compositions of plinths, flights of stairs and seating possibilities.
The case study also contains an *indication of time and change*, through historical descriptions of the transformation of these spaces from railway tracks and wasteland, into new urban spaces with new functions and programmes.

Observations in situ provide definite knowledge about how the urban spaces are *occupied and used* by different user groups. The observations show the employment of the urban spaces by the users, among other things how young students use the large and small spaces, how cyclists act etc. The observations show both the *interaction of the users* with each other and their interaction with the performative elements in the urban spaces, such as the sound-wells, the water-wall and the mists of vapour.

The subject of discussion is performative urban space, which may derive from the theatre and its world of artistically staged performance, but it is not an actual artistic performance. The squares are not the result of a work of art, but of a design process, which has the aim of creating space for everyday life. Thus the children's play with the mist does not show a scene from the theatre world, but on the contrary a scene from daily life. It shows how children through their play forget themselves and physically experience the space and the mist. Via their interaction with both underlay and mist they create their own space with its own rules (Rasmussen 1957). The older man is a spectator to the scene, like the researcher. Each of them creates images of the atmosphere in the space.

Even though performative architecture and urban design set the stage for the experiences to be created through personal interaction, it is nevertheless essential for architects and urban planners to know what creates the aesthetic experience and how projects and works are perceived. In the process of clarifying this rather vague question, inspiration can be found, among other places, in the phenomenological work by Merleau-Ponty.. With perception as one of his main fields, Merleau-Ponty draws attention to the importance of our senses as the way through which we experience our surroundings. At the same time he considers the senses as a significant part of the body. This implies that individuals do not only experience, but also actually create space and their surroundings via the body and the senses. The bodily presence creates and defines space. The space acquires significance and meaning (Merleau-Ponty 1994). Solbjerg Plads acquires meaning for the two cycling boys, through their playful exploration of the coverings and performative elements of the space. They create their own space.

Furthermore, the mood can influence the experience. As we also saw in the case study regarding how the lighting of trees and water created a new change of backdrop. The users were different and so was the atmosphere. Many artists and architects work consciously with creating a particular ambience or mood. In his research related to mood as aesthetic concept, Gernot Böhme defines atmosphere as follows:

"Atmosphere is something between the subject and the object, therefore an aesthetic of atmosphere must mediate between the aesthetic of reception and the aesthetic of the product or the production."
(Böhme 1998)

Atmospheres fill spaces and places. They can be highlighted with many different adjectives, like a joyful atmosphere, tense, sad, obscure etc. In other words, we experience atmospheres as:

"Quasi-objective, whose existence we also can communicate with others. Yet they cannot be defined independently from the persons emotionally affected by them; they are subjective facts." (Böhme 1998)

Even so, many architectural studios still attempt to create designs which promote certain atmospheres, or where the spatial experience, the view or the experience of a detail are pre-determined. Research involving more systematic mapping of parts of the urban atmosphere in the form of smell and noise are also well known. In the field of geography researchers for instance map 'smell scapes' in different urban places and neighbourhoods (Porteous 1985), while others focus on sound scapes. In the field of psychology a new approach to how we as humans experience the urban environment has it own field called urban psychology with an interdisciplinary theoretical approach (Valsiner 2004).

Conclusion

As we saw in the case study, atmosphere can be produced via intentional designs and via different arrangements with sound, light and water. This is performative urban design, as it is understood in this article. The designer has worked with different moods and experiences of moods. Some are free and others more regulated and orchestrated. The physical form and architecture of a place can be revealed, its historical transformation can be traced and presented, just as behaviour can be observed and recorded.

It is difficult to give an adequate picture of how the individual experiences place bodily and in terms of atmosphere, however it is possible to reach an understanding through personal storytelling about the place supported by photos, films, poetry etc. It is also possible to reach an understanding by using a mix of approaches. In this article an analytical approach developed by Edward Soja has been used. It involved architectural analyses, observations in situ and indications of time and change.

The case study in this article has been done in connection with the research project Experience City – hybrid culture projects and performative urban spaces 2007 – 2011.

References

Augé, M. (1995) *Non-places – An introduction to Supermodernity*. New York: Verso.

Böhme, G. (1994) ´Atmosphere as an Aesthetic Concept´. In: *Daidalos: Architecture Art Culture*: Constructing Atmosphere, # 68 June 1998: 112-116.

Goffman, E. (1966) *Behaviour in Public Places: Notes on the Social Organisation of Gatherings*. New York: The Free Press.

Hajer, M. and Reijndorp, A. (2001) *In Search of new Public Domain*. Rotterdam: NAI Publishers.

Ifversen, K. (2010) ´Plads til forførelse´. In: *Politiken*, October 1.

Kiib, H. (ed.) (2010) *Performative Urban Design*. Aalborg: Aalborg University Press.

Marling, G. (2003) *Urban songlines - hverdagslivets drømmespor*. Aalborg: Aalborg University Press.

Marling, G. (2005) *Urban Songlines – Lifestyle, Urban Spaces & Territories*. Aalborg: Department of Architecture & Design # 3, Aalborg University.

Marling, G., Kiib, H. and Jensen, O. B. (2008) ´Designing the Experience City – the role of hybrid cultural Projects´. In Marling, G. (Ed.) *Designing the Experience City*. Trondheim: Nordic Journal for Architectural Research, 1.

Marling, G., Kiib, H. and Jensen, O. B. (2008) *Experience city.dk*. Aalborg: Aalborg University Press.

Marling, G. and Kiib, H. (2011) *Instant City@Roskilde Festival*. Aalborg: Aalborg University Press.

Merleau-Ponty, M. (1994) *Kroppens Fænomenologi*. Copenhagen: Det lille Forlag.

Porteous, D. (1985) ´Smell Scapes´. In: *Progress in Physical Geography*, 9 (3): 356-378.

Rasmussen, S. E. (1957) *Om at opleve arkitektur*. Copenhagen: Arkitektens Forlag.

Soja, E. W. (1996) *Third space. Journeys to Los Angeles and Other Real-and-Imagined Places*. Oxford: Blackwell Publishers.

Valsiner, J. (2004) ´The Street´. In: *KHORA II #5: Mind Land & Society*. Barcelona: Escuela Tecnica Superior de Architectura de Barcelona.

Interviews

Interviews with architect Stig L. Andersson and art historian Martin Søberg, SLA arkitekter, May 14, 2008.

Interview with chief gardener Karsten Klintø, Frederiksberg Kommune, June 4, 2008.

A Case Study of Mediated Urban Architecture: Red Pavilion 2010

Esben Skouboe Poulsen, Hans Jørgen Andersen, Ole B. Jensen & Mads Brath Jensen

Introduction

Today the city has become the dominant 'scenery' for everyday life, as such it presents even greater design challenges for an improved urban spatial performance. In particular we are interested in a social performance of public architecture that explores how an extended mediated architectural expression can afford, or inspire, people to engage differently in everyday life settings. We acknowledge that today's urban spaces are sites of movement and interaction that hold underutilized potentials (Jensen 2009), (Jensen 2010b), and that public spaces are 'stages' for a multitude of interactions (Goffman 1959). By exploring how such 'stages' are used in terms of human social practice and occupancy patterns we can get an idea of both what sites are used for, as well as how they may be enriched by a changing program, redirecting flows or proposing new social interaction affordances. An understanding of interaction practice and choreography will allow us to enter into discussions on how different mediated urban environments 'stage' everyday interaction practices in public space. By approaching performance space from an analytical and experimental perspective, we can explore new situationally and interactionally sensitive approaches to urban design (Jensen 2006), (Jensen 2010a).

As a secondary research trajectory the authors of this paper were key actors in the design and realisation of the experimental stage Red Pavilion (figure 1). The design initiative challenges parametric design practice (Woodbury 2010), and the development of new digital design tools to sketch and realize advanced geometries using automated computational techniques. This design strategy addresses geometries as informed design systems (Brandt 2010), consequently presenting new questions of structural and geometrical performance qualities (Kolarevic and Malkawi 2005). To enrich the link between the overall social visions, it was essential to link the parametric architectural concept, with one of mediated social performance. To meet these challenges a double-layered grid structure solution was developed. The depth of the grid and the steel pyramids were controlled by a low surface in relation to the position of the projector, increasing the projection area. The steel pyramid component was perforated on one side allowing light emitted from the exterior and the interior to blend creating interesting relations and light effects. Furthermore the parametric model was key in the control and effectiveness of the CNC-manufacturing technique.

Social Atmospheres in Public Spaces

"The atmosphere is like a cloud hanging in the air, which has the potential for changing your mood" (Böhme 2011)

In continuation of philosopher Gernot Bohme's metaphor of atmosphere as a cloud hanging in space, we see potential for constructively affecting the social characteristics of the "cloud". As the cloud reflects temperature, humidity, smell, light intensities, sounds, it also reflects social mechanisms such as group pressure, engagement, sadness etc. We must acknowledge that the experience of atmosphere has an emergent nature and is partly man-made. Everyone in the space persistently shapes the atmosphere (some more than others), therefore we can approach atmosphere as a construction, and we can thereby introduce a more or less socially *productive* atmosphere - producing certain kinds of preferred conditions. Hence architecture organises the boundaries of public space, thereby framing or staging everyday life, it becomes an essential character in the shaping of public atmosphere. Traditional architects have a series of tools to affect the atmosphere of a public space, but often the tools are bound to a material reality. However new dynamic light technologies allow architecture to perform in different ways (Kolarevic, Malkawi 2005), (Kronenburg 2007). In the experimental Red Pavilion, the authors set out to explore how different performance protocols could afford more or less social interaction.

To approach social relations in public spaces is a complex affair. In order to frame the methodology, the authors have employed observation techniques inspired by the sociologist Erving Goffman (1959). These observations should indicate if different performance protocols could affect social relations between people. In Goffman's writings he describes how people constantly radiate social cues, and how we constantly interpret these signals to calibrate and adapt ours in response. These mechanisms are practiced as a series of events of micro exchange during our everyday mobility ride though the city. We constantly fade in and out of small temporal groups also called 'mobile withs' (Jensen 2010b), (Jensen forthcoming 2013), producing temporal social enclaves of togetherness e.g., waiting, sitting, shopping etc. To make life easier, we have developed a range of different interactional rituals or nonverbal languages, which allows us to practice and communicate intentions without speaking. It is by reading and understanding these social signals we can adapt our behaviour in relations to the situation. The process is a kind of second order interaction, described by Goffman as a face saving practice. He believes that because we are aware that others expect a certain kind of behaviour and because we do not want to lose face or see others lose face, we behave in a certain way (Goffman 1959). Exchange happens in this kind of double interaction presenting interactions in public space as an important social phenomenon. It is this *sidewalk ballet*, where dancers constantly feel each other's position to make the best possible next act (Jacobs 1961) we can observe from a distance, and it is this practice we often refer to as the real culture of a place. Goffman uses the theatrical metaphor of front stage performance to describe how we vary detailed work to underline our social roles: "Front is the expressive equipment of a standard kind intentionally or unwittingly employed by the individual during his performance." (Goffman 1959) Our front includes: insignia of office or rank, clothing, sex, age and racial characteristics, size and looks, posture, speech patterns, facial expressions, bodily gestures, and the like (Goffman 1959). It is by receiving and sending these signals we can navigate through our everyday social life. Erving Goffman calls this social dynamism role-plays (Goffman 1959) and he describe how we constantly adapt to the situation - how we practice different 'masks' or take different roles to adapt to a specific social situation. It is this framework of interaction rituals and face practices we can observe from a distance.

Experimental Setup

The pavilion site was situated on the edge of the newly renovated harbour front in the centre of Aalborg, Denmark. As an example of a typical Danish September day, the climate was windy, cloudy and the temperature fluctuated between 10 degrees at night to 22 degrees during the day. By placing 2 shell structures towards the west and southeast, the pavilion became a shelter from the wind and established a more private stage space opening up towards the fjord and the sunset. Five seating arrangements and a stage furnished the interior of the pavilion, while projectors, computers, loudspeakers and interior lighting made up the media toolbox of the building. The site was located in a flow trajectory where people passed by hand-in-hand or in their individual catwalk poses. The site was also located in the centre of the city - one of the preferred ex-

1: THE PAVILION, VIOLIN PLAYER AND ELECTRONIC MUSICIAN PRESENT MUSIC WHILE A VJ PAINTS THE SHELLS WITH COLOURS

cursions in Aalborg. On sunny days it is a very popular place because of the water and the small public park. However the site placed on the edge of central flow lines connects the harbour front with the centre of the city. The space encapsulated by the 2 shell structures became a semi-private pool very close to the primary flow lines, and as such it had great potential to communicate with a wide range of people passing by, and maybe offering intimate, sheltered spaces.

The 2 shell structures were placed as shown in illustration figure 2.

As illustrated on the map, seating facilities were distributed in a circle of 8 meters around the scene; some were placed sheltered from the western wind, and some placed with a view to the water. The orientation affords very short distances between performer and spectator, which facilitates an intimate frame for the performances. As shown on the drawing, 2 projector towers were placed to illuminate the 2 shell structures from the exterior. Furthermore a *Digital Mapping* - a process of overlaying physical structures with detailed mapped projections was carried out on the mem-

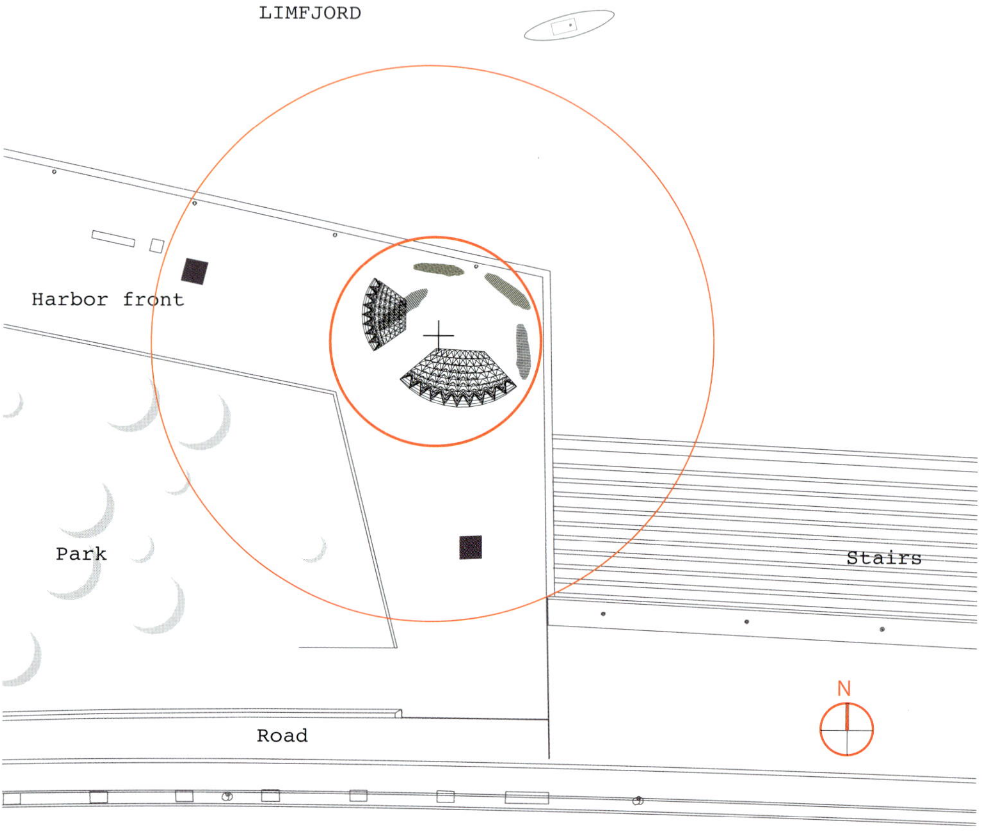

2: PLAN OF SPATIAL LAYOUT FOR THE RED PAVILION

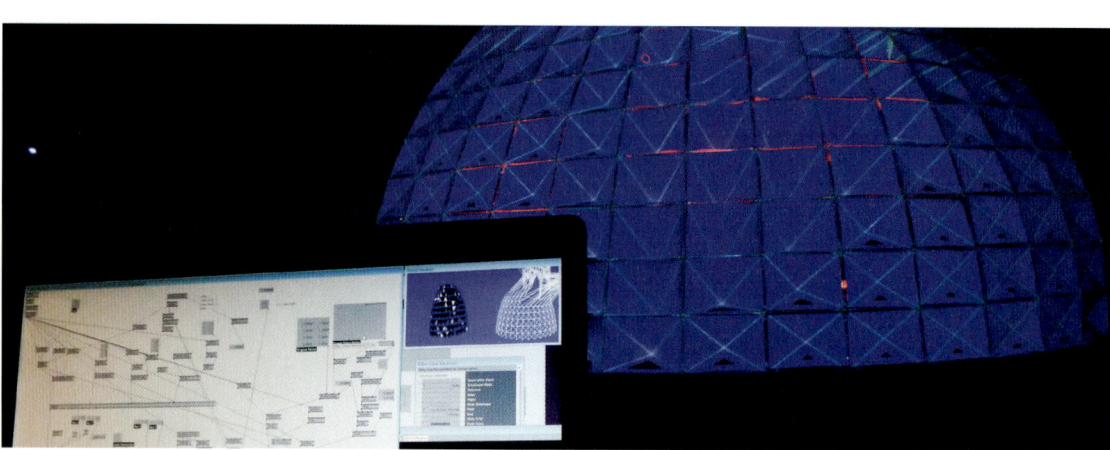

3: EVERY FACE IS ILLUMINATED INDIVIDUALLY

branes using software and allowing for very detailed dynamic light control of each face. Furthermore 5 multi-coloured luminaires illuminated the shell structures from the inside, producing an interesting blend effect between interior and exterior lighting. (See figure 4) The pavilion became a performance instrument for dynamic light performance as well as music performances during the day. The integrated design solution between structure and exterior and interior lighting allowed light designers to dynamically change the shape and colour of the pyramids causing interesting animated patterns. Sometimes a dynamic light designer would develop generative graphic patterns in relation to the music. (See figure 4) Now it was essential to study how different people adapted to the changing musical and architectural performance.

To approach the experimental challenge, exploring how public architecture can afford more socio-productive spaces, the experiment investigated 3 different architectural performance settings: participatory, performing and idle.

- Participatory setting: A musician developed a show inviting passers-by to be part of the musical performance and thereby create a collaborative musical composition that would afford a strong feeling of attachment among the performers. Furthermore we anticipated that more extrovert-oriented people would participate in the creation of the musical event, while others would observe from a distance.

- Performing stage setting: A musician and a dancer were placed very close to the passing audience, as such building a scenography where spectators could observe an intimate relation between musician and dancers, and fellow occupants. The intimate performance would make people stop and the architectural performance would be a catalyst of new 'withs' and an object for discussion, ultimately producing a new discourse.

- Idle state: No human actors, but autonomous changing light patterns on the membrane in relation to ambient music and the activity levels of people.

Observations

In situations without music performance, the semi-private seating facilities became a small inlet in the primary flow space. People stopped and used the seating facilities, they consumed their home brought bread or took a sip of a cold beer - seen from the flow path it became an intimate space where people rested from the very hectic and public life. As seen in figure 5, the three meter wide opening between the 2 shells be-

4: LIGHT PATTERNS AND INTERIOR LIGHT

5: A VIEW FROM THE PARK

6: NIGHTLIFE IN THE PAVILION

7: COLLABORATIVE MUSIC EVENT

came essential. When people passed the pavilion 'this place' afforded the first experience of life inside the shells. It became the place to get the answer to *"what is going on here?"* This then was the place to decide at which level you wanted to perform; ignoring the activities, keeping your distance as a spectator or moving into the semi-private zone being part of the 'mobile with' of the setting. When musical performances were happening, this was also the place to decide the level of participation you would engage in.

The different spatial zones shifted dramatically according to climatic conditions, e.g., excessive wind, rain or low temperatures. Not surprisingly the urban microclimates presented different determining factors for social interactions, the dynamics in the pavilion changed dramatically when the climate changed. A kind of urban 'dress code' was experienced, with small jackets, umbrellas and very impractical shoes – the clothes were designed to keep the rain, cold and wind out for as long as took to run to the nearest café. The relationship between urban microenvironments and comfort zones were not systematically annotated, but the need for such a study was acknowledged, as it could help to qualify better planning strategies in the future.

When the sun slowly slid under the horizon in the west the artificial lights were turned on. The shells changed their expression from the white and clean structure to a mediated structure of colours, giving the skin of the pavilion its own life and causing dramatic effects in the 'image' of the pavilion. The light could be seen from a distance and it was evident that people changed their route to study the newly illuminated structure at close hand. When approaching the illuminated pavilion the common reaction was to touch the membrane in order to try to understand *'how it worked'*. It was not an atmosphere that afforded play, but more of a silent fascination, or an investigating atmosphere where people used the situation as a photo opportunity. Normally people spent 10-15 minutes in and around the pavilion before continuing on along the harbor front.

During the experiment 2 kinds of musical performances were carried out in the pavilion: *a traditional musical performance and a participatory musical performance*. It was essential to study the role-play dynamisms in the two different types of social atmospheres. The participatory event was a daytime performance. One musician and 10 young girls from the local church choir were musical mediators and they used the steel structure itself, as well as waste steel from its construction, as percussive instruments to make rhythmical 'stump'-like music. It became almost like a *ritual*, where people passing by could choose their role in the tribe. Some people engaged directly, while others needed time to adapt or synchronize to the atmosphere. But it was evident that the 'natural' route into the participatory performance was through the different steps of participatory hierarchy: from the distant spectator getting an overview, to the active dancer making a significant contribution to the collective experience of the space. In figure 7 one can see a dancing lady in the center of the picture. It turned out that she was a visiting tourist and a professional dancer. She suggested contributing to the event as a spontaneous initiative and became a significant contribution to the performance. As a result of her initiative more passers-by gathered their courage to change roles from being a distant spectator to an active participant in the dance performance. As such, the space afforded engagement and participation, during the time the musician and 10 young girls guided the event – their actions became mediators for the spatial performance, and one could ask if mediated architecture would have these qualities?

During the nighttime performance a Visual Jockey (VJ) used projectors and laminators to create a very detailed digital overlay on the pavilion's physical structure. Combined with the soundscape, the light patterns had a significant impact on the atmosphere by 'painting' the experience and the aesthetic character of the space. People stopped to study the structure, moving around it to see how the interior and the exterior light

9: AVANT-GARDE AND 'STRANGE' DANCE PERFORMANCE PRESENTED AN EXCLUSIVE ATMOSPHERE

10: THE PAVILION AND AALBORG HARBOR FRONT

melted together. Many people went very close to touch the metal faces and to investigate the light source. Throughout the experiment period, the pavilion was the subject of extensive examination and the focus of many talks and wonderings. Also, the different light patterns as well as the performer's skills in animating and impressing the crowd challenged the aesthetic taste of the visitors. The coloured light was visible at a distance of up to a kilometer and thereby attracted people from a far distance. The detailed mapped dynamic light patterns and the coloured light affected the amount of time peoples were in the space, it also made people stop on the street, driver slower in their cars, make a spontaneous stop on the bike. The question arises whether some of the findings from the daytime participatory scenario could be implemented into the mediated architectural concept, thus using light as a mediator for different and new types of participatory and engaging urban spaces.

Conclusion

The case study of the Red Pavilion 2010 shows that by manipulating light and soundscape around a piece of temporary urban architecture, one can affect and shape the atmosphere dramatically, thereby presenting new trajectories for role-play in public spaces. Indeed the mediated architecture has proven to hold a significant social potential as a central driver for participatory events. In the experiment musicians, dancers and light designers contributed to the creation of three very different performance protocols; hence they intuitively were able to closely navigate the feelings and moods of the crowd. As a part of the participatory session, we observed how passers-by spontaneously took different roles motivated by the performance protocol; occupants became more engaged in the production of the temporary atmosphere, hence they became active contributors in creating sounds, some even took the role of dancer on the public stage. Generally we observed how extroverted people took part in the performance and how more introverted people assumed the role of observers, but also how people (on the fly) could decide to change roles from spectator to performer and become a co-producer of the event. These social dynamics afforded a tribe-like behaviour, creating a strong temporary 'with' (Goffman 1959). In the case of the performance stage setting, people did, as we anticipated, take the role of observers. The performing character of the event did cause many different people to stop, look at each other and exchange a smile, shake their heads or clap; hence the performing urban stage became a mediator for micro exchanges, events which would not have happened without the setup. We can conclude that urban architecture through the means of stage activities can create meaningful events. On the basis of these studies we can also conclude that the window between private and public spaces is of significant importance. It is in this window people group and where decisions are made about roles and engagements – the *first impression* of the architectural space. In the last case of the Idle state (figure 6), it is apparent that dynamic lighting relating to the level of occupancy is something many from Aalborg never had seen before. We can conclude that the object became the reason for many pointing gestures, exchanges of words, conversations, touching and photographing. Many people used their Smartphone to take snapshots and some even presented them as profile pictures on Facebook (see figure 13). One could say that the role-play continues into the networked social realm and that the architecture extends the experienced effect as a symbol of life into the edge of the avant-garde. The dynamic illuminated pavilion became an object of concern and the mediated quality of the lighting did add a significant quality to the experience of the harbour front - something 'new' and a challenge for people to comprehend, which

11: WINDOW IN BETWEEN PERFORMANCE SPACE AND FLOW SPACE

is why we could observe all the attention, photo shootings and spontaneous stopping in front of the pavilion. Hence the pavilion presented a 'news' value, on the everyday mobility ride, but maybe most important is the fact that we observed how changing light made people reflect differently on the environment and question the logic and materiality of response.

After the experiment was finalised and the pavilion was removed from the harbour front, however, evidence of the building can still be witnessed. By coincidence, Google's Streetview photo-car technology drove by the pavilion under the construction phase – consequently making the temporary experiment of the Red Pavilion part of the global image of Aalborg City (figure 12). The pavilion is now displayed every time potential tourists take a virtual walk down the streets of Aalborg's' new harbour front.

Future Challenges and Discussions

This short article presents initial case studies of public architecture that acts in relation to 3 performance protocols; hence this is a prototype enforcing human actors to take the roles of mediators. But in scenarios in the near future, we might see architecture that senses the temporary atmosphere and self-organises its performance protocol appropriately. If we, through the use of sensor technologies, can develop automated systems that can track certain atmospheres, then we open up new possibilities for design strategies that respond. One could think of different tools and techniques that could be utilised to instrumentalise architecture as a social catalyst that affords more exchange, use and creates more specific architectural expressions, which underline, emphasise or contrast the existing atmosphere. However quantifying a subjective phenomenon as atmospheres is part of our future challenges. In relation to the participatory setting, we could see that some people did enjoy the collaborative effort, and that it did formalise tribe-like behaviours. This social quality of collaboration among strangers or groups of strangers is unique and does motivate new ways of thinking urban performance space as a place where some people actually want to express themselves in relation to others. In the case of Red Pavilion, a musician did mediate the relations, but one can ask if we could imagine an architectural performance which developed collaborative events such as games, music etc.?

In relation to the stage-setting scenario, one could speculate on an architectural infrastructure that automatically mobilised the many actors in the city to utilise public space as a showroom. Can one imagine a public stage setting where local actors book 'show-times' like they book training sessions in the gym, utilising architecture as a public stage to mobilise expressions and cultures on the street?

In the case of the idle scenario we find the mediated materiality very interesting to investigate further. We believe that only the top of the iceberg has been seen and new responsive strategies have the capacity to underline or complement atmospheric characteristics in the field of architectural studies. This will open up the theoretical toolbox to interaction design and visions such as the 'open work' presented by Umberto Eco (Eco 1989). If light and media content are not only something we present on screens, but use information as dynamic performance qualities embedded into the lighting or the décor of the building, then media architects could begin to develop tools and methodologies that allow for new participatory architectural performances in public spaces.

Acknowledgements

The authors would like to thank the following people and organisations for support during the project: Visual artist Sune Petersen, Musicians: Dan Overholt and Christian Skjødt, Architecture and Design students: Thiru Manickam, Kenn Clausen, Aste Ploug Henriksen, Jens Jakob Møller Pedersen, Aalborg Municipality, Martin Light Professional and colleagues on Electrotexture Lab. and Aalborg University.

References

Albrecht, K. (2006) *Social intelligence: the new science of success*. San Francisco: Jossey-Bass Press.

Brandt, R. (2010) *Design informed: driving innovation with evidence-based design*. Hoboken, New Jersey: John Wiley & Sons.

Benfold, B. and Reid, I. (2009) ´Guiding Visual Surveillance by Tracking Human Attention`. In: *Proceedings of the 20th British Machine Vision Conference*. London, U.K.

Böhme, G. (2011) 'Urban Atmospheres: Concept and Criticism of Making Atmospheres'. In *Atmospheres, Architecture, and Urban Space: New Conceptions of Management and the Social*, Conference at the Department of Management, Politics and Philosophy, Copenhagen Business School (author's notes).

Eco, U. (1989) ´The Poetics of the Open Work`. In: *The Open Work*. Cambridge Massachusetts: Harvard University Press, 1-24.

Goffman, E. (1959). *The presentation of self in everyday life*. Garden City, NY: Doubleday Anchor Books.

Goffman, E. (1967) *Interaction ritual: essays on face-to-face behaviour*. Harmondsworth: Penguin.

Hall, E. (1973) *The silent language*. New York: Doubleday Anchor Books.

Jacobs, J. (1961) *The death and life of great American cities*. New York: Random House.

Jensen, O. B. (2006) ´Facework, Flow and the City: Simmel, Goffman, and Mobility in the Contemporary City`. In: *Mobilities*, 1 (2): 143-165.

Jensen, O. B. (2009) ´Flows of meaning, cultures of movement - urban mobility as meaningful everyday life practice`. In: *Mobilities*, 4 (1): 139-158.

Jensen, O. B. (2010a). ´Erving Goffman and Everyday Life Mobility`. In: Jacobsen, M. (Ed.) *The Contemporary Goffman*. New York: Routledge.

Jensen, O. B. (2010b) ´Negotiation in Motion: Unpacking a Geography of Mobility`. In: *Space and Culture*. 13 (4): 389 402.

Jensen, O. B. (2013) ´Staging Mobilities`. In: *Mobility*. 4 (4): 139-158.

Kronenburg, R. (2007) *Flexible: Architecture That Responds to Change*. London: Laurence King.

Kolarevic, B. and Malkawi, A. (2005) *Performative architecture: beyond instrumentality*. New York: Spon Press.

Whyte, H. (1988) *City. Rediscovering the Centre*. Philadelphia: University of Pennsylvania Press.

Woodbury, R. (2010) *Elements of Parametric Design*. London: Routledge.

12: SCREENSHOT FROM GOOGLE MAPS

13: PROFILE PICTURE FROM FACEBOOK

Kulturator 27 - A Time-Based Design

Mikkel Stensgaard & Simon Wind

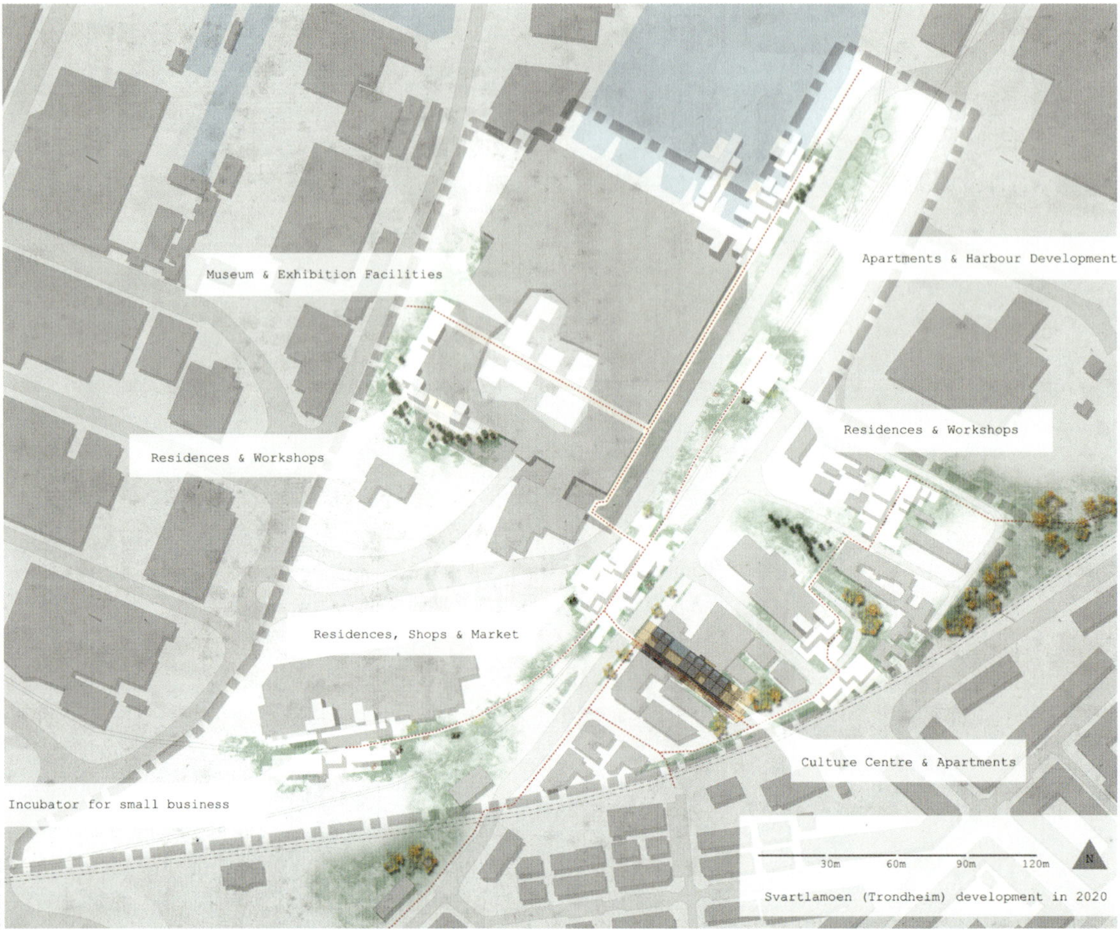

SITE PLAN

This master thesis took its point of departure in the EUROPAN 10 competition and a site located in Trondheim, Norway. The scope of the competition was an architectural solution for a small infill site and an urban solution for the whole project area. The vision of the project was to strengthen the cultural environment at the project area in Trondheim and to create a new cultural institution intertwined with dwellings through a time based urban acupuncture strategy. Through the project different themes such as time based design, revitalization of the harbor, and wood as a sustainable building material have been processed.

SOUTH FACADE OF KULTURATOR 27 DEVELOPMENT

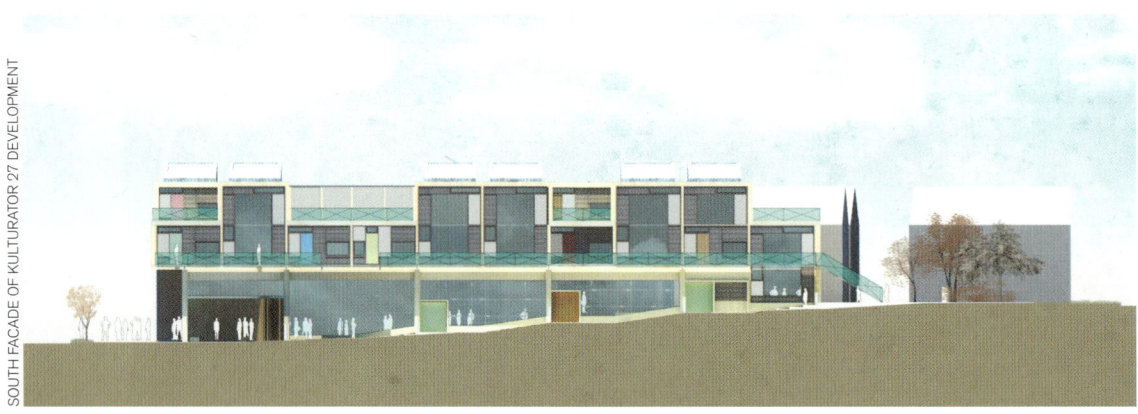

A FRAMEWORK FOR CULTURE - INTERIOR SPACES OF KULTURATOR 27

KULTURATOR 27 IN ITS' PHYSICAL CONTEXT

Selected student project / Master Thesis 2009 / Supervisor: Lasse Andersson
Performativity

Encountering Chernobyl - design interventions in the city of Pripyat
Daniel Bejtrup & Dina Brændstrup

NATURE TAKING OVER

The project introduced seven design interventions in the city of Pripyat where 50,000 inhabitants were evacuated after the explosion in reactor 4 at the Chernobyl nuclear power plant in April, 1986. The area has in recent years become more open to visitors and tourists. Through research, analysis and a theoretical discussion, we defined our vision for the area: to emphasise the social and environmental consequences that followed the accident. The intention with the designs is to enhance the visitors' physical and bodily experience when visiting the city - urging them to reflect, wonder and question the course and extent of the accident.

DESOLATION

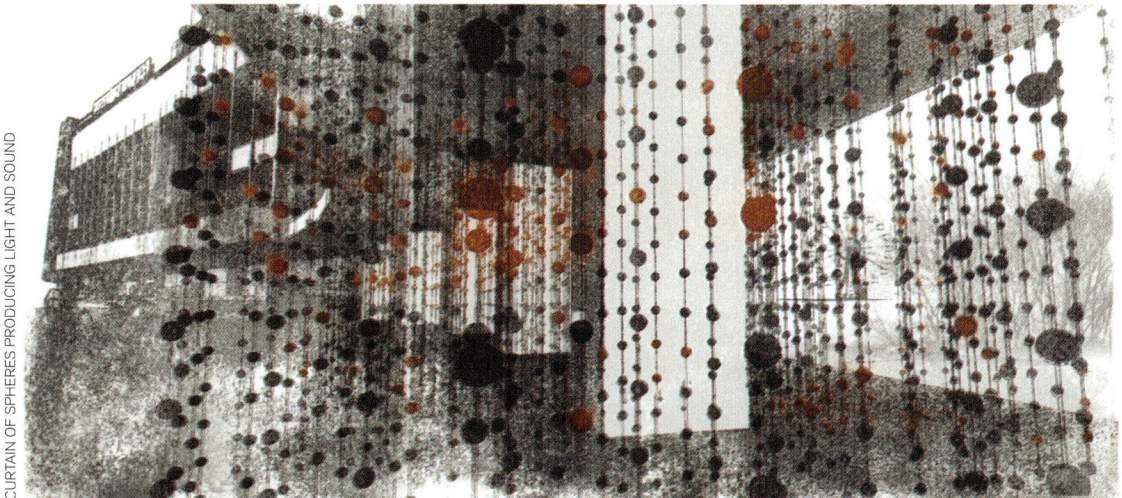
CURTAIN OF SPHERES PRODUCING LIGHT AND SOUND

CIRCULATION PATH THROUGH AND AROUND THE DESERTED 16-STOREY HOUSING BLOCK LEADING TO A VIEW INTO AND OVER THE DESOLATION

Selected student project / Master Thesis 2010 / Supervisor: Gitte Marling
Performativity

The Sensuous Stories of Urban Space
Helena Kaae

The project puts forward a concept for Randers harbour pier and an urban spatial design that generates sensuous experiences based on the stories of the river, the valley and the harbour. By exploiting the stories of the place itself as points of departure for the urban spatial design, an identity specific to the place is promoted. The atmosphere is experienced by the person, and the sensuous experiences emphasize the relationship between person and place. Greenery, water, materials, lighting and the relation between these plus the changeability which time and weather contribute, are used as tools to develop the sensuous experiences and stories of the place.

PLAN VIEW OF THE NEW URBAN SPACES, RANDERS HARBOUR PIER

DEVELOPMENT PLAN

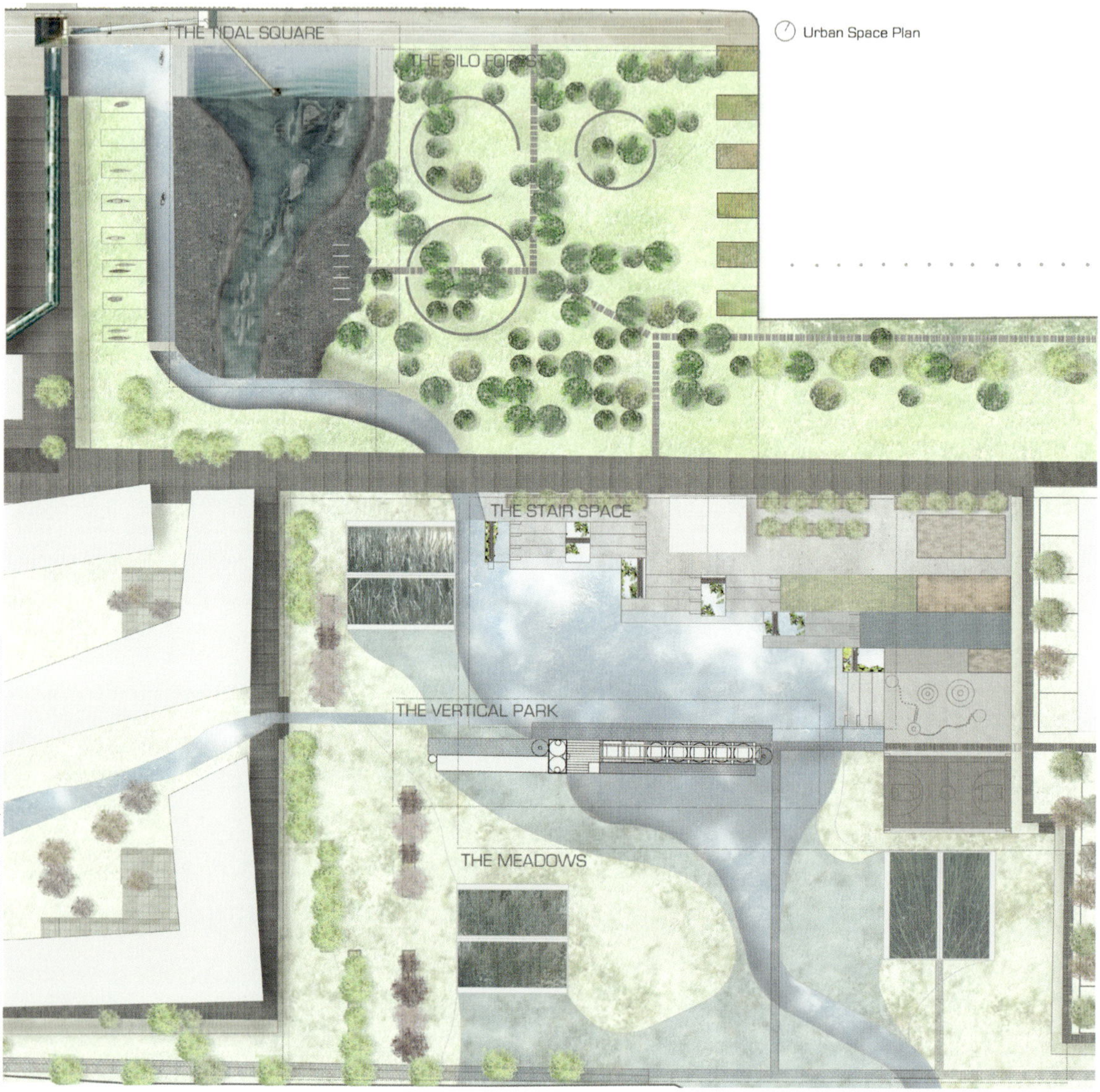

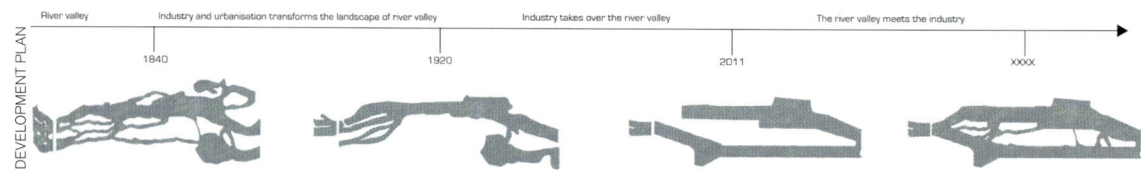

VIEW OF THE TIDAL SQUARE

SPACES OF THE VERTICAL PARK

Selected student project / Master Thesis 2011 / Supervisor: Gitte Marling
Performativity

Lindholm Strandpark - a cultural hub in Aalborg
Nicolai Hagbarth Hansen

Based on visual and material references to Aalborg's industrial port, a park has been created which underlines the division between the park and the fjord. This division is made by laying a grid over the park/fjord overlap area within which volumes are determined, realized and varied. These volumes in the context of this project can be seen as concrete columns and surfaces you can move between and on, and are 'centred' around a Cultural building. As juxtaposition to the concrete columns a cherry orchard is planted and when you move through the area between the cherry trees and the concrete columns, where the natural axes are located on the site, you will see how the Cultural building forms the Point de Vue.

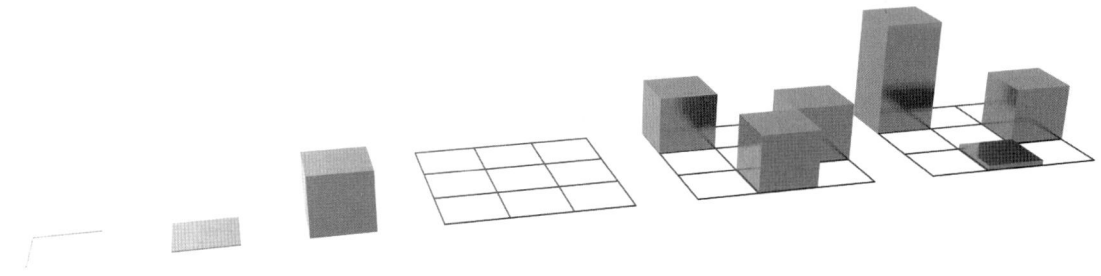

CONCEPT

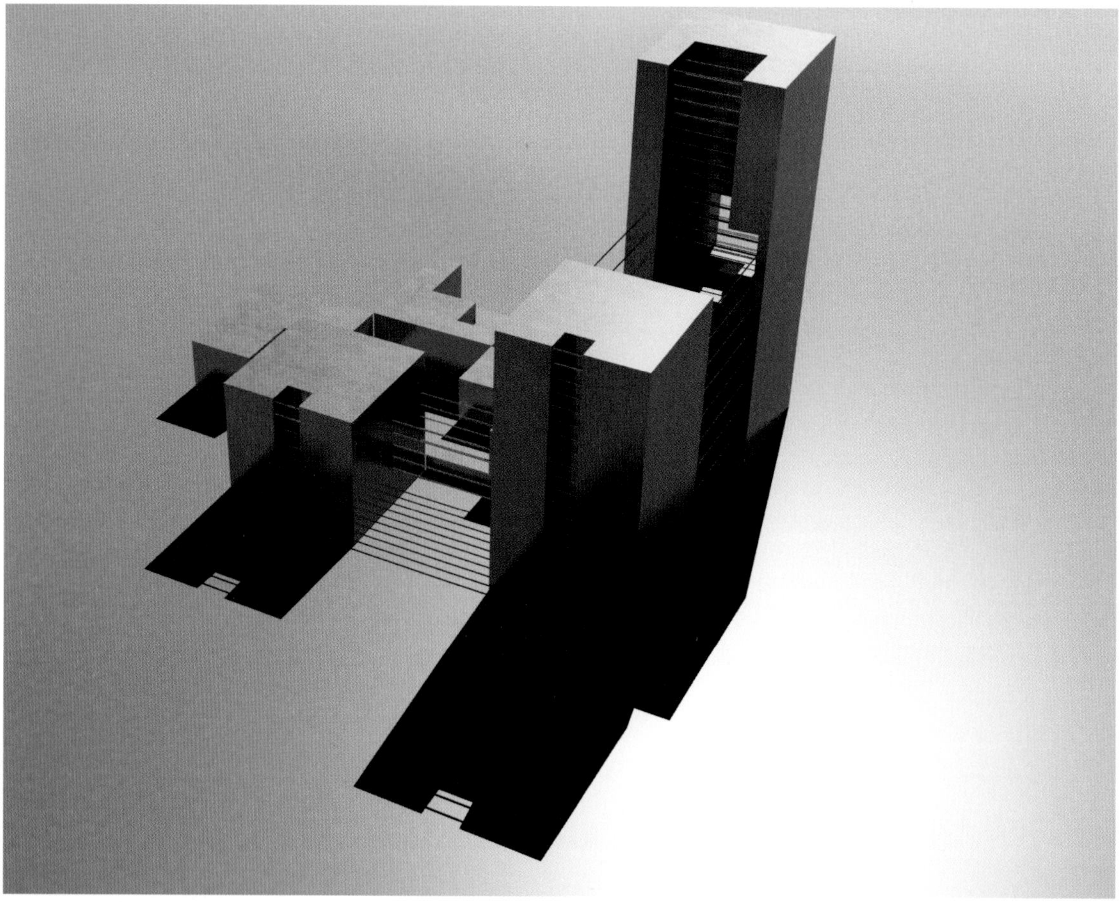

PARKOUR STRUCTURE

SITE PLAN

CULTURAL LANDSCAPE TO BE MOVED ON, IN AND THROUGH

Selected student project / 3rd BSc 2010 / Supervisor: Shelley Smith
Performativity

Bumps in the Road – mobility and spatial experience through the lens of parkour
Shelley Smith

ACT I: Road map
The Urban Mobile

Contemporary urbanity is characterised by a number of factors: globalisation, dissolving borders, sprawl, large scale – but involved in, if not the cause of all of these, is mobility. Mobility has reigned supreme in the effect it has had on urban development – not only in regard to the physical environment, but also regarding the mental environs of our self understanding. Our built environment is comprised of larger and larger areas, many of which are sparsely filled, and through which we move and travel. The organization and planning of our urban settlements is dictated to by the structuring of our infrastructure. These are areas so vast that we are most often dependent on 'movement assistance' in our traversing of them. And our mental mobility allows us, in this contemporary urban society, to see ourselves in a myriad of different roles, settings and situations – often simultaneously. However, mobility has also challenged the everyday spaces of the urban and how we live, act, react, interact in – and with - the built environment – and ultimately how we experience it.

This article will examine how the concept of space and the perception and experience of space have been altered by contemporary urban development, particularly as characterised by mobility, and how the art of movement – i.e. parkour - can be used as a lens through which to view this and a point from which to discuss experiential potential.

Our Spatially Challenged Existence

"Much of the ambiguity of the term 'space' in modern architectural use comes from a willingness to confuse it with a general philosophical category of 'space'. To put it slightly differently, as well as being a physical property of dimension and extent, 'space' is also a property of the mind, part of the apparatus through which we perceive the world." (Forty 2000: 256)

Without a doubt the 'dimension and extent' of space has increased as a result of mobility, but of interest here is what, in the contemporary urban, this change in the cartographic spatial has meant for the perceptual spatial.

Architectural historian and critic Sigfried Giedion's epic Space, Time and Architecture, was first published in 1941. Giedion indicated that as a result of the time-space continuum, the concept of space changed from earlier perceptions and understood models. Moving from spatial perception based on enclosure and the hollowing out of volumes seen as interior space, spatial understanding had moved into more fluid concepts which saw a correlation, and movement, between interior and exterior and which included in the spatial a temporal element. Already here, mobility had begun to change the face of the city and our perception of its spaces.

"Today we must deal with the city from a new aspect, dictated by the advent of the automobile, based on technical considerations, and belonging to the artistic vision born out of our period – space-time." (Giedion 1941 (1967): 822)

The artistic vision Giedion refers to is that of Cubism, which represented a radical departure from the perspective dominated spatial perception that had prevailed for centuries. Cubism linked space with time through a simultaneity of views. Giedion's observation of new characteristics involved in the development of the city were further elaborated to perceptual experience:

"The space-time feeling of our period can seldom be so keenly felt as when driving, the wheel under one's hand, up and down hills, beneath overpasses, up ramps, and over giant bridges." (Giedion 1941 (1967): 831)

Giedion spoke of objects and landscape – physical elements which were the objects in time and space. However, since the writing of Time, Space and Architecture, the physical environment has changed significantly. In the contemporary urban landscape, the proportional relationship between vertical and horizontal planes in the city has changed and created a situation in which the force of the vertical plane is diminished in an abundance of horizontality. Contemporary urbanism is thus characterised by a primacy of space rather the more traditional primacy of form which was based on the strength of the architectural gesture. (Pope 1996), (Smith 2003) "As proposed many times, from Garden Cities of Tomorrow, to the New City, to Learning from Las Vegas, to S,M, L, XL, it is not built form which characterised the contemporary city, but the immense spaces over which built form has little or no control. Theses spaces, which overwhelm the architectural gesture, ultimately dominate the contemporary urban environment." (Pope 1996: 2)

1: THE NEED FOR MOVEMENT ASSISTANCE

2: DRIVING

Bumps in the Road - mobility and spatial experience through the lens of parkour
Mobility

57

3A: IN THE ZOOMSCAPE

3B: IN THE ZOOMSCAPE

3C: IN THE ZOOMSCAPE

Giedion spoke of objects and landscape – physical elements which were the objects in time and space. However, since the writing of *Time, Space and Architecture*, the physical environment has changed significantly. In the contemporary urban landscape, the proportional relationship between vertical and horizontal planes in the city has changed and created a situation in which the force of the vertical plane is diminished in an abundance of horizontality. Contemporary urbanism is thus characterised by a *primacy of space* rather the more traditional *primacy of form* which was based on the strength of the architectural gesture. (Pope 1996), (Smith 2003)

> "As proposed many times, from Garden Cities of Tomorrow, to the New City, to Learning from Las Vegas, to S,M, L, XL, it is not built form which characterised the contemporary city, but the immense spaces over which built form has little or no control. Theses spaces, which overwhelm the architectural gesture, ultimately dominate the contemporary urban environment." (Pope 1996: 2)

Contemporary urban form has deviated from traditional patterns of development and this has made it difficult for us to 'think' the city, i.e., to understand it in a physical way, but also as a mental construct of perception. (Pope 1996), (Forty 2000)

We have become estranged from the physical environment in part because our views have become mediated taking place in motion via train, plane or car, or via media, but also because we do not 'see' our surroundings or experience them in ways that entail an interface with them.

Much of the urban environment is taken for granted, either because there is so much of it that it exceeds comprehension (Smith 2003), or because the focus has changed and it no longer holds meaning for us. The city is seen – or not seen as the case may be - in a removed view – at a distance and without actual contact.

> "...a brutal world of collective neglect, very nearly dropped from the consciousness of its inhabitants. Viewed from the window of a train or plane, on the edges of televised newscasts, or through the ubiquitous windshield, what passes for the city has been not so much forgotten or deliberately ignored as it has remained unseen." (Pope 1996: 2)

These are views based on infrastructural or 'infostructural' vantage points – and given the prevalence of the technologies behind them and our dependence on them, this is the way in which the contemporary city is often seen and most commonly perceived.

This strikes a chord with the notion of Zoomscape (Schwarzer 2004), which describes a situation in which transportation and camera technologies have changed the perception of our physical surroundings. The Zoomscape represents a new perceptual model that, although difficult to define because it contains pretty much everything: architectural pearls, no-name structures, engineering feats, highways and roads, cities, suburbs, skylines, in short, cultural landscapes, it has as one of its key features the disintegration of the building into parts, and as part of the infrastructural network that moderates the views of it.

> "We are experiencing architecture within a technologically expanded visual field – not just as objects in continuous space, but also as variable assemblages in intermittent space." (Schwarzer 2004: 21)

This architectural experience entails a 'liberation' of the built object from its fixivity, its site – but it also entails a 'liberation' from the body, in that sensory perception, most specifically the sense of touch is not present. Instead, the visual is the only sense activated and it is often then at a distance and with speed. (Schwarzer 2004)

> "We have become used to seeing architecture through abrupt shifts of viewpoint and via unexpected juxtapositions. Vehicles zoom our sight across great distances at tremendous velocities. Cameras zoom our sight beyond the capacities of our bodies, and usually rupture the continuum of space and time." (Schwarzer 2004:12)

Returning to Giedion at this juncture, the change between Giedion's time-space continuum experienced while driving through the landscape, on bridges, ramps and overpasses is striking. In the span of fifty odd years we have moved from a perspective rife with the potential of moving through space that resounds with the experience of 'keenly feeling', to a perspective that speaks of a complete lack of contact with and regard for the city, the capacity of the body exceeded, the architectural gesture overwhelmed and a rupture of the time space continuum.

We have moved from the landscape to the Zoomscape. We still need to deal with the city in regards to the automobile and technology, and in regards to time and space in new aspects, but it seems that the increases in urban mobility since Giedion's writing may have occasioned the loss of the perceptual content in their experience. Giedion prefaced the elements of his urban context with a complexity of prepositions that is absent from descriptions of the contemporary picture: Giedion's movement in space is up and down (hills), beneath (overpasses), up (ramps) and over (bridges) (Giedion 1941 (1967): 831), rather than just through. Perhaps the contemporary urban mobile is focussed on time at the exclusion of space.

The focus on time in contemporary urban societies is exemplified through efficient approaches to the urban – in business proposals for types of urban development. The shift to a mobile culture, according John Kasarda, an American business professor who has developed and globally promoted the *aerotropolis* concept – a business plan that encourages urban development based on proximity to aviation sites, has suggested that the age old real estate adage of 'Location! Location! Location!' has now been replaced by that of 'Accessibility! Accessibility! Accessibility!'(Kasarda 2002) Implicit here is the shift from a stationary, defined and static position – from the localizing of location to a spatial flow that focuses not on the interrelationship between time and space, but on the ability to get somewhere and the efficiency with which this can be accomplished.

This is a focus solely on the temporal aspect of mobility, and represents a kind of 'diet' form of movement – one concerned with time reduction, rather than on the experience of moving – or on the spaces moved through. Although it might get you somewhere fast – there is no up and down, no around here - maintaining this focus alone paves the way for an impoverished spatial experience.

In this primacy of space, when the focus is on getting there efficiently, the intention is on the absence of friction, on the desire for seamless movement. Given that the architectural gesture has little effect in the primacy of space, and that contact with the city and sensory experience of the spatial seem to be extremely diminished, one could ask, does seamlessness seems like less? Should all our dealings with the urban be all that smooth and frictionless, or are we missing some of the experiential qualities of space by focussing just on getting through it? Could alternative models of movement give some clues regarding the experience of space in contemporary urbanity?

INTERMEZZO: The Art of Movement - A Bump in the Road

An alternative model and a lens through which to view the contemporary urban situation *characterised* by an abundance of unseen or unexperienced space could be found in *the art of movement* – otherwise known as the practise of parkour.

Parkour entered my theoretical existence quite by chance in 2007 at a GAM3 conference in Copenhagen. The conference addressed Sport in Public Spaces and one of the presenters, Streetmovement, an organisation of parkour practitioners and teachers presented City Surfers - a film they had been a part of making. And there it was, a graphic representation of contemporary urban theory traced in the lines of the art of movement – a representation that accessed a real and physical attachment to urban space that so

4: THE CITY AS 24/7 ARENA FOR MOVEMENT

5: PHYSICAL AND MENTAL – A SENSORY CAPACITY

Bumps in the Road - mobility and spatial experience through the lens of parkour
Mobility

much contemporary theory lacked. Parkour opened up a whole new facet of public space – of real and mobile public space, seen and felt and in need of navigation, and it raised questions especially regarding how we see space, how we use the city and in particular, it challenged stiff and static views of the city and its spaces. In the years since a co-operation has emerged with Streetmovement that interchanges and exchanges practice and theory and that discusses the sensed physicality of urban spatiality.

Inextricably linked to the urban today, the city in its entirety provides the 24/7 framework for the practise of parkour – freeing it from the restraints of opening times and rules dictating types of equipment and usage. The city is always open for business as an arena for movement. The practise of parkour in its urban locality changes the focus, finds a new and not necessarily easier path and has at its core the desire to exceed borders – both spatial and personal - and in an uncanny combination of the 2, becomes itself a spectacle for the observation of space unfolding in new and sensory charged ways.

Parkour is a physical discipline that has become more visible through its exposure in film and YouTube entries of cell phone videos. In this context it is the spectacle of extreme movement that is often highlighted – how high, how far, how dangerous. However, the everyday practise of parkour has a much different focus. Originally developed as a military training method - an obstacle course; *parcours du combattant* – parkour stemmed from a holistic philosophy that took its point of departure in the movements that the human body made naturally e.g., running, jumping, hopping, swinging, walking on all fours, with the main function being that of moving forward. Its' intent was to hone the soldier's ability to negotiate the jungles of Vietnam as efficiently and quickly as possible using what they always had at hand – their own bodies.

Parkour as an urban practise is quite another thing and although forward propulsion by leaping between, and rolling and swinging around urban objects occurs, the body and mind-present experience in the spaces to be traversed is what establishes the core of the practise. Parkour in its more down to earth, everyday form is still inherently based on overcoming barriers – both physical and mental - and in this sense it is mainly concerned with practicality and efficiency in its interaction with the environment – similar to other forms of contemporary mobility. But in the case of parkour, this comes about with the complete involvement of the sensory.

The engagement in both the physical and mental capacity of relating to space makes parkour an interesting optic as it has the ability to address both the cartographic and the perceptual aspects of moving through space - an interrelation with surroundings that covers stances, but that is reliant on the senses. In this regard the alias of parkour, i.e., the art of movement, introduces an aesthetic capacity – and a connection to a sensory approach in that the Greek, *aisthesis* – the etymological root of aesthetics – means to sense.

Parkour turns the stasis of the built environment into flux, into a series of connections between previously unconnected objects, making the once unseen spaces between visible. The *traceur* – the practitioner of parkour – literally *draws* non-programmed routes through the city, is a creator of connections and a finder of paths.

In the act of observing the traceur, new spatial connections and flows are made available to non-practitioners – space becomes traced out – visually accessible. In this sense, the traceur also draws new spatial constructs and creates new narratives for the observer. Parkour invokes the traversing of distance via an editing process that occurs in motion – one that chooses some parts and deletes others, that clips and re-pieces, that weaves together continually new stories and narratives from the same set of component parts making up the city.

In the practise of parkour the movement is fluid through space, but punctuated by points of contact that serve to accentuate the experience of space. These points of contact are like bumps in the road – not so much interruptions of flow as they are changes in perception. Points of contact make themselves known – jolting us, even just momentarily – out of a fixation with the smoothness of flow.

ACT II: Road savvy
Foreground and background -
Urban Depth of Field

The combination of the movement through space and the points of contact that takes place in the practise of parkour results in the occurrence of scalar shifts. To describe the city as e.g., an amalgamation of built and not built, could speak of form and space, or as mentioned earlier in a discussion of the primacy of the one over the other, space contra form. However this does not directly address the perceptual potential of the city, and in particular ways in which the city is seen. To explore this, concepts used in the visual arts, namely those of foreground, *middle ground* and *background* are activated here, and in particular a relation of these to the practise of parkour.

Parkour is a graphic representation of a kind of spatial perception that through movement accesses both the large scale and the small scale – and moves constantly back and forth between them. This contains an enormous perceptual capacity and one that links space with experience via contact. The presence of the practitioner traversing space occasions shifts and connect-

6: FOREGROUND AND BACKGROUND

ions between these 2 very diverse scales; the large-scale, or *background* and the small-scale, or *foreground*. What comprises the background is the urban context with all of its trappings: buildings, infrastructure, in betweens – not as individual objects, but as a texture made up of these things seen together. The foreground interestingly enough, is also comprised of texture, but here it is the texture of materials.

The middle ground, traditionally the auspices of the primacy of form, is the location of the architectural object. The objects found here lend themselves to both the background and the foreground, and seen through the lens of parkour, transition into texture in both instances - disappearing and relinquishing their presence as individual objects in the act of doing this.

A primacy of space is emphasised as space to be, and being, moved through – the urban context comes into focus in the one moment, while in the next moment, neither form nor space, but materiality comes into focus. Contact is made in the close-up, perhaps introducing the possibility of a new primacy - *a primacy of the senses*. In the change of optics, the architectural object is out of focus – lost in the movement of transition – its gesture overwhelmed as it either fades into the background context, or emerges as material in the foreground, either smooth or rough, or dull or shiny. This is not an impoverished perception. There is a dynamic movement in this scalar shift - a jolting of focus that hones the sensory in the large scale and connects the sensed in a flow of space.

The 'scale of parkour' is a scale in flux - encompassing the vast scale of the urban and the minute scale of materials - and constantly shifting between the two. This can be seen as being related to the change in optics that puts one thing out of focus in order to bring another into focus - in photography, *the depth of field*.

Depth of field is the range of distance within which an object appears sharp, i.e., is in focus. The focus doesn't change immediately, but rather through a gradual movement from sharp to unsharp, from being in focus to being out of focus. In between focus and out of focus in this realm of transition is a blur. When objects are no longer sharp, they are in, in photographic terms, in the *circle of confusion*. The movement between the large scale of the urban context and the materiality of the detail, describes the activity of the traceur and is an indication of a depth of field in urban spatiality – constituting a perceptual definition outside of the circle of confusion.

Connecting the dots

The art of movement is a tactile art. The movement of parkour is a serial movement mitigated by touch-down points - literally. These are dots of contact that ground the movement in the overall space of the urban context – the larger scale framework of movement, bringing to the sensory foreground surfaces comprised of material that can be smooth or rough, too slippery, too sharp, just right. The meeting of skin and building, of sole and infrastructure is a rare meeting in a world where the most common urban optic is on space defined by, and experienced through speed and enormity through a mediated view.

The perception of space through parkour can perhaps be likened to connecting the dots. Or in some ways perhaps a reversal of the activity found in books intended to keep children occupied – interestingly often in the back seats of cars - in which the known and recognisable figure emerges only when the dots are connected. However, parkour doesn't disclose the familiar and recognisable figure - on the contrary the joining of the parkourian dots invents a new picture that, while made up of existing dots, disregards their original locations and instead connects them with dots that were previously on completely different pages of the book. The dots and the spaces between them can change and in this way new stories are told in which new players – new dots - take part.

Using parkour as a vantage point from which to view a type of movement through space brings awareness of the tactile, of the sensory into the picture at the same time that it facilitates the possibility to view contemporary urban spatial surroundings in new ways – but 'up close and personal' as ever-changing narratives, relocated and restructured elements strung together by movement and made more complex by the shifts in scale it occasions and the opening it makes for a larger vocabulary of prepositions. There is room for up and down, for beneath and around and for over. Parkour makes visible a new choreography of standard urban catalogue elements – railing, curb, window sill, paver, ledge, asphalt – by bringing them to the forefront of vision and touch. Separated from their context, these elements re-enter new contexts comprised of other bits and pieces – 'dots', and combine to create new totalities in their sudden connection to each other. The concept of space in contemporary urbanity doesn't necessarily need to be characterised by the remote view, the distanced glance or an impoverished spatiality. We need not be satisfied, either as practitioner or observer, with a lack of experiential content.

The practise of parkour reminds us to remember the sensory, particularly the tactile, to embrace new spatial, and perceptual, connections in motion - and to welcome the bumps in the road as opportunities to keenly feel.

References

Forty, A. (2000) *Words and Buildings*. London: Thames and Hudson.

Giedion, S. (1941)(1982) *Time, Space and Architecture – The Growth of a New Tradition*. Cambridge: Harvard University Press.

Hajer, M. and Reijndorp, A. (2001) *In Search of th New Public Domain*. Rotterdam: NAi Publishers.

Kasarda, J. (2002) *Airport Driven Development*. University of North Carolina.

Pope, A. (1996) *Ladders*. New York: Princeton Architectural Press.

Schwarzer, M. (2004) *Zoomscape – architecture in motion and media*. New York: Princeton Architectural Press.

Smith, S. (2003) *Beyond Big – an examination of contemporary space*. Aarhus: PhD Thesis AAA.

Smith, S. (2009) 'A Hop, Skip and a Jump Away – examining the experiential potential in contemporary urban public space'. Conference paper at: *City Stages conference*, Aalborg.

Smith, S. (2010) 'Parkour as Spatial Connectivity in a World in Motion'. Conference paper at: *Cultures of Mobility Conference*, Aalborg.

Smith, S. (2010) 'Potential and Alternative Uses of Public Space'. Conference paper at: *Street movement Conference Health, Movement and City Development*, Copenhagen.

Smith, S. (2010) 'Discovering Urban Voids and Vertical Spaces'. In: Kiib, H. (Ed.) *Performative Urban Design*. Aalborg: Aalborg University Press.

7: CONNECTING THE DOTS

8: THE MATERIAL FOREGROUND

Bumps in the Road - mobility and spatial experience through the lens of parkour
Mobility

65

Critical Points of Contact – between urban networks and flows

Ole B. Jensen, Simon Wind & Ditte Bendix Langg

"The trunk of the tree, which establishes the path of movement of thousands of tubes, diverging in the branches and delivering the chemicals necessary for growth to the leaves, can be linked to a city's movement systems. Water acts as the vehicle to propel the chemicals to the leaves, and in turn it evaporates into the air. The point of change from water for vapor is the place where the flowers and fruit develop. So in cities the points of connection between systems should be places of special emphasis and design enrichment." (Bacon 1967: 35)

Introduction

Busses, bikes and cars pass by. They make a stop, and speed up again. People cross the street and reach the station; the southbound train must be coming in. On the benches at the square a couple of women chat. Behind them the cinema façade displays images of the movie coming up. People at the bus stops have grocery bags from the nearby supermarket standing at their feet. This could be a daily scene of many an urban environment, where different functions lie side by side, people and vehicle networks intersect and engage in dynamic processes of interaction and exchange with each other and with the physical setting. When we elucidate such sites through the lens of urban design, we have a determined aim of understanding and describing the urban complexity that is found. Often, we even want to make ourselves capable of designing cleverly for this complexity. To do so we need concepts and methods.

In this brief article, we shall illustrate the application of the analytical and interventionist concept of 'Critical Points of Contact' (CPC) through a number of urban design studios. The notion of CPC has been developed over a span of the last three to four years and is reported in more detail elsewhere (Jensen and Morelli 2011). In this article we will only discuss the conceptual and theoretical framing superficially, since our real interest is to show and discuss the concept's application value to spatial design in a number of urban design studios. The 'data' or the projects presented are seven student studios made in the 1st semester of the Urban Design Master Programme in the fall of 2009 and 2010. The CPC concept is double edged since it both provides the stepping-stone for analysis as well as a scaffold for intervention and re-design. Thereby, it fits the underlying philosophy of teaching in urban design at Aalborg University, where urban design consists of both an analytical and an interventionist field of operation. Furthermore, the content of the CPC concept links to research in mobilities, the network city, and urban design. These are among the core pillars of both the masters programme curriculum as well as the urban design group's research.

We have only included a sample, rather than complete studio submissions, as space in this article is limited. Naturally, the criterion for selection have been the studios ability to illustrate the underlying ideas and potential of the notion of CPC. This obviously gives a slightly biased picture of what one single studio submission may look like. Instead we have chosen the concern communicating the key rationales and ideas behind a new concept, rather than give full justice to all the student works we draw upon.

After this short introduction we shall, in the following section, present the key ideas behind the CPC. In the section afterwards, we will present the studio work in a fairly descriptive fashion. We will address the issue of usefulness of the CPC concept when applied, as well as point towards future perspectives within teaching and researching in relation to CPC in the final section.

'Where the Rubber Meets the Road' – Introduction to the Notion of Critical Points of Contact

This section is based upon the paper presenting the CPC in more detail (see Jensen and Morelli 2011). In contemporary urban societies multiple networks and systems interact, overlap, exist in parallel, converge, conflict etc. creating unheeded complexity. By exploring how layered networks of physical movement, service information, goods delivery, commercial communication etc. are connected (and disconnected) we get a much better understanding of how to design and intervene regardless if we are thinking about public spaces in the city or transit systems of the network city. Conceptually we lean on a number of contemporary urban and mobility theories. However, we may start out by simply looking into the *'Oxford Advanced Learners Dictionary'*. In here one may note the notions of 'Interface', 'Node' and 'Network' as crucial components of a CPC. Accordingly we see each of these definitions as important:

Interface: 'The point where two subjects, systems, etc. meet and affect each other'

Node: 'A point at which two lines or systems meet or cross: a network node'

Network: 'A complicated system of roads, lines, tubes, nerves, etc. that cross each other and are connected to each other'

CPCs are to be understood as nodes where points in a network interface in such a manner that mutual exchange between networks and systems are established (this may be in all sorts of ways e.g. economic transactions between market systems, ecological metabolism between systems of ecologies, communication exchanges between social agents or even non-human agents such as software driven interfaces). The many networks orchestrating and facilitating contemporary everyday life are dependent on the strategic sites where these networks meet and establish contact. As for example when Castells discusses the role of 'switches' in the network society:

'Switches connecting the networks (for example, financial flows taking control of media empires that influence political processes) are the privileged instruments of power.' (Castells 1996: 471)

Moreover, such switches work as CPCs creating complex and over-layering geographies of power that signifies a new urban landscape of networks, sites and flows (Graham and Marvin 2001). The key idea behind the notion of CPC is thus to facilitate network thinking and analysis, as well as network design. In coining this concept much inspiration has been found in the theories of the network city (Graham and Marvin 2001) (Sumrell and Varnelis 2007), the Network Society (Castells 1996), Actor Network Theory (Latour 2005), Assemblage Theory (Dovey 2010) (Farias and Bender 2010), Non-representational theories (Thrift 2008), and the so-called mobilities turn (Cresswell 2006) (Jensen 2009a) (Jensen 2009b) (Urry 2007). We see the CPC concept closely related to the notion of assemblages in general and of 'urban assemblages' in particular:

"The notion of urban assemblages in the plural form offers a powerful foundation to grasp the city anew, as an object which is relentlessly being assembled at concrete sites of urban practices or, to put it differently, as a multiplicity of processes of becoming, affixing sociotechnical networks, hybrid collectives and alternative topologies. From this perspective, the city becomes a difficult and decentered object, which cannot any more be taken for granted as a bounded object, specific context or delimited site. The city is rather an improbable ontological achievement that necessitates an elucidation." (Farias 2010: 2)

Seeing the CPC as a part of an 'urban assemblage' furthermore relate quite well to the notion of 'networked ecologies', which according to Varnelis is:

"...a series of co-dependent systems of environmental mitigation, land-use organization, communication and service delivery ... [being] networked, hypercomplex systems produced by technology, laws, political pressures, disciplinary desires, environmental constraints and a myriad of other pressures, tied together with feedback mechanisms." (Varnelis 2008: 15)

We cannot possibly do justice to these complex theories, in the context of this chapter, but rather encourage the reader to consult the literature. The initial work in defining the concept and framing mobility in the network city in light of CPC may be described as follows:

"The many networks orchestrating and facilitating contemporary everyday life are dependent on the strategic sites where the networks meet and establish contact. Thus we argue for the usefulness of the notion CPC to deepen our understanding of the actual 'life within networks' ... CPCs are sites of difference. They become critical when the one system changes/influences the conditions of the other as where entities, flows and qualities are modified as a consequence of the CPC (e.g. as when I become a passenger by a function of the CPC of the metro station and my economic resources and other capabilities to embark)." (Jensen and Morelli 2011)

The idea that a node and a network connection may be critical is illustrated with Scollon's metaphor 'where the rubber meets the road' (Scollon 2008) as a way of stating that sites may be 'critical' depending on a particular 'point of view'. This may, for example, be according to profit, new services, social in- or exclusion, efficiency or a host of other underlying values that will shape the evaluation of a CPC as either underperforming, doing well or other types of assessments. The work on CPC is based on the many theories referred to above in general, but in more specific terms also by the work of authors like Keller Easterling who has been writing about architecture and networks for more than a decade (Easterling1999 2011) and who speaks about 'network architectures' as a site where powerful protocols organise interplay, adjustment and timing among 'ecologies of circuitry' (Easterling 1999:1). In accordance with the perspective underpinning CPC, infrastructures should therefore be understood as much more than technical systems:

'While infrastructure typically conjures associations with physical networks for transportation, communication, or utilities, it also includes the countless shared protocols that format everything from technical objects to management styles of the spaces of urbanism – defining the world as it is clasped and engaged in the space of everyday life. Infrastructural space is, as the word suggests, customarily regarded as a hidden substrate – the binding medium or current between objects of positive consequence, shape, and law – yet it is also the <u>point of contact</u> and access, the spatial outcropping of underlying laws and logics.' (Easterling 2011: 10, our emphasis)

The particular kind of 'network thinking' that the CPC seeks to foster is related to a specific way of thinking about mobility and transit as more than instrumental movements from A to B (Jensen 2009a, 2009b). Mobility is culture and the sites of movements are often locations with much more potential than is being granted in the everyday life routines. Furthermore, infrastructure is related both to 'hardware' and 'software' as mobility and transit networks oscillate between geometry (hardware) and protocol (software).

There are no fixed scales for defining a CPC. Depending on the 'point of view' of the analysis this may be a switching board, a street corner, a terminal building, an Internet web hotel etc. From earlier work Jensen argued that even a metro station might be seen as a CPC:

"So trains, trails, stations, platforms, escalators, metro staff, travellers, signs, commercials, musicians, homeless, police force, tickets, ticket machines, power supplies, newspaper stands, coffee shops, customers etc. are assembled into socio-technical systems producing the lived mobility of metro travellers in London, Paris and Copenhagen. The specific assemblage within the socio-technical system is 'what makes metro mobility' by means of sorting, filtering, circulating, and orchestrating mobilities ... The story of how the socio-technical metro systems in London, Paris and Copenhagen produces lived mobilities is obviously a story of friction versus flow. It is a story about the merging of the social (e.g. regulations, people, and cultures) and the technical (e.g. trains, platforms, and tickets). But furthermore it is a window into the socio-spatial processes of organising flow that creates the everyday life situation to the contemporary urbanite. By exploring the production of lived mobilities within these socio-technical systems we get an insight into how cities create and shape 'European Metroscapes." (Jensen 2008, see also Jensen 2012)

Much more could be said about the CPC, and more rigour needs to be exercised in order to frame the notion in a fully theoretically coherent manner. But as it stands, it has the status of being a heuristic tool that may lend itself to both analysis and intervention in a fairly practical manner. In order to illustrate this point, we shall end this section with briefly showing the 'five steps of CPC', which describe the process that students, in the studios working with CPC, have been following. We may argue that it is difficult to capture a design process in strictly defined steps and therefore some of the phases overlap or return in iterative loops when doing an analysis and intervention/re-design studio assignment. However, for the sake of simplicity, we will present it as five serial steps in a working process:

- Identify a site of two or more intersecting systems performing as CPC
- Map technical, social and aesthetic dimensions of the identified CPC
- Make an analytical judgement of the CPC in terms of a chosen point of view/research question (e.g. technical functionality, social exclusion etc.)
- Identify a potential for social and economic value that has not been fulfilled by the CPC (e.g. a service not catered for, a user group not included etc.)
- Make a first tentative proposal for a re-design catering for the identified potential

As the topic of concern is urban design, the key to exploring the CPC concept is to utilize it in uncovering how design may facilitate 'life in networks'. The notion of 'point of view' suggests that any intervention in the city is based upon a more or less explicitly articulated set of norms and values. So for the sake of the argument let us imagine that a group of students in the urban design studio has chosen a transit hub like a Copenhagen metro station. One of the key features about the Metro in Copenhagen is that it facilitates flow at almost 100%, but it does not accommodate any other urban programs such as shops or public spaces where interaction may occur (there are no benches only leaning devices for that same reason, see Jensen 2012).

Now, a five step CPC process might begin by selecting a particular station (the site specific context of the station being very important to its potentials).

Step two would then be to map the site in terms of how it performs as a technical node of urban infrastructure (e.g. volume of traffic and transit etc.), how it is performing as a social space (e.g. how it is designed to either cater for interaction or the reverse), and finally register how the aesthetics (in terms of the design code and the architectural spaces) facilitates a 'life in networks'.

The third step is then to make an analytical judgement of how the chosen CPC may perform in accordance to a 'yardstick' or value. This could for example be how the Metro station accommodates public interaction.'

If the analysis points at this to be a underutilized field of intervention, step four then has to do with articulating this in a more explicit manner; how do we want our Metro Station to invite to social interaction, between whom and why?

This leads to the fifth and final step of the process, which is about proposing design parameters and starts with the first tentative re-design proposals. In the case of a Metro Station underperforming as a public space this could concern how to make room for seating, how to facilitate interaction by means of public

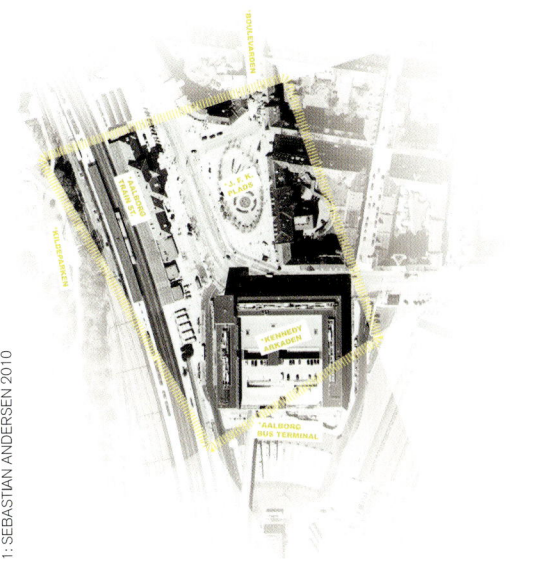

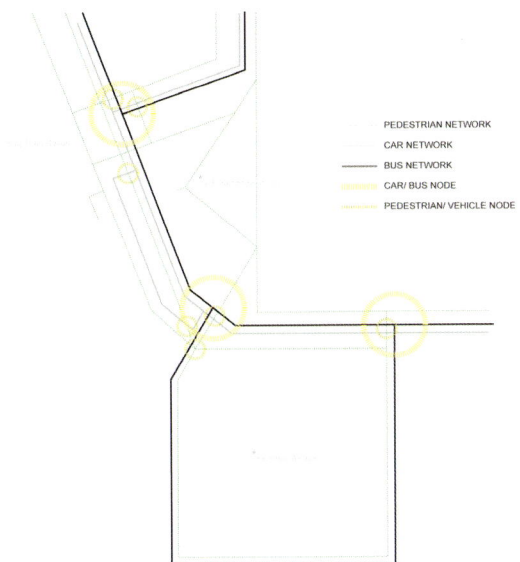

programmes, or even new digital media. In this short space we have not been able to detail the five step CPC approach. Hopefully it is comprehensible that it works as a pedagogic tool for connecting theoretically informed thinking to design intervention in a process that we acknowledge to be iterative and non-linear. However, for the sake of a manageable learning situation the process is treated as linear.

The proof is in the pudding however, so let us move toward a few concrete examples of how students have worked with the CPC notion in the urban design studios we have taught.

Critical Points of Contact in the Heart of Aalborg - Urban Design Studios

In this section we will provide some tangible examples of engaging the CPC thinking in urban design studios. The section describes student works seeking to operationalise the CPC concept and use the five step model described above. In their studios, the students have treated a wide array of different CPC locations in the city centre of Aalborg and produced various analyses and tentative proposals for design intervention. The section is arranged according to the five step framework.

As the first step, students were asked to identify a site performing as a CPC. Here, we have chosen to display submissions dealing with the location most commonly chosen by the students, the J.F. Kennedy Plaza area. This area is characterised as a complex site of intersecting systems: physical, virtual and social networks associated with the central traffic functions of the area (Aalborg train station and the main bus terminal), the shopping facilities of the commercial centre (Kennedy Arkaden) and the public square (J.F.K. Plads). These functional elements are shown on the aerial photo (ill. 1). The perspective photograph (ill. 2) gives an impression of the urban space between buildings.

At the second stage of the process the students began to dissect the complexity of the area in order to map technical, social and aesthetic dimensions. Many students took their point of departure in the transit situation, emphasizing traffic flows and nodes where the separate traffic networks cross each other (ill. 3). There is a particular effort towards the organisation and appeal of the area to the pedestrian´s point of view. This finds expression in illustration 4(ill. 4) where the main concern is for the significance and communication of the façade of the shopping arcade to the pedestrians and arriving bus passengers. This project also illustrates another general effort among the students: the attention towards semiotic aspects in the form of building architecture and signage (ill. 5).

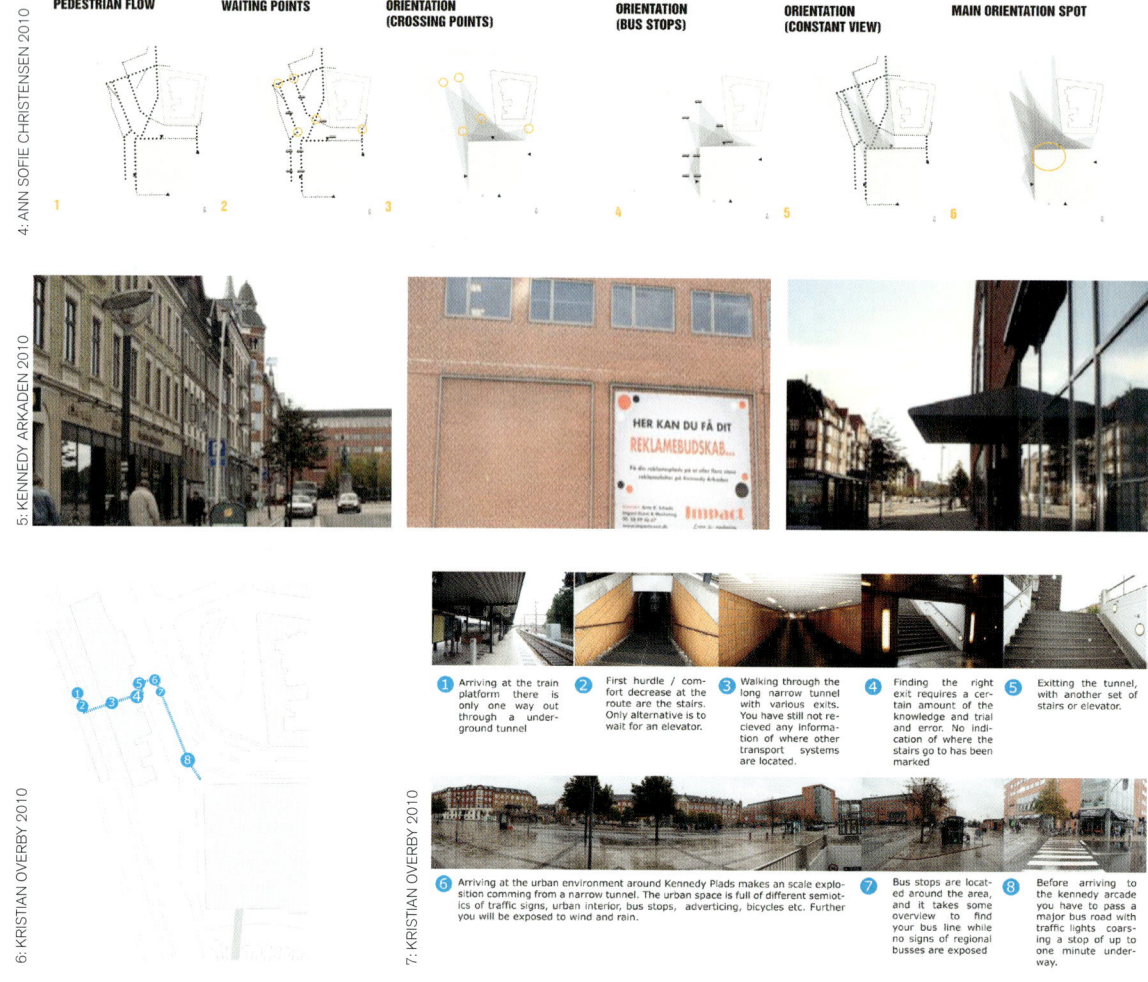

Through their analyses the students have described a somewhat confusing meeting between the 'pedestrianised' traveller and the numerous infrastructural systems, characterised by vague organisation of important infrastructural nodes, and massive yet unclear signage. This concerns e.g. the person in transit moving by foot from the train platforms to the bus terminal, as described in illustrations 6 and 7, where this short journey is depicted through a series of images representing the sequence of spatial encounters. The key aspects in the students´ analytical judgement (the third step of the CPC framework) are therefore inaccessibility and illegibility of the area from the pedestrian´s perspective.

In the analysis of the CPC the students have sought to explore and identify unseen potentials for social and economic value that have not been fulfilled by the CPC. In this fourth step of the process, many of the students identified economic potential, either through the optimization of the infrastructure systems (time as a currency) or enhancing commercial aspects of the Kennedy Arcade. Other students found an underused asset of social value primarily through the notion of the Kennedy area as a ´public domain´ (Hajer and Reiijn-dorp 2003) as can be seen on illustrations 8, 9 and 10 where the presence of multiple people in the same space is emphasised as a potential for social interaction.

The CPC studio encouraged re-designs that challenge the existing city design and urban discourse. In the last step of the process, where the task was to make a tentative proposal for a re-design catering for the identified potential, many of the students worked with enhancing or optimizing infrastructure. Drastic changes in direction and regulation of flows and reconfiguration of the transport systems were proposed, e.g. as shown on illustration 11 the creation of rolling sidewalks and improved information system to create frictionless travel. Other students focused their re-design on enhancing the site as a public domain as mentioned above. These proposals included the reconfiguration of the entire area, expressed in illustrations 12 and 13 suggesting moving and reshaping the shopping arcade in order to create new physical links and meeting places. They also included small strategic interventions, e.g. in the form of robot inspired urban furniture as a platform for growth of public domain, identity and improved legibility, see illustration 14.

8: BERGITTE HATTELUND 2010

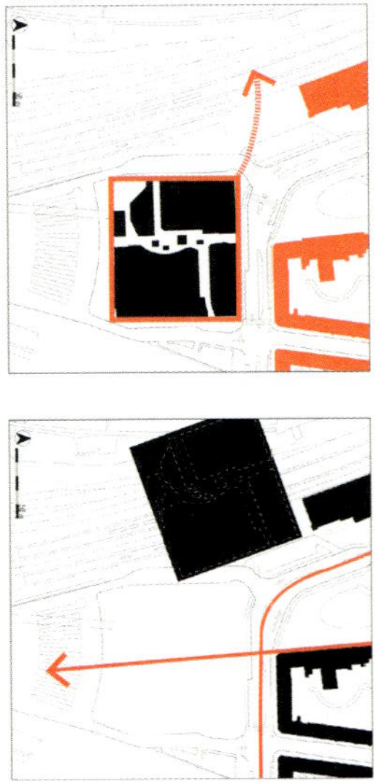

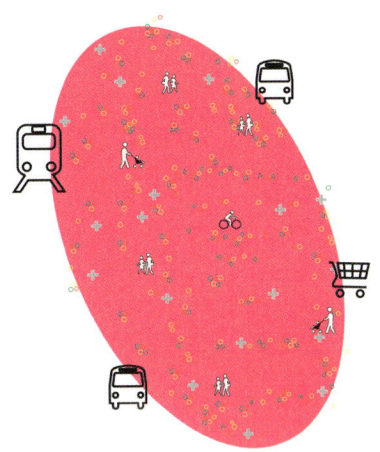
9: JEPPE FINK 2009

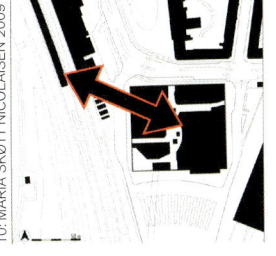
10: MARIA SKØTT NICOLAISEN 2009

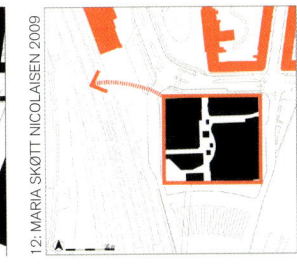
12: MARIA SKØTT NICOLAISEN 2009

11: KRISTIAN OVERBY 2010

Critical Points of Contact – between urban networks and flows
Mobility

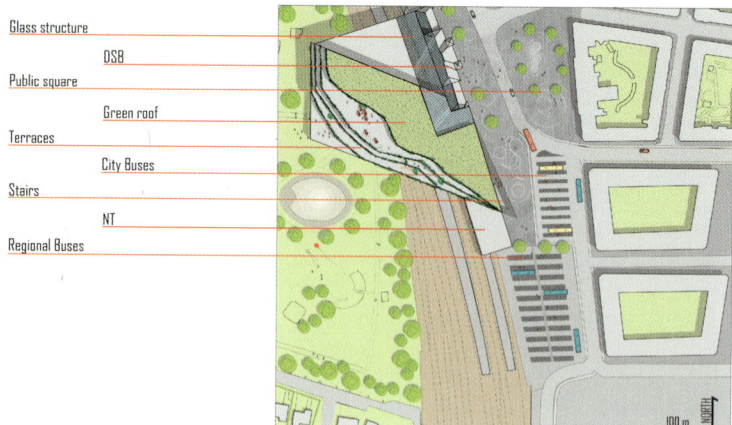

Towards Further Development of the CPC as a Design Method

Through the CPC concept the students have engaged with understanding and designing networks and flows in the city. The hypothesis was that it is possible to activate underused potential and optimize the city through re-design by dissecting, analysing, understanding and re-assemble the networks and flows of the city in new configurations. So what happened when coupling the CPC concept with the student's projects? Two main conclusions can be drawn.

Firstly, the outcome of the student studios, namely a collection of varying, imaginative and daring (urban) re-designs, shows that the CPC concept provides a productive gaze on the networked urban environment by focusing the urban complexity to an approachable size while not losing track of this as part of a larger complex networked urban context. The major strength of the CPC methodology is exactly this; it can identify and make multiple layered networks visible, but also serve as a mind-set for dissecting and focusing only on the critical networks. Surprisingly, this also seems to be a potential pitfall for some students. The challenge is the necessity to formulate a point of view to specify what is critical without losing track of what lies outside the point of view. A redistribution of the urban environment always comes at a cost, and it is the understanding how to balance this that creates the successful re-design. As mentioned earlier, the goal of operationalising the CPC concept in the design studios is to get one step closer to understand how the complex networks are spatially and socially organised, how they intersect and affect one another and thereby exactly provide insight for balancing a potential re-design.

This brings us to discuss the second conclusion from the experience of operationalising the five step framework. Following the working processes of the students and assessing the results of the studios two main issues can be raised. Firstly, the design process is seldom accomplished as a linear process, but rather as a looping between steps in several iterative cycles. While the five step framework did give the students an overall understanding of the process, it was in many cases less helpful for the students when they had to engage with their own project because of the simplistic nature of the steps. The downside in reaching for simplicity in the case of the five step framework, is the inability to, at the same time, open the 'black box' of the design process. Further development of the framework to guide the complex process of getting from the analytical level to the re-design is therefore needed. Secondly, the framework needs to better capture the substance of the CPC concept to actually create meaning and progression in the process for the designer. As it stands, the five steps are relatively generic, and thus, not encompassing the full capability and potential of the CPC approach as a viable design method. To claim this, the focus within the method could be shifted from instructions for the obvious steps, to what lies in between, thereby uncovering the intermediate calculations and pry open the black box.

This brings us back to the notion of the CPC as a double-edged concept entailing both an analytical and an interventionist dimension. The strength of the CPC framework lies in its potential ability to identify critical sites for re-design and in its analytical capacity to inform the design process. The five step framework should therefore be understood as a way to engage in two complex processes, bringing the analytic and the design process into one unifying framework. The CPC approach thereby holds the potential to encompass a new network oriented vocabulary, an analytical gaze, and a design tool. This enables us to start unravelling the complexity of the network city, and furthermore, gives the potential to be able to engage with creating network-based design in the city. The CPC approach addresses the city as an organic, living system, as shown in the opening quote of this article – Ed Bacon´s metaphor of the ecosystem of the tree. It guides us to realise where the urban systems interconnect in important and strategic places of special emphasis, and it guides us to work spatially with analysis and design for these critical points of contact in the network city.

Acknowledgements

We would like to thank the students from the Urban Design master programme Sebastian Andersen, Ann Sofie G. Christensen, Kristian Overby, Maria Skøtt Nicolaisen, Jakob Charmoth Nielsen, Bergitte Hattelund and Jeppe Fink for contributing to this article with illustrations from their studio submissions.

References

Bacon, E. (1967) *Design of Cities*. London: Penguin.

Castells, M. (1996) *The Information Age: Economy, Society and Culture, vol. I. The Rise of the Network Society*. Oxford: Blackwell Publishers.

Cresswell, T. (2006) *On the Move. Mobility in the Modern Western World*. London: Routledge.

DeLanda, M. (2006) *A New Philosophy of Society. Assemblage Theory and Social Complexity*. New York: Continuum.

Dovey, K. (2010) *Becoming Places. Urbanism/Architecture/Identity/Power*. London: Routledge.

Easterling, K. (1999) *Organisation Space. Landscapes, Highways, and Houses in America*. Cambridge Mass.: MIT Press.

Easterling, K. (2011) ´Fresh Field`. In: Bhatia, N. et al. (Eds.) *Coupling Strategies for Infrastructural Opportunism*. New York: Princeton Architectural Press.

Farias, I. and Bender, T. (Eds.) (2010) *Urban Assemblages. How Actor-Network Theory changes urban studies*. London: Routledge.

Graham, S. and Marvin, S. (2001) *Splintering Urbanism*. London: Routledge.

Hajer, M. and Reijndorp, A. (2003) *In Search of New Public Domain*. Rotterdam: Nai Publishers.

Jensen, O. B. (2008) ´European Metroscapes - the production of lived mobilities within the socio-technical Metro systems in Copenhagen, London and Paris`. In: *Proceedings of the 'Mobility, the City and STS' Conference*. The Technical University of Denmark (DTU), Copenhagen.

Jensen, O. B. (2009a) ´Flows of Meaning, cultures of Movement – urban mobility as meaningful everyday life practice`. In: *Mobilities*. 4 (1): pp. 139-158.

Jensen, O. B. (2009b) ´Mobilities as Culture`. In: Vannini, P. (Ed.) *The Cultures of Alternative Mobilities: Routes Less Travelled*. Farnham: Ashgate.

Jensen, O. B. (2012) ´Metroens Arkitektur og Bevægelser`. In: Andersen, J. et al. (Eds.) *Byen i Bevægelse. Mobilitet – Politik – Performativitet*. Frederiksberg: Roskilde Universitetsforlag.

Jensen, O. B. and Morelli, N. (2011) ´Critical Points of Contact - exploring networked relations in urban mobility and service design`. In: *Danish Journal of Geoinformatics and Land Management*, 46 (1): pp. 36-49. (in press).

Latour, B. (2005) *Reassembling the Social*. Cambridge: Cambridge University Press.

Oxford Advanced Learners Dictionary 7th Edition (2005). Oxford University Press.

Scollon, R. (2008) ´Geographies of Discourse: Action Across Layered Spaces` In: *Proceedings of the Space Interaction Discourse Conference*, Aalborg University, 12-14 November.

Sumrell, R. and Varnelis, K. (2007) *Blue Monday. Stories of Absurd realities and natural philosophies*. Barcelona: ACTAR.

Thrift, N. (2008) *Non-Representational Theory. Space. Politics. Affect*. London: Routledge.

Urry, J. (2007) *Mobilities*. Cambridge: Polity.

Urban Design and the Tracking of Secondary School Students in the Urban Landscape

Henrik Harder, Peter Bro & Anne-Marie Sanvig Knudsen

Recent developments in the global positioning system (GPS) and the global system for mobile communications have enabled an increasingly simple and cost-effective tracking of human activity in urban areas through the use of mobile telephony for the collection of vast amounts of location-based data.

From an urban design perspective, location-based datasets concerning collective or individual spatial behaviour in urban areas are highly interesting. By combining the data with existing information on urban elements such as the location of plazas, shops, etc., infinitely detailed mappings of the interplay between users' individual behaviours and urban elements can be gathered, but this requires accessible ways of representation. Further questions should address other, value-based choices concerning urban design.

In the following we demonstrate a number of ways in which the collected data enable statistical analysis of urban activity, such as citizens' time spent in various locations. More complex analyses are also undertaken by breaking down the data into male and female cohorts, and specific activities at several places of interest. We aim to demonstrate that urban designers are now able to utilize such studies as the basis for the regeneration of urban areas.

Background: The Aalborg Case 2009

The study took place in the municipality of Aalborg. With 122,461 inhabitants (2009), the city of Aalborg is Denmark's fourth largest city.

We combined data from the GPS-tracking of respondents' outdoor activities with their self-reported movements in urban spaces. We also employed radio-frequency identification (RFID) for activity tracking in both indoor and outdoor spaces. For the respondents' daily reporting of their activities, a GPS unit connected to a central server/database was used. Additional qualitative data were collected using a combination of web-based questionnaires and interviews after the GPS data had been harvested.

We present here the major results of the Aalborg Case 2009. The respondents in the study were defined as young adults living in the municipality of Aalborg who attended one of urban Aalborg's upper secondary schools directed at academically gifted students aged 16 to 20 years. The schools all required daily attendance. The study thus recruited not only a group of very active users but also one that represents the future users of Aalborg's urban spaces. This population was furthermore chosen because of its easy accessibility through school administrations, a circumstance that made the survey logistically and economically feasible.

The present account is based on three surveys, only two of which are reported here, and only partially. The first survey was a large-scale web-tracking of more than a thousand students, while the second survey combined the results of the web-tracking with GPS data on the movements of a smaller student cohort. The respondents entered a report of their day-to-day activities into a web database. The third survey was based on supplementary qualitative data gleaned from 18 face-to-face interviews.

The shared point of departure for all three surveys was an interest in how young adults spend their time in urban areas and the possibility of working with 'urban living' on the basis of GPS-generated data. The objectives of the surveys were to:

- supply a detailed illustration of themes concerning young adults' attitudes and priorities in relation to Aalborg's central city areas.
- collect data for a survey of the study group's spatial behaviour at three levels: the central city, the larger urban area of Aalborg, and the entire municipality.
- demonstrate that the collected data enable urban designers to take a new approach to work in areas such as Aalborg city.

Ultimately we aimed to create a more evidence-based approach to urban design.

Web Surveying 1073 Students

The first part of the survey was conducted between 2007 and 2008 using web-based technology. In a unique effort to follow the movements and activities of a whole population segment through detailed, second-by-second electronic tracking, the entire population of students attending youth education programmes was contacted by email. The 7,277 young adults thus comprised the whole spectrum of students from both academically and vocationally oriented programmes (Statistics Denmark 2006). Positive responses were received from 1,073 persons (463 males and 610 females), most of whom studied at the academically oriented schools. We therefore decided to restrict the study so that the sample was fully representative of

2: AALBORG HARBOR FRONT

Aalborg's population of upper secondary students between 16 and 20 years, while it was only partly representative in respect to the following parameters: the type of school attended, gender distribution, and home address in the municipality. Denmark's upper secondary schools are comparable in terms of their academic level, but for historical reasons, separate institutions cater to traditional academic studies, technical studies, and commercial studies, respectively.

One of the central questions of the survey was:

> "What do the following elements mean to you as you move around in the central city and park spaces of Aalborg?"

Participants were asked to respond by indicating their rating of the significance of a number of parameters, as they reflected on the question in retrospective. Their answer options were: "Very important", "Important", "Less important" and "Slightly important". Only the 858 responses for 'Very important' are given here (response rate 80%) (A test inspired by Gehl's 12 key quality criteria (Gehl et al 2006)).

Table 1 shows that respondents gave strongest emphasis to the statement "Feeling protected from crime and violence". In an urban design perspective, it may be argued that a sense of security is supported not only by urban design elements but also by a number of other conditions, such as the frequency and types of behaviour in the areas frequented by the respondents and other users of the city space. Second priority was given to the statement "Being able to walk through a green area, for example a park", which indicates a more direct relevance of urban design considerations. The complexity of the subject is indicated by the fact that Gehl did not include a similar factor in his 12 key quality criteria (Gehl et al 2006). We chose to include the 'green element' in the questionnaire because we believe that its value in the urban area is underestimated.

In an attempt to elucidate the respondents' priorities in relation to the future, the following question was asked: "What do you think will be important to you in the future as you move around the central city and park spaces of Aalborg?" As Table 2 shows, highest priority was given to elements which are only indirectly related to urban design; such elements took only fourth place. Only the 858 responses for "Very important" are given here (response rate 80%) The respondents reaffirmed their emphasis on 'the green element'.

It appears that the results of such studies may give urban designers the opportunity to reflect on the types of urban design elements and design interventions under consideration.

TABLE 1: SIGNIFICANCE OF A NUMBER OF PARAMETERS IN RETROSPECTIVE

What do the following elements mean to you as you move around in the central city and park spaces of Aalborg?	Men	Women	Total	Diff.
1. Feeling protected from crime and violence	39%	65%	54%	25%
2. Being able to walk through a green area, for example a park	33%	38%	36%	4%
3. Being able to watch other people and go window-shopping, etc.	26%	43%	35%	17%
4. Being able to enjoy the weather, e.g. the sun, or stand in the shade	29%	34%	32%	5%
5. Having the opportunity to talk to others or listen to what they are saying/low noise level	28%	32%	30%	4%
6. Feeling safe in traffic, for example from cars, etc.	24%	34%	30%	10%
7. Being able to move freely across roads, pavements and plaza pavements	24%	27%	26%	2%
8. Finding urban space smartly designed	24%	20%	22%	-4%
9. Having the opportunity to sit down on a bench, etc.	18%	23%	21%	5%
10. Finding that urban space suits me and is not too cold or too big	22%	20%	21%	-2%
11. Having the opportunity to stop and stay in a place	15%	24%	20%	9%
12. That the city and park spaces I move around in do not have strong winds or rain	21%	19%	20%	-2%
13. Being able to jog, play, jump, skate or run	15%	11%	13%	-3%

TABLE 2: SIGNIFICANCE OF A NUMBER OF PARAMETERS IN RELATION TO THE FUTURE

What do you think will be important to you in the future as you move around the central city and park spaces of Aalborg	Men	Women	Total	Diff.
1. Feeling that parks, streets and plazas are kept clean	44%	56%	51%	12%
2. Feeling that parks, streets and plazas are well maintained	40%	46%	43%	6%
3. Feeling that parks, streets and plazas have an authentic atmosphere	31%	40%	36%	8%
4. That there will be more trees and bushes in the city spaces	24%	26%	25%	2%
5. That others do not feel bothered by me and my friends	23%	24%	23%	1%
6. Being able to use city and park spaces for more than just walking around	20%	23%	21%	3%
7. That there are other people of my type in the areas that I visit	23%	17%	20%	-6%
8. At I am not being bothered by others in the city and park spaces	21%	19%	20%	-2%
9. Being able to walk in covered areas (for example in a mall)	15%	21%	18%	6%
10. Being able to jog, etc., in city and park spaces, for example in streets and parks	13%	16%	15%	3%
11. Being able to e.g., go swimming in the cityside bay	13%	12%	12%	-2%

GPS- and Web-Surveying 169 Students

This part of the Aalborg study was conducted through a combination of GPS-tracking and web-surveying involving students at eight schools, with data collection taking place over four months leading up to, and following the summer holiday period of 2008, and in April the following year.

The focus was on temporal and spatial behaviour and activity in both physical and virtual environments. By utilizing cross-disciplinary research methods such as surveys based on quantitative and qualitative set-ups, the aim was to allow for a broad discussion of interrelations and interactions between respondents and spaces. Data were charted for the respondents' current position, current activity and its duration, and their motivation for undertaking the activity. In other words, the data showed where they were, what they were doing, how long they had been doing it, and why they did it. We assumed that such information would be useful for urban designers in their design work on for instance the central city area in Aalborg.

It should be noted that Aalborg's urban spaces (defined as physical, typically open spaces with public access) represent only one of several opportunities for young adults to socialize in and communicate with their peers or with other people. The Internet, social networking sites and mobile telecommunication, etc., represent technologies that may be conceived as part of the 'urban space' that young people use for social and other purposes. This takes place for example through www.facebook.com, www.hotmail.com, www.youtube.com, which represents new types of virtual meeting places that compete with physical urban spaces for respondents' time. It should also be noted that the mappings reproduced here do not directly reflect respondents' actual behaviour, but are the result of several procedures. The collected data were thus processed at three levels and over seven procedures in preparation for the mapping shown here:

A. Data processing at respondent level:
1. Actual behaviour
2. GPS-logged behaviour
3. Web survey-logged behaviour

B. Data processing at database level:
4. Correction for discrepancies between GPS-logged behaviour and reported behaviour (see 2. and 3. above; priority given to the former)
5. Correction for behaviour in data-cleaning processes
6. Analysis of corrected reported behaviour (e.g. for trips/stays)

C. Data processing at map/analysis level:
7. GIS square visualizations of behaviour, in maps.

The potential number of daily GPS updates for all 169 respondents was 110,728,800 seconds for the seven days that the respondents participated in the survey while the actual number of recorded GPS updates was no larger than half of that.

The GPS datasets were created through updates at 5-second intervals from the GPS unit, which were afterwards interpolated to 1-second GPS points. Considered in isolation, our relatively simple recording set-up based on GPS updates and the corresponding GPS points has several potential sources of error, which are described briefly here. In principle, errors may occur both in connection with the collection and the subsequent processing of data.

Data Collection

The great majority of the respondents obliged fully with requirements, but for a variety of social or technical reasons data may occasionally have been lost. For instance, if respondents had forgotten to recharge or pick up their GPS unit before going out, or if, during the GPS survey period, they deliberately avoided carrying it for certain occasions such as parties or the spring carnival (a major event involving over 20,000 young people over one day). The tendency to forget or avoid using the device seems to have increased over the seven-day period. Other reasons included GPS breakdowns, battery failure or connection failures to the central database. As a result, GPS point updates were incomplete and not fully representative of the individual respondent's behaviour. Such discrepancies are not given further treatment here, but as an example, the number of GPS updates declined during nights, probably due to battery failure.

Data Processing

In preparing the maps and data sets for this survey, some of the scatter originating in the raw GPS-generated data was removed. Scatter is defined here as GPS updates showing substantial deviation from what was deemed to be feasible, such as updates that could not be explained as a result of statistical discrepancy, or updates that would have presupposed that respondents had moved with improbable speeds. GPS updates were also discarded as scatter on the basis of other considerations, such as weather conditions, satellite positions, signal obstruction from buildings, or because the quality of GPS hardware and software was insufficient.

The Respondents

The respondents were asked to carry a pocket-size GPS unit for seven consecutive days. Using the unit's Google Maps, every evening they were to complete a travel diary logging the GPS waypoints visited during the preceding 24 hours.

In practical terms, the eight partial surveys were organized on a staggered schedule in which the devices were handed out to respondents at each school for the following week. The start of each partial survey was designated as "Survey Day 1", beginning at 12:00 and ending on "Survey Day 8" at noon, after which the participants were instructed to immediately hand in the GPS units to the school secretariat. They were then collected by the person responsible for the partial survey.

Partial Survey Periods and Schools Involved

Survey 1: Aalborg Studenterkursus. 2008-03-06 to 2008-03-13 (year-month-day)

Survey 2: Aalborg Katedralskole. 2008-05-07 to 2008-05-14

Survey 3: Aalborg Tekniske Gymnasium, Øster Uttrup Vej. 2008-05-19 to 2008-05-26

Survey 4: Aalborg Tekniske Gymnasium, Sankelmarksgade. 2008-05-28 to 2008-06-04

Survey 5: Hasseris Gymnasium. 2008-08-14 to 2008-09-21

Survey 6: Aalborg Handelsskole. 2008-08-25 to 2008-09-01

Survey 7: Nørresundby Gymnasium. 2008-09-03 to 2008-09-10

Survey 8: Aalborghus Gymnasium. 2009-05-04 to 2009-05-11

Maps in Urban Design Work

To inspire urban designers in their future work, the visual material shown here gives partial results of the analyses of accumulated time use for all 169 respondents in the GPS survey. The examples may also serve to highlight some of the challenges encountered in using such maps in urban design processes.

The harvested and processed data served as a basis for the construction of several maps in three different scales. The central city of Aalborg covers approximately 1 x 1 km. The official city limits of Aalborg is designated the urban area, which is approximately 10 x 10 km. Finally, the whole municipality of Aalborg measures approximately 50 x 40 km. The table below gives the number of loggings within these boundaries, before and after the processing of data, respectively.

TABLE 3: TOTAL AND AVERAGE TIME SPENT, BY AREA (SECONDS)

Area	Before correction	After correction	Average per respondent
Central city	3,992,458	3,967,948	3,354
Urban	34,881,310	34,861,922	29,469
Municipal	52,829,973	52,818,008	44,648

Time Spent According to Area

Figures 4, 5 and 6 show images of maps based on data analyses of time spent in the municipality as a whole, in the urban area, and in central city, respectively. Times before and after correction for scatter are given. In preparing the maps, several challenges had to be overcome, the most important being to secure that our analyses were based on data of adequate quality and quantity. The following analysis concentrates on the central city area.

Calculations on the basis of the times given in Table 3 indicate that the average respondent spent approximately 56 minutes per day in the central city area of Aalborg, 491 minutes in the urban area, and 744 minutes in the municipality (later figures include the former).

As all respondents lived in the municipality of Aalborg, the total time logged on school days should be close to 24 hours, or 1,440 minutes, but in reality no more than approximately 52 % of respondents' time was recorded. When subtracting from the 56 minutes the time spent in the respondents' school areas and the homes of those who lived inside the area (26 minutes), the average approximate time spent in the central city of Aalborg was 30 minutes per day.

Time in 'Flow' and in 'Stay'

The maps shown in Figures 7A and 7B give two-dimensional images of the respondents' time spent in the central city area, divided between time spent in movement and staying at a location, respectively. The two modes are designated as 'flow' and 'stay'. The average was approximately 12 minutes per day spent in movement, or flow, while approximately 44 minutes were logged as stationary per day. The map thus gives a survey of the location of central Aalborg's typical 'flow' and 'stay' areas, as indicated by the density of plotting. Unsurprisingly, respondents' homes and school grounds, followed by parks, were the areas that scored the highest figures for stays.

Gender Differences

Figure 8A and 8B shows the distribution of time as it was spent in central Aalborg by males and females, respectively. The differences between the maps reflect the fact that, in general, females spent longer time in central Aalborg, with an average 30 minutes per day compared to the approximately 26 minutes spent by males per day (red circle: location of school – blue circle: location of respondent's home). A gender difference was also seen in behaviour patterns with respect to the time spent in different areas, with the females spending more time than the males in the central, east-west-oriented pedestrian streets. Both young women and men moved along the central north-west oriented street known as Boulevarden, but the women also stayed there for longer. For the parks, such as Kildeparken close to the central train station, gender differences were negligible. See also the park map in Figure 10.

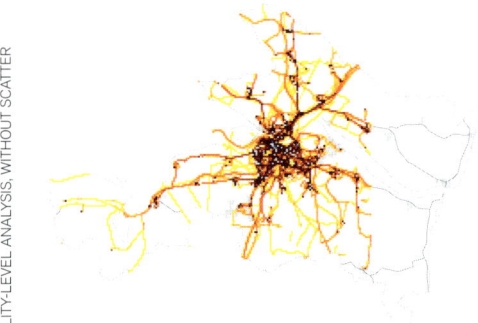

4: MUNICIPALITY-LEVEL ANALYSIS, WITHOUT SCATTER

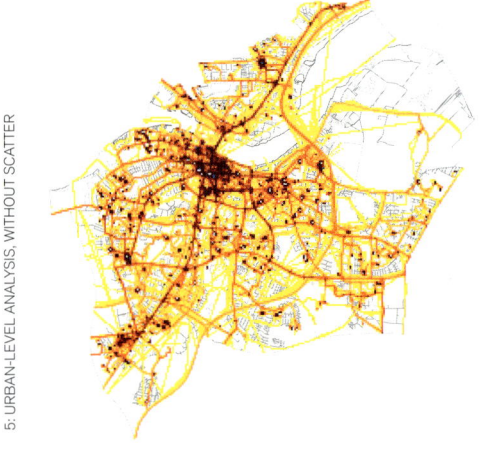

5: URBAN-LEVEL ANALYSIS, WITHOUT SCATTER

7A: CITY-LEVEL ANALYSIS WITH TIME SPENT IN STATIONARY

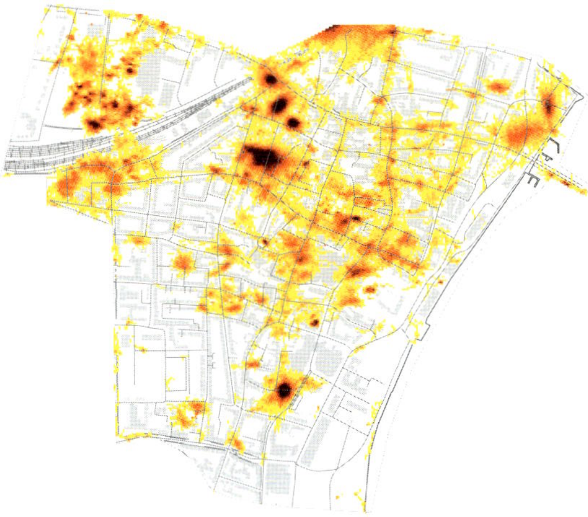

6: CITY-LEVEL ANALYSIS, WITHOUT SCATTER

7B: CITY-LEVEL ANALYSIS WITH TIME SPENT IN MOTION

8A: CITY LEVEL ANALYSIS SHOWING TIME SPENT BY GENDER

8B: CITY-LEVEL ANALYSIS SHOWING TIME SPENT BY GENDER

Urban Design and the Tracking of Secondary School Students in the Urban Landscape
Mobility

In Plazas and Streets

The map gives a three-dimensional image of respondents' time as spent in the central plazas, motor vehicle streets and pedestrian streets in central Aalborg (blue circle: location of school – red circle: location of respondent's home). It appears that very few of the young respondents stayed in one place for longer periods of time. Two of the longest stays were recorded for the home address of a respondent (indicated by a red circle). The respondents spent approximately 7 minutes in plazas and streets per day. Most of the remaining areas hosting longer stays were close to bus stops. Longer continuous stays were recorded for parks than for plazas, cf. Figure 10.

In Parks

The time spent by respondents' in central Aalborg's park areas is shown in three dimensions in Figure 10. The map shows that one park in particular, the Kildeparken, is popular with the respondents. They spent approximately 6 minutes in Aalborg's park areas per day (blue circle: location of school – red circle: location of respondent's home). The other smaller park areas show a use pattern resembling that of the streets, i.e., primarily as thoroughfares. During one of the tracking periods a carnival took place, a major event involving over 20,000 young people over one day – in fact some of the highest dark columns reflect areas and times corresponding to the carnival activities.

Window-Shopping

The map shown in Figure 11 gives a three-dimensional illustration of the amount of time spent window-shopping by respondents in the central city area of Aalborg (blue circle: location of school – red circle: location of respondent's home). The activity was defined as "stays" outside shops and restaurants in a circle with a radius 5 meters; the respondents spent approximately 4 minutes in these areas per day. The highest figures appear for the broad mosaic pavement outside of a fast-food restaurant. In general, the shops in the pedestrian streets and those situated closest to Aalborg's commercial centre attracted the respondents for longer times when compared to shops with more peripheral locations.

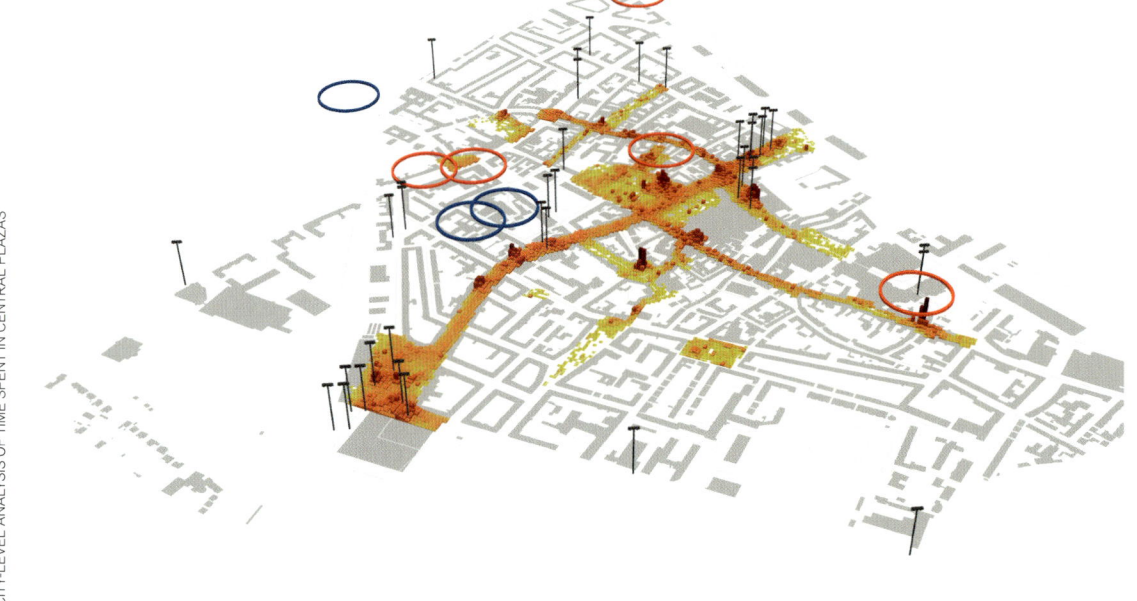

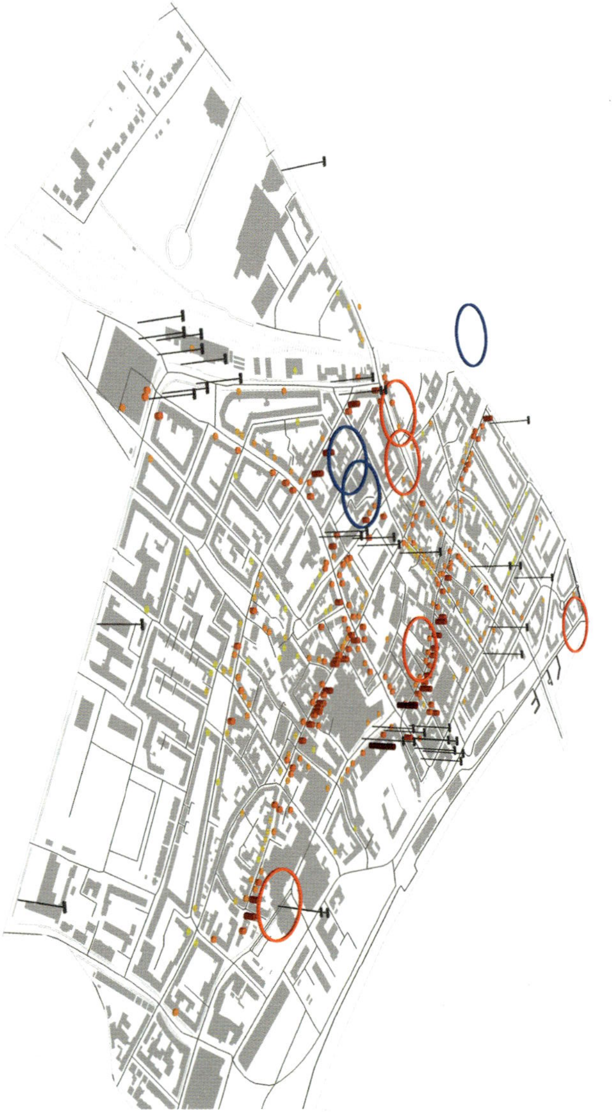

10: CITY-LEVEL ANALYSIS OF TIME SPENT IN PARKS

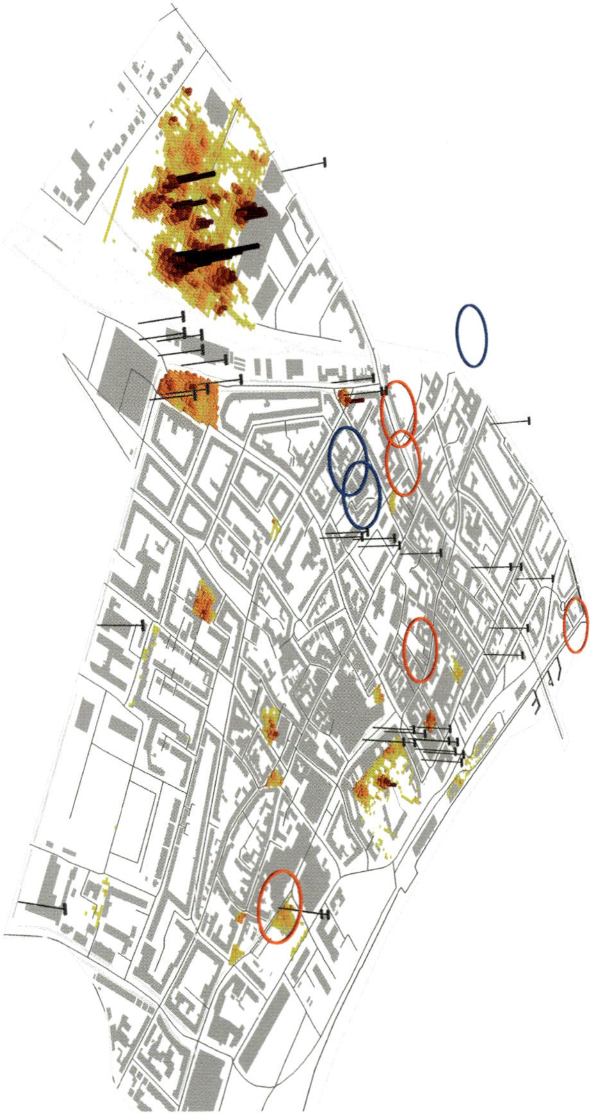

11: CITY-LEVEL ANALYSIS OF TIME SPENT WINDOW-SHOPPING

Urban Design and the Tracking of Secondary School Students in the Urban Landscape
Mobility

Conclusions

The results of the first survey seem to indicate that the immediate physical urban design elements are not foremost in the minds of the young respondents when they assess the central urban area. Via their responses to the questions "What do the following elements mean to you as you move around in the central city and park spaces of Aalborg?" and "What do you think will be important to you in the future as you move around the central city and park spaces of Aalborg?", we show that respondents do not unambiguously ascribe major importance to physical design elements of the cityscape. They give the highest rating to the city's 'green element', a somewhat underexposed theme in research into urban design, as exemplified by Gehl (Gehl et al 2006). This raises the question whether urban designers and other professionals working with the design of city spaces give adequate emphasis to this element.

The second survey was based on a unique sample of movement data on 169 partly representative 16 to 20-year-old young adults. The respondents were GPS-tracked over a period of seven days in 2008-2009 to plot their use of Aalborg's central city area. It is demonstrated that the map-based data enable statistical analysis of urban activity, such as the time spent in plazas, parks, window-shopping, etc., and the results illustrate the relevance for city planners of GIS- and location-based datasets on collective and individual spatial behaviour in urban areas. By combining the data with existing information on physical elements in the cityscape, we are offered extremely detailed information on the interplay between users' individual behaviour and urban elements. New technologies thus allow easy retrieval and animation of information on urban activity.

While the maps presented here offer much information of a quantitative nature, such as the amount of time and the patterns in which it is spent, etc., we are left with the realization that urban designers and other professionals are faced with a rather complicated task of making useful and generally accessible comparisons among those categories.

We therefore propose that analyses of the huge datasets should be seen as giving only part of the answers to essential questions concerning urban users' motivations for their activities and urban designers' aim to deliver solutions. In order to glean such information, planners and researchers continue to rely on, for instance, the traditional in-depth interview to track other important parameters, such as the needs and motivations behind city user behaviour.

References

Gehl, J. et al. (2006) *New City Life*. Copenhagen: The Danish Architectural Press.

Harder, H. et al. (2008) *Det mangfoldige byrum: aalborg 2008 - byrumsundersøgelse_del 1*. Aalborg: A&D skriftserie (18), Aalborg Universitet.

Harder, H. et al. (2008) *Det mangfoldige byrum: aalborg 2008 - byrumsundersøgelse_del 2*. Aalborg: A&D skriftserie (18), Aalborg Universitet.

Harder, H. et al. (2008) 'Experiences from GPS tracking of visitors in Public Parks in Denmark based on GPS technologies'. In: van Schaick, J. and van der Spek, S. (Eds.) *Urbanism on Track. Application of Tracking Technologies in Urbanism*. Amsterdam: IOS Press.

Kwan, M. (2009) 'GIS Methods in Time-Geographic Research: Geocomputation and Geovisualization of Human Activity Patterns'. In: *Geografiska Annaler: Series B, Human Geography*, 86 (4): 267–280.

Nielsen, T. A. S. and Hovgesen, H. H. (2005) ´Urban fields in the making: new evidence from a Danish context´. In: *Tijdschrift voor Economische en Sociale Geografie*, 96(5): 515-528.

Van der Spek, S. et al. (2009) 'Sensing Human Activity: GPS Tracking'. In: *Sensors* 2009, 9:3033-3055.

The New Nørreport

Ann Sofie Christensen, Kristian Overby, Sebastian Andersen & Thomas Oxvig Håkonsson

TRANSIT SPACE AND PUBLIC DOMAIN

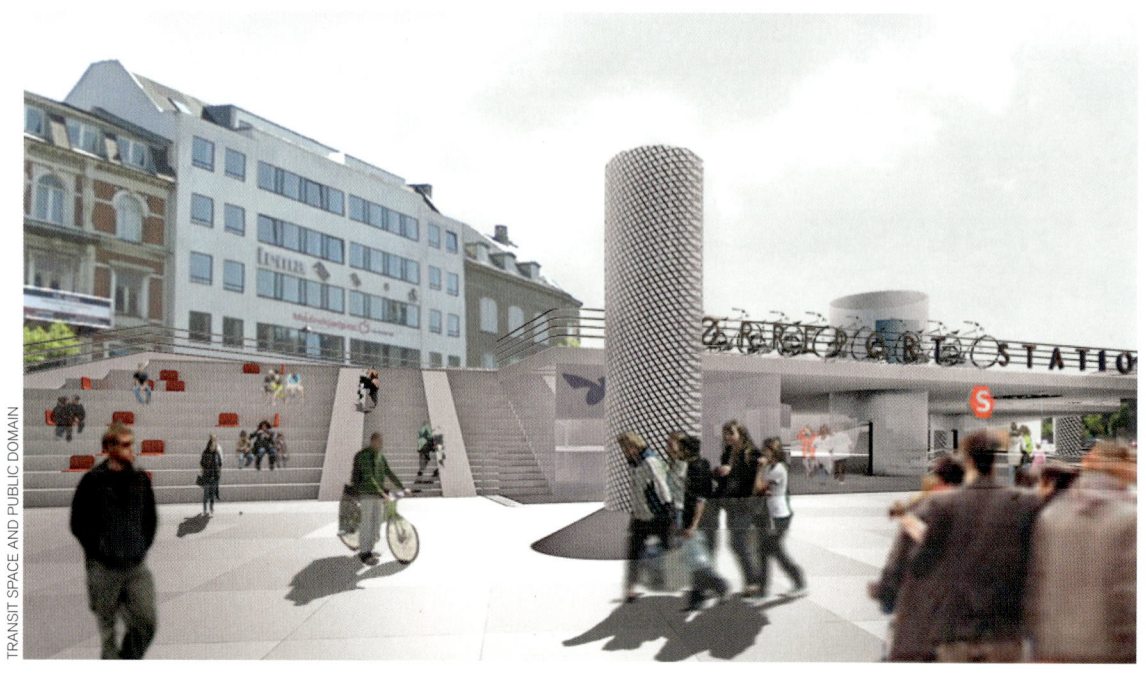

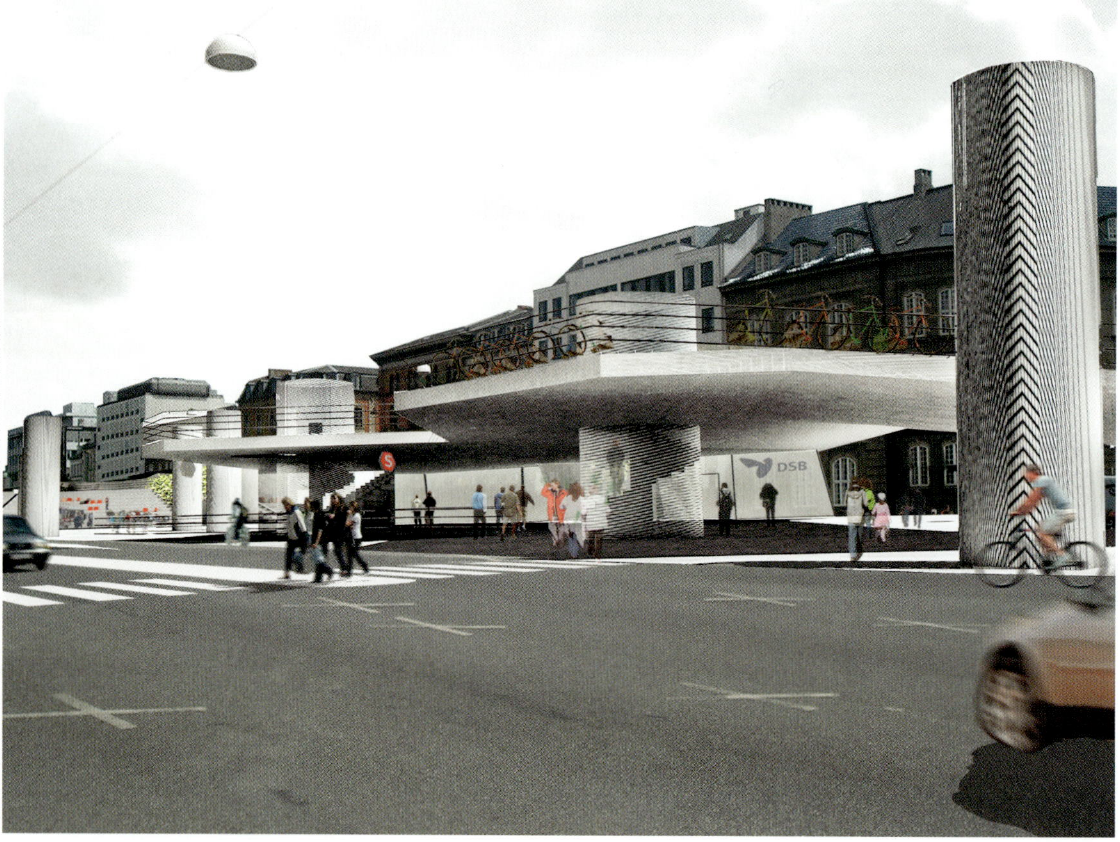

NØRREPORT STATION AS A PART OF THE FLOW OF MULTIMODAL TRANSPORTATION

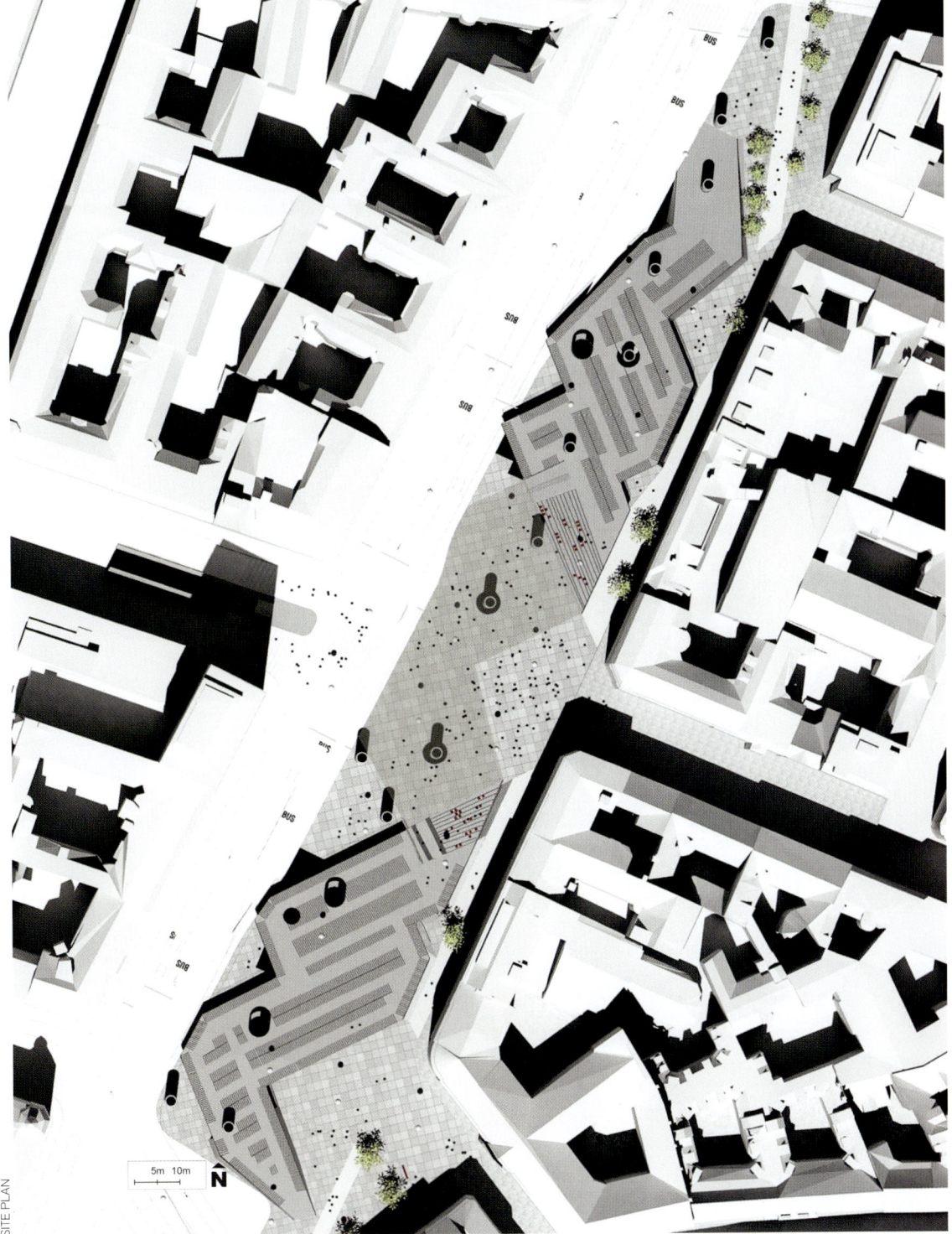

SITE PLAN

Nørreport Station, Copenhagen, is a complex facility to use with its multiple modes of transportation. To accommodate this it was the intention to create as seamless an experience as possible. The challenge is that places designed for seamless travel easily get so generic and streamlined, that people have a hard time relating to them. Concurrently the station serves as one of the greatest potentials for public domains in Copenhagen metropolitan area. The concept of this project was to create the greatest possible compromise between the two by merging seamless flows and facilities of recreation for the public domain in such a way that they do not conflict with one another.

A Matter of Planning? - with the light rail towards a new Aarhus

Line Morsing Nielsen & Maria Vestergaard Jensen

The Municipality of Aarhus aims at having 75,000 new citizens, 50,000 new dwellings and jobs, and 10,000 new student residences by 2030, as well as a new light rail connecting downtown Aarhus and the northern suburbs. These aspects of development have been the point of departure for this master thesis, which challenges concepts of sustainability and station-related urban development with the light rail as a catalyst for urban growth in a local, municipal and regional context. The project offers an illustration of how this may be accomplished through two design scenarios boasting the development of new dense, beautiful, and diverse sub-centers along the light rail – both in relation to built-up areas as well as un-built ones.

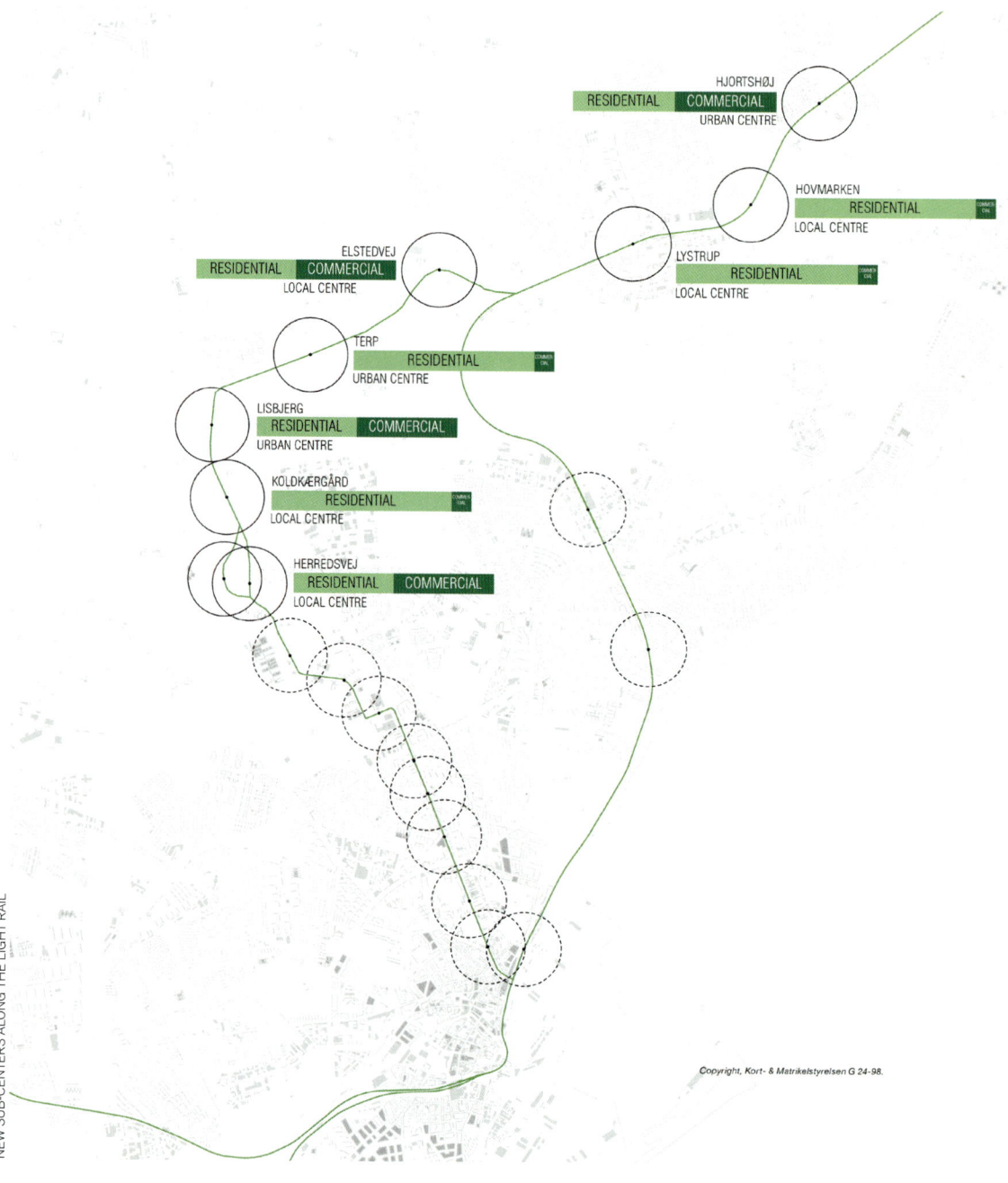

NEW SUB-CENTERS ALONG THE LIGHT RAIL

CENTRAL SQUARE OF SUB-CENTRE

Selected student project / Master Thesis 2009 / Supervisor: Henrik Harder
Mobility

Consequences at local scale.
Copyright, Kort & Matrikelstyrelsen G 24-98.

Consequences at municipal scale.
Copyright, Kort & Matrikelstyrelsen G 24-98.

Consequences at regional scale.
Copyright, Kort & Matrikelstyrelsen G 24-98.

CONSEQUENCES BY SCALE

Dynamic Eastern Jutland – a vision
Sille Christiane Linnet & Lisa Gedsø

Increased private traffic has given way to an expansion of buildings along the Danish highways and therefore the landscape is receding. The result is a monotonous traffic experience. Eastern Jutland was used as case, and an analysis of the highway between Randers and Kolding was made. The number of buildings along the highway proved to be more extensive than first expected. Additionally, areas for sale were reserved for trade buildings. A vision of future land use along the highway was designed with the main goal being to create a variety of traffic experiences and to prevent the areas along the highway from becoming even more densely built.

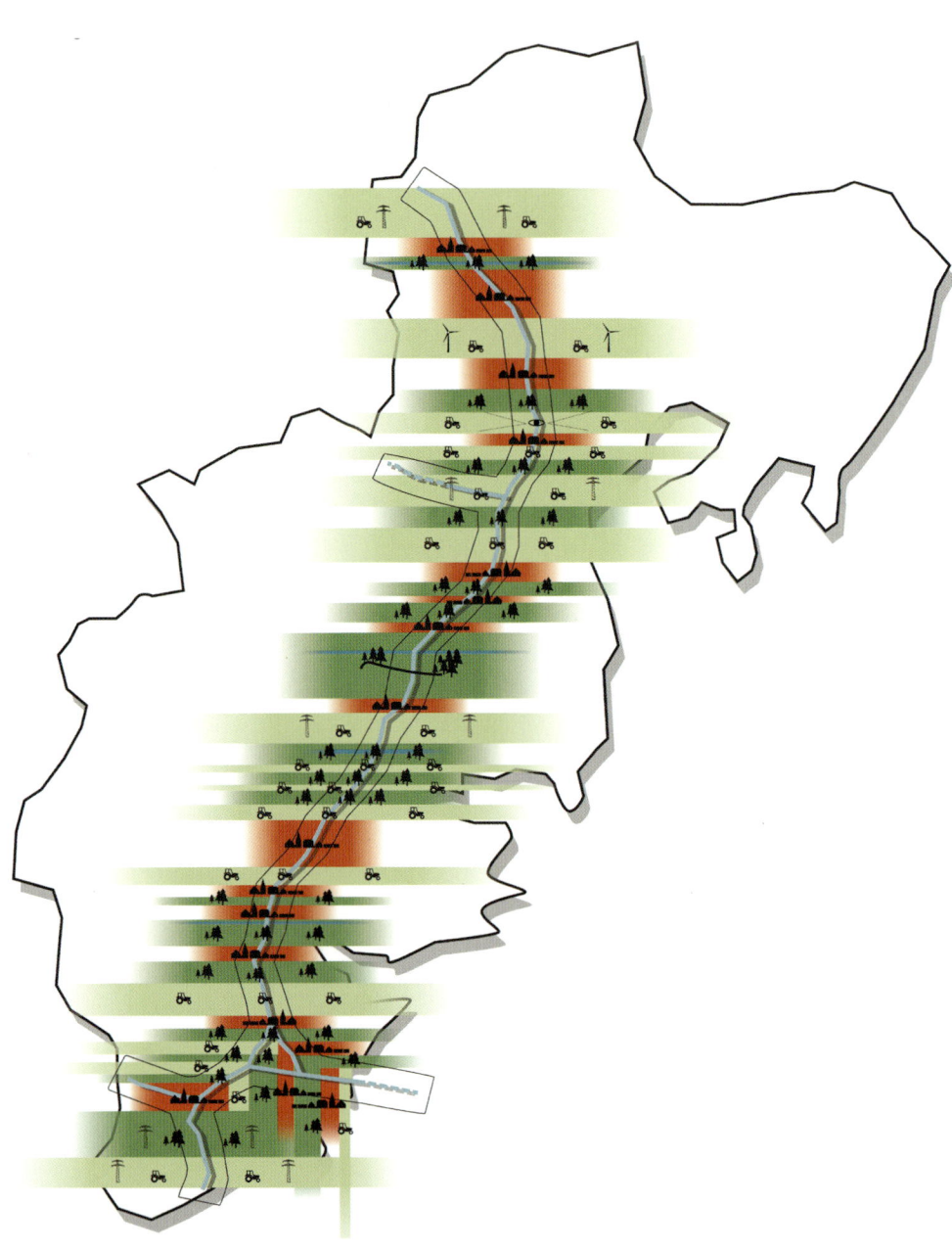

IN MOTION ANALYSIS

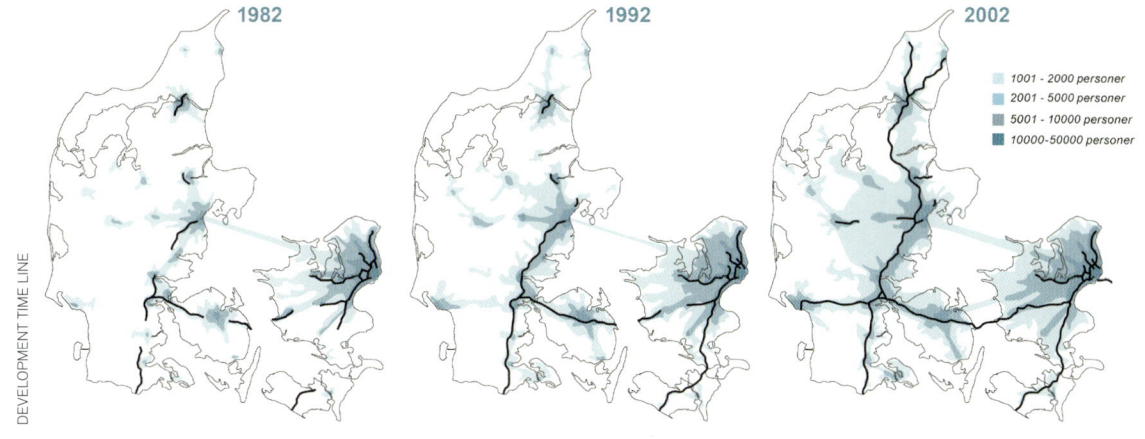

DEVELOPMENT TIME LINE

DESIGN CASE, CLUSTER OF WINDMILLS AHEAD

DESIGN CASE, AVENUE OF WINDMILLS DEFINING THE ROAD

Selected student project / Master Thesis 2009 / Supervisor: Henrik Harder
Mobility

Transforming Vestergade Vest into a Ludic and Shared-Use Space

Victor Andrade, Ole B. Jensen, Henrik Harder & Jens C. O. Madsen

1: VESTERGADE VEST: A SHARED USE SPATIALITY

Introduction

During the last century, motorized vehicles have dominated the streets. However, the emergence of the debate about sustainability and its relation to the urban environment has influenced urban designers to rethink the role of the streets and their spatiality. Pedestrians and cyclists are gaining space, not only for moving to a specific destination, but also space in which to play and stay.

Taking into consideration the formal structure of our cities, streets are critical to urban transformation and are strategic in terms of restructuring urban flows and the quality of urban life.

This paper aims to explore and discuss shared spatiality as a design strategy to enhance street life and non-motorized modes of transportation. This research is part of a project titled Bikeability – funded by the Danish Research Council. The overall purpose of the Bikeability project is to investigate and document relations between cycling motivation from different socio-demographic groups and distinct design characteristics related to the urban environment and cycling infrastructure. Under the umbrella of the Bikeability research project, this paper describes the result of an in-depth case study of the urban transformation of a street in the centre of Odense – Vestergade Vest.

Firstly, this paper presents the notion of shared-use streets – including a brief historical context and a debate about the design characteristics of shared-use streets and their role in enhancing street life. Secondly, it presents a creative and low budget design solution that transformed Vestergade Vest (located in the centre of the Danish city of Odense) into a ludic and shared-use space. Vestergade Vest was originally a stream of cars infiltrating the core of the city; it has now been closed to motorized traffic and is a strictly reserved shared space for everyone from cyclists to pedestrians, families and youths. As a result, Vestergade Vest has became a very vibrant and diverse space encompassing cafés, entertainment, restaurants, shops and playful elements (see Figure 1).

Bridging research and practice, the findings of this research project can also support pedestrian and bike-friendly design and a more vibrant street life.

Shared-Use Streets

Decisions on transportation projects are typically based on the potential for the project to contribute to broad public policy goals. In this context, streets are valuable public spaces that do not only provide the space for traffic movement and access to buildings. Streets have the potential to function as spaces of diversity wherein several roles are developed at the same time. Shared-use space has always been a common concept when designing streets and still is in many parts of the world today. Until the nineteenth century, most streets could be defined as shared-use spaces. Conditions were not necessarily comfortable, but the street certainly created an arena where people interacted with each other to negotiate their way forward.

However, during the last century mainstream urban design segregated motorized vehicles, vulnerable modes of transport and pedestrians in terms of space for the sake of speed, safety and efficiency (Hamilton-Baillie 2008). Therefore the majority of the public realm was occupied by motorized vehicles.

Moreover, design solutions have commonly prioritized motorized traffic at the expense of pedestrians and vulnerable modes of transport, which include bikes, skateboards, wheelchairs, etc. (Patton 2007). Streets usually have a design whereby motorized vehicles are prioritized and the concept of dedicated lanes for each street user has become the general design solution. Consequently, streets have large motorized vehicle lanes and narrow pavements where there is no space for alternative activities, which results in urban environments lacking or suffering from a shortage of attractive public space.

An inflexion in the design of streets occurred in the 1960s. The contemporary solution of shared-use streets was developed in the Netherlands where the woonerf concept was developed and implemented in Dutch residential suburbs at the end of the decade. Woornef is the concept of lively street where the needs of motorized vehicles are secondary to the needs of vulnerable modes of transport and pedestrians. The main goal is to create a shared-use space for pedestrians, playing children, cyclists, etc. (Appleyard 1981; IHIE, 2002; Quimby and Castle 2006).
Later, the concept was brought to the core of several North European cities. There is currently a renaissance of lively streets through urban design interventions that reclaim the public realm from the dominance of motorized vehicles, thus transforming segregated traffic spaces into shared use and lively spots.

Gillies (2010) points out that the space in a street must be shared like any other limited resource. Shared space integrates pedestrians and other road users and usually eliminates traditional street design elements such as traffic lights, pedestrian barriers and dedicated lanes.

A growing body of literature indicates a link between the establishment of a shared-use space and the improvement of safety (Van den Broecke and Rijkswaterstaat 1980; Shared Space 2005; Velde and Bos 2008). A shared space creates ambiguity and also gives users a higher perception of risk, which leads them to behave more cautiously.

Shared-Use Space and Lively Streets

There is no precise definition of the notion of shared-use streets and there are several terminologies – civilized street, single surface street, street renaissance, etc. – which are directly related to this notion. However, there is a consensus that the concept of shared-use streets is based on a vision of social integration, high quality multi-purpose spaces and diversity of street life.

Reid (2009) understands shared space as a design approach rather than a standard type of design. Therefore shared-use streets cannot be generalized and they cannot be understood as something generic. The rationale of shared-use streets is that they are essentially unique and have characteristics that are intrinsic to their locations. However, Reid (2009) also suggests that three design parameters directly influence the performance of such streets: connection to the traffic system, surface, and the speed of the motorized vehicles. When designing shared-use streets, it is paramount to create a design for human interaction, public life and slow movement. In this context, streets should be seen as an arena to facilitate social activities and not the opposite, which often happens in traditional segregated streets.

The design of shared-use streets has some peculiarities that differ from those applied to streets where motorized vehicles are hegemonic. For example, signage is primarily designed to answer the demands of the slow-moving users. Moreover, there are often times when experimental and playful solutions are applied in which an intimate connection with the street user is intended (Hamilton-Baillie 2008). There are big differences between the street environment with hegemony of low and high speed. The different traffic modes are usually in conflict because of the differences in speed. This conflict has been highlighted by urban designers and has become an important theme on the agenda of several local governments.

Method

The main element of the case study is a questionnaire amongst users of the three infrastructures allowing determination of the socio-economic characteristics of the users and effects of the infrastructure in terms of the use of bikes. Furthermore, the users were asked to assess the infrastructure project as well as to describe what specific design element most motivated them to travel by bike. Furthermore, field studies and observation methods were applied. A number of instructed research assistants observed the space and its functionality as well as conducting the questionnaire survey at the site.

The Transformation of Vestergade Vest

Vestergade Vest is a very progressive shared-use space created on a very low budget of only DKK 500,000, which has helped to push imagination even further into a fusion of creativity. It is also a very temporary and flexible space where experi-mentation can take place.

One of the main challenges for contemporary urban designers is to enhance public life in our cities. Being engaged in this debate, Danish urban designers have been searching for alternatives to enhance the public realm and life in the streets.

In this context, Vestergade Vest can be seen as a valuable experience to better understand possible alternatives in order to enhance public life in the streets.

The transformation of Vestergade Vest is part of an overall strategic plan to improve the quality of urban life within the core of Odense as described in the Traffic and Mobility Plan 2008 (City of Odense 2009).

As background to the strategic plan, a study conducted by Gehl Architects indicated that the number of pedestrians in the core of the city was decreasing. One of the reasons mentioned was the increasing level of competition between street-based retail and large commercial shopping centres located in the outskirts of Odense – for example the shopping centre called Rosengårdscenteret, which has 100,000 m2 of shop floor space.

In this context, the City of Odense has implemented several physical interventions in order to promote a lively urban core – including the transformation of Vestergade Vest into a shared-use street, although without cars. According to an interview with Dorthe Råby and Rune Bugge Jensen (urban designers from the City of Odense who worked directly with the transformation of Vestergade Vest), one of the main targets

3: CYCLISTS RIDING THEIR BIKES TO WORK AND SLOWING DOWN WHEN APPROACHING A SPEED BUMP AT VESTERGADE VEST.

of these interventions is to improve the quality of the experience of walking and cycling.

Formerly, Vestergade Vest had more than two hundred buses passing every day causing noise pollution, air pollution and also inhibiting a more friendly space for pedestrians, cyclists and other potential activities in the public space. (see Figure 2).

On 1st August 2010, Vestergade Vest was closed to motorized vehicle traffic and the urban transformation began. The approach to changing the street was done in a somewhat untraditional manner.

Due to the tight municipal budget, the technicians had to develop a proposal at a cost of only DKK 500,000. The small budget limited opportunities for structural changes in the materials and surfaces of the street. This limitation forced the technicians to come up with a creative solution, preserving the street surfaces and materials and using temporary elements that made it possible to rethink the design concept during the entire project period. The street profile was completely preserved. However, its spatial logic was radically transformed into a shared-use space. The former street made crowded by motorized vehicles was transformed into a shared-use space for pedestrians, cyclists and a future central electric bus ring – allowing access of motorized vehicles carrying goods, as well as cars of local residents. All the buses were rerouted to parallel streets nearby and taxis were permitted in the area from 10pm to 6am (City of Odense 2009).

After the urban transformation, the street changed its profile completely – enhancing walking, cycling, shopping, eating and playing in a shared user space. The urban transformation has enhanced a discussion about public domain and has also regenerated the image of Vestergade Vest to that of a lively street (Andrade et al. 2011).

The entire urban transformation took only 14 days to complete and the official opening was held on 14th August 2010. During these 14 days the street was closed to vehicles, but the former car lane and pavements remained intact. Several elements were then inserted into the streetscape – plastic guiding markers, bicycle parking racks, ping-pong tables, etc. – and Vestergade Vest began to look more like a flexible and informal street which was open to different experiences.

Moreover, there are also signs which are integrated into the design of the street. These signs give information about the use of the space in a more playful way: For example, symbols of a footprint and bicycle wheels painted onto the pavement (Figure 5).

There are no signs in the street defining speed and behaviour, but that is also the concept of shared-use

4: MULTIPLICITY OF USERS, USES AND TRANSIT MODES

5: LUDIC INTERVENTIONS

space. The playful elements supply the street with a more lively and relaxed atmosphere and enhance the concept of a shared-use space (Figure 3 and 4).

The project is not yet finalized, which is indeed its precise intention: to be a dynamic intervention that can be improved over time and adapted to new demands. More elements will be added over time, in addition to the fact that evaluations of the space may change the layout over time. The intervention made it possible to implement new changes at a low cost. After the first month, the technicians from the municipal authority received feedback from users – pedestrians, cyclists, shopkeepers, people out dining, etc. – after which re-arrangement of the mobile equipment took place and plastic markers were relocated. Vestergade Vest can be seen as a laboratory where temporary interventions were made in order to understand how the population would react to new experiences and the public space. The pavements and levels of the former street were retained and elements were inserted into the streetscape to indicate pedestrian-only paths along facades and shared space in the middle of the road.

Rune Bugge Jensen and Dorthe Råby emphasized how important it is to improve urban life experience in the core of Odense. With regard to the intervention at Vestergade Vest and Mageløs, he stated:

"I wanted to push the limits from what experiences people have in the public space and I also wanted to make them start to question and reflect for what a public space could be used for… It has been very provocative to put ping pong tables on the former motorized vehicle lanes… It has been a challenge to reinvent the former motorized vehicle lanes into a space for urban life, play and exercise"
(interview with Rune Bugge Jensen, 2nd of September, 2010).

Shared-Use Space and Speed

The flow of cyclists and pedestrians at Vestergade Vest moves in multiple directions with the main flow of cyclists along the middle of the street. Traffic flow in the morning is relatively calm as there are no pedestrians congesting the space, which allows cyclists to flow freely. Cyclists are focused and know exactly how to navigate and avoid other cyclists. In the morning the street is not occupied by shop signs or café tables as is the case in the afternoon, making it possible for cyclists and delivery vans to move swiftly and unobstructed through the street.

In order to slow the speed of the cyclists there is a speed bump placed at one of the most critical points of the street where many programmes such as a café, ping-pong tables and shops are placed side-by-side (Figure 6).

6: LUDIC URBAN FURNITURE (E.G. TENNIS TABLE) AND TRAFFIC CALMING FOR BIKES

7: LUDIC SIGNAGE INDICATING THE STARTING OF THE SHARED USE SPATIALITY

In the morning, cyclists try to avoid the speed bump by making a detour onto the pavement instead of continuing in the road. In the afternoon it is more difficult for the cyclists to avoid the speed bump because of the crowded pedestrian flow on the pavements.

The flow structure in the afternoon is thus completely different from the morning flow. The street is more crowded, which produces a more congested and chaotic flow. However, cyclists still persist in riding at high speeds, but they are disturbed by pedestrians moving in multiple directions and at a slower pace. It means that the cyclists sometimes have to brake suddenly or come to a complete stop and carry their bike through the space.

In the afternoon the street is transformed into a multiple shared space, and therefore the flow is somewhat more congested. The pedestrians begin to occupy the shared-use space in the middle of the street, thus disturbing the flow of eager cyclists. Conversely, there are many pedestrians crossing the street while cyclists and pedestrians are moving in many different directions, thus creating a complex situation. Additionally, there are several other uses in the shared area – including people sitting at restaurant tables and kids playing. In the evening the shops close at 6 pm and people begin to bounce around the space in multiple directions crowding the infrastructure – some going out for dinner, others going out to party. At the same time, cyclists are eager to ride fast through the street, which creates a complex and chaotic zone where cyclists need be aware of crossing pedestrians – whilst pedestrians need to be aware of fast-moving cyclists.

In the evening the street is calmer and there are not as many people on the street, so cyclists can go a lot faster. To prevent cyclists from going too fast a speed bump has been built into the street, although as mentioned previously many cyclists go onto the pedestrian path to avoid the speed bump. By creating a shared-use street where pedestrians, cyclists and drivers explore new spatial and social relations, the innovative design of Vestergade Vest enhances new speeds and flows in the streetscape of Odense.

Final Remarks

This paper aims to present the relationship between shared-use spaces and public life. In doing so it highlights the implementation of shared-use space as one strategic key to enhancing public life.

The theoretical underpinning of this research is partly derived from the nexus of traffic planning and urban design in general. However, at a more profound level we are inspired by the 'mobility turn' (Urry 2007) and its insistence on seeing mobility and sites of mobility as much more that just instrumental acts of movement from A to B. We understand mobility as an important social and cultural activity that transforms and affects how we understand ourselves, others and our environment (Jensen 2009). From this understanding it also makes sense to open up the design agenda in the direction of re-thinking streets and public spaces as sites for playful interaction and social exchange.

Shared-use spaces are not common in Denmark, but they can be an alternative way of creating more lively urban spaces enhancing a variety of experiences. However, this may depend on a longer process of appropriation within a traffic culture that has been extremely regulated over many decades. The open and dynamic situations of shared spaces may be seen as out of touch with the Danish experience of detailed and highly regulated traffic design (for research on the differences in cycling culture see Furnness 2010; Jensen 2007; Mikkelsen et al. 2011). Further research must document whether the Danish context is less open to appropriating the shared- space planning doctrine than other nations.

The outcomes of this research may be propagated and used by decision-makers, urban designers, city planners and traffic engineers committed to promoting more vibrant public life.

References

Andrade, V. et al. (2011) 'Bike Infrastructures'. In: *Architecture and Design*. 37. Aalborg: Department of Architecture and Design, Aalborg University.

Appleyard, D. (1981). *Liveable Streets*. Berkeley, CA: University of California Press.

Furness, Z. (2010) *One Less Car. Bicycling and the Politics of Automobility*. Philadelphia: Temple University Press.

Gillies, A. (2010) *Is the road there to share? Shared space an Australian context*. PhD Thesis. University of South Wales.

Hamilton-Baillie, B. (2008) 'Shared Space: Reconciling People, Places and Traffic'. In: *Built Environment*, 34: pp.161-181.

IHIE (2002) *Home Zone Design Guidelines*. Institute of Highway Incorporated Engineers, England.

Jensen, R. (2010) Interviewed by Kristian Overby, 2 September.

Jensen, O. B. (2009) 'Flows of Meaning, Cultures of Movements – Urban Mobility as Meaningful Everyday Life Practice'. In: *Mobilities*, 4: pp.139-158.

Jensen, O. B. (2007) 'Biking in the Land of the Car – clashes of mobility cultures in the USA'. In: *Proceedings of the Conference Trafikdage*. Aalborg.

Mikkelsen, J., Smith, S. & Jensen, O. B. (2011) 'Challenging the 'King of the Road' – exploring mobility battles between cars and bikes in the USA'. In: *Proceedings for the 4th Nordic Geographers Meeting*. Roskilde, Denmark.

Odense Municipality (2009i) *Trafik og mobilitetsplan*. Available from: http://www.odense.dk/Topmenu/Borger/ByMiljoe/Planlaegning/Trafikplan.aspx (Accessed 18 November 2012).

Patton, J. (2007) 'A pedestrian world: Competing rationalities and the calculation of transportation change'. In: *Environment and Planning*, 39 (4): pp.928-944.

Quimby, A. and Castle, J. (2006) *A Review of Simplified Streetscape Schemes*. Published Project Report 292, Transport for London.

Reid, S. (2009) *Appraisal of Shared Space. Report for the British Department for Transport*. United Kingdom.

Shared Space (2005) Shared Space: *Plads til alle – en ny vision for det offentlige rum*. Leeuwarden: Interreg IIIB project Shared Space, Province Fryslan.

Urry, J. (2007) *Mobilities*. Cambridge: Polity.

Van den Broecke, Rijkswaterstaat (1980) Belevingsonderzoek demonstratie-fietsroutes Den Haag – Tilburg. Samenvattend rapport. Netherlands

Velde, R. and Bos, E. (2008) *Shared space Haren, Evaluatie en integratie, Concept*. Grontmij, Haren. Netherlands.

Enhancing the landscape - architectural installations in the Landscape
Lea Louise Holst Laursen

In the Nordic countries the more sparsely populated rural areas are facing difficulties. The small communities within are facing a decline in economy and population, which has become evident in the exodus of young people, the increasing number of elderly people, an increasing number of vacant buildings and declining employment opportunities. At the same time, structural changes are emerging in the rural landscapes, as they evolve from being primarily utility landscapes of production (fishery, foresting and agriculture) to increasingly becoming leisure landscapes of recreation and experiences. This transformation can be seen as a way of responding to the difficulties these rural territories are undergoing; a transformation where the rural landscapes are given a new and different role. The French Architectural theoretician Sébastien Marot points to the importance of dealing with the rural landscape in new ways:

> "The preservation of the legacy of these agrarian communities, the care of their resources, and the adaptation to new, changing economies demand true intervention in the form of innovative landscape projects" (Sébastien Marot 1999: 49)

This suggests that an important task lies within developing the landscape on all scales from local public spaces to extensive multifunctional landscapes (Laursen 2011), (Laursen and Andersson 2011). Thus the accessibility and/or attractiveness of the local landscape could be a decisive factor in the development potential of individual localities (Tietjen and Laursen 2008). This means seeing the landscape as a valuable asset that can be used proactively in these shrinking rural areas (Laursen and Andersson 2011).

This increased focus on the landscape and its inherent potential in the development of rural areas is related to a site-specific approach currently prevailing in Nordic peripheral rural areas. This approach involves identifying and using the inherent potential present within the site and using this potential as an engine for development. In this respect, the landscape is often used due to the number of scenic landscapes present in Nordic rural landscapes. In Denmark one of the first site-specific landscape initiatives was the establishment of five national parks, the first one being Thy National park, which opened in August 2008. The purpose of the national parks was to protect and develop the valuable cultural and natural landscapes, but also to make the landscapes more accessible to locals and tourists. Finally, the national parks have a role in contributing to regional economic development through, for example, increased tourism, and with the national park as an incentive for local business activity, the possibility of launching special "national park articles" like food, tourism, trade (Danish Forest and Nature Agency 2008).

Another Danish initiative is the initiatives of the private foundation Realdania regarding peripheral Danish rural areas. Through a number of initiatives, the foundation focuses on site-based development possibilities; firstly in the land of possibilities campaign (Danish: mulighedernes land) and most recently in the site matters campaign (Danish: stedet tæller). In the 'site matters' campaign the goal is to develop and exploit the site-based potential, which can then boost quality of life in peripheral areas (stedet-taeller 2012).

In Norway the Norwegian Highway Authority is head of a project called the National Tourist Routes Project, a project that aims to make Norway a more attractive tourist destination, thus boosting business and the living environment in peripheral areas in Norway. This is done through determined work with the existing landscape and the staging of the landscape by making it more accessible (this project will be used as a case later in the paper). What these projects and other related projects in the Nordic countries have in common is a focus on the site-specific landscape potential. They seek to find landscape potential and exploit it, often by working with physical spatial installations, and thus create some kind of surplus value that apparently adds to an increased leisure and experience economy in the peripheral rural areas.

With a point of departure in perceiving the landscape as a potential in creating a surplus value in peripheral rural areas, I will, in what follows, endeavour to investigate the potential of creating installations in the landscape that combine architecture and landscape, thus creating an enhanced experience of the landscape. By using the aforementioned case of the National Tourist Routes Project in Norway, I will look into the integration of built structures and the rural Norwegian landscape, in addition to which the project has used the potential of the landscape combined with architecture to create new or renewed identities in a field that is characterized by its scenic landscapes as well as its negative development forecasts. Can determined work with landscape plus architecture be a new identifying element in rural landscapes, contributing to the production of a specific identity of place that can in turn contribute to increased economic revenue?

1- STEGASTEIN LOOKOUT, AURLAND, NORWAY. ARCHITECTURE MEETS LANDSCAPE CREATING SPECTACULAR VIEWS OVER THE FJORD LANDSCAPE © NILS VIK

Enhancing the landscape - architectural installations in the Landscape
Transformation

Methods

The intention of this paper is thus to explore site-specific landscape installations regarding both the relationship between landscape and architecture and how architecture can enhance the landscape and vice versa, as well as looking into these site-specific landscape installations as a means of creating not only a spatial and aesthetic surplus value, but also creating an economic surplus.

In order to develop this theoretically, the subject of landscape is investigated in order to get closer to what site-specific landscape projects are and in order to grasp which landscape concept is present in contemporary landscape architecture. Furthermore, the relationship between landscape and architecture is investigated to get closer to what landscape and architectural installations can contribute within the peripheral rural areas.

With the purpose of exemplifying site-specific landscape installations, one main case that can help to exemplify the theoretical findings has been chosen. The case is, as mentioned earlier, the Norwegian National Tourist Routes Project. In Norway, the Norwegian Parliament and Ministry of Transport and Communications have commissioned the development of the National Tourist Routes Project, which by the end of 2020 will hopefully have created 18 routes throughout the Norwegian landscape enhancing the landscape and accessibility to the landscape for tourists and visitors. The project is placed under the auspices of the Norwegian Highway Authority and has a total budget of 3.4 billion Norwegian Kroner (Stenbro 2011). The purpose of the project is to develop and market high-quality tourist attractions (Evensen 2006).

Theories of landscape

"What we denote as nature is often culture: a man-made, societal, historical phenomenon. It is a long time since we have recognized that moor, common and pine-forest are a result of a particular way of cultivation. To realize that nature is usually the work of man is a simple necessity" (Hauxner 2011:10) (the author's own translation from Danish to English)

The quotation by Professor Malene Hauxner states that nature and culture are not a dichotomy, but rather two closely related terms that mutually influence one another. This recognition makes us question whether there is such a thing as natural nature. Architect Rem Koolhaas uses the term super-nature in his book Delirious New York from 1994 in order to stress that there is no such thing as natural nature. In later works by Koolhaas he switches to using the term landscape in the same way as super-nature. Here landscape marks the dissolution of the dichotomy: nature versus culture. Hence, the landscape is to be understood as more than just a traditional pastoral understanding of green areas. This holistic scope of the concept of landscape is evident in the European Landscape Convention from 2000, where the landscape is understood as a whole where natural and cultural components are perceived together (Thompson and Herlin 2004), (Council of Europe 2000). Thus landscape reflects society and its history (Holden 2006: 19). Moreover, landscape can influence the shaping of modern culture (Corner 1999) and the landscape can be seen as a moulder of culture.

"Underlying this aim is the belief that landscape has the capacity to critically engage the metaphysical and political programs that operate in a given society, that landscape architecture is not simply a reflection of culture but more an active instrument in the shaping of modern culture." (Corner 1999: 1)

Landscape architect James Corner thus sees the landscape as an enricher and producer of culture, and by working purposefully with the landscape new meanings can arise within the landscape. This means that the landscape is not perceived as something that needs to be preserved at any cost, but as something that continuously develops and is transformed with respect to the characteristic potential of the specific site.

The Danish architect Jørgen Bo argued in 1963 that it is not enough to make decisions about what must not happen with the landscape (Jørgen Bo in Hauxner 2003: 48) (Jørgen Bo's statement is repeated in Malene Hauxner's book Open to the Sky from 2003, but originally the statement is from Jørgen Bo's article Landskabsbehandling, published in the journal Byplan vol. 84 in 1963 on page 31). Jørgen Bo states that to a large extent it is necessary to preserve the landscape, but that we also have to take constructive action and to evaluate and develop landscape values in order to ensure the correct use and management of the landscape (Jørgen Bo in Hauxner 2003: 48). Thus we have to be aware of the balance between considering the landscape as nature to be preserved and considering the landscape as a medium for artistic treatment (Hauxner 2003: 49).

Developing site through landscape and architecture

"Of course, every site is already unique. The topography, surface material, scale, and light peculiar to a particular place creates a special character. This character is built up in layers – from the bedrock, through chalk and clay sediments, to the Ice-Age deposits of stone and gravel that have been subject to the influences of climate and the actions of human settlement for centuries. These endless combinatorial possibilities provide the basis for the essential to be deduced. Local conditions of material, light, space, and structure ought to inspire and generate

new forms of design as needs and desires change." (Høyer 1999: 72)

The landscape is unique for each site where the climate and other local conditions affect the landscape and shape it. These differences in the landscape can be worked with where *"local phenomena such as light, weather, topography, horizon and earth provide clues as to how we might create new landscapes on the basis of what exists in a given location"* (Høyer 1999: 74).

Thus the reading of the landscape, its programme, history, materiality, etc., become extremely important when designing the renewed landscape and when introducing, for example, architectural installations within the landscape. Thus determined work with the landscape using its inherent potential seems to create a specific identity of place. By exploiting the potential of the landscape, it seems possible to stand out from the crowd and brand an area as a unique locality, creating an attractor in itself. Moreover, however, the use of architectonic installations within a landscape can create distinction in the landscape and thereby emphasize that the landscape can be enhanced by working with it from an architectonic perspective.

A case in point is Peter Zumthor's Thermal bath in Vals built in 1996. Here Zumthor uses local materials – stone from a local quarry – to achieve this local landscape narrative. Even more interesting in a landscape perspective is the way in which he integrates the building into the mountain landscape, making the building look like a grass-covered mountain. Zumthor thus exploits the qualities of the specific landscape – raw materials and topography – where the thermal bath is designed as an interplay between building and landscape trying to establish a special relationship between the building and the mountain landscape (Zumthor 1997).

"Mountain, stone, water, building with stone, building into the mountain, building out of the mountain – our attempts to give this chain of words an architectural interpretation, to translate into architecture its meanings and sensuousness, guided our design for the building and step-by-step gave it form." (Zumthor 1997: 11)

As mentioned above, the intention is to perceive the bath as a large grass-covered mountain stone coming out from the slope (Zumthor 1997). This huge monolithic structure is then hollowed out and provided with *"caves, sunken areas and slots for a variety of uses (which) also helped to define a strategy for cutting up the stone mass towards the top of the building, to bring in light."* (Zumthor 1997: 13)

This unique interplay between building and landscape indicates a determined use of the potential of the landscape, and this hybrid between landscape and building

3: STEGASTEIN LOOKOUT, AURLAND, NORWAY. THE INSTALLATION GIVES THE VISITOR THE POSSIBILITY TO FULLY EXPERIENCE THE DRAMATIC LANDSCAPES OF AURLAND FJORD © TODD SAUNDERS

becomes a brand, giving the place a special character in relation to other places.

However, Nordic architectural tradition is famous for its: *"interplay between building and landscape, where the landscape is used to form and structure the buildings, and the buildings play an active part in the landscape treatment"*. as expressed by, among others, Jørn Utzon, Alvar Alto and Jørgen Bo (Hauxner 2003: 54).

Here there is a gentle interaction between landscape and architecture, where the landscape influences the architecture and vice versa. Looking at Alvar Alto's work, he deliberately works with horizontality and verticality when building houses in the landscape.

> *"Placing vertical and horizontal planes into the sloping terrain was an important part of Alvar Alto's language."* (Hauxner 2003: 34)

This deliberate use of horizontal and vertical planes resulted in Alto's characteristic squares and flights of steps or, as at Alto's art museum in Aalborg, an amphitheatre and a sculpture garden *"which like a broad, grass-covered stairway cuts into the slope supported by vertical white walls."* (Hauxner 2003: 34)
Here there is a gentle interaction between landscape and architecture, where the landscape influences the architecture and vice versa. Looking at Alvar Alto's work, he deliberately works with horizontality and verticality when building houses in the landscape.

This particular Scandinavian architecture is strongly influenced by Frank Lloyd Wright and his deliberate work with the relationship between building and landscape. Looking for instance at Lloyd Wright's *Falling Water* built between 1936 and 1939, Lloyd Wright builds upon a waterfall and integrates the landscape within the building and thereby creates a unique building. The building adapts to the landscape, but it also enriches the landscape. In relation to Lloyd Wright's architectural activities, he has claimed that it was only after the house had been built accentuating the lines of the landscape and reflecting the textural oddness of his choice of site-specific materials that people could see the characteristic beauty of the place (Langkilde 1959: 204).

The examples thus show that the use of architecture can determine the specific place and its physical qualities (Solá-Morales 1997). The architecture brings an aesthetic dimension to space; the architectural installation, with its composition of landscape, use of materials, textures, surfaces, furniture and so on, can create an experience in itself as it may add a certain expression to space which can be enjoyed and turn it into a place (Larsen and Laursen 2012). It is thereby emphasized that within a site-specific landscape approach the inherent potential of the site has to be considered a decisive element and incorporated as an active and acting partner (Stenbro and Christoffersen 2008), in addition to the fact that architectonical structures can influence the landscape and an architectonic restructuring of existing sites can even create new meanings for its users – making new sites (Larsen and Laursen 2012). This restructuring of sites by using architectural features will be investigated in the following through the case of the National Tourist Routes Project, which looks at landscape-specific architectural installations.

Case Study of the National Tourist Routes Project

The National Tourist Routes Project has been under construction since 2002, and so far six routes have been approved and have obtained the official label of National Tourist Route; the remainder will be established in the years ahead. More than 100 picnic areas and vantage points have been established, and more than 50 architects, landscape architects and artists have been engaged in the project (Innovasjon Norge 2011). Apart from a couple of projects developed by architect Peter Zumthor and artist Louise Bourgeois, only Norwegian architects and artists have designed the different spots, and in fact many of these are young up-and-coming architects and artists (Stenbro 2011).

Every route has its own identity, but is still part of the full 18-route project. The key elements are fjord, mountain and coastline, and these elements will be addressed in different ways in order to highlight the distinctive character of each route (Evensen 2006). The different projects within the routes vary, ranging from small installations such as preserving a line of sight and the construction of toilet facilities to the more spectacular and radical projects such as vantage points hanging out from a cliff. The project mainly deals with the transformation of already existing vantage points and picnic areas, and many of the spots are already famous for their magnificent views (Stenbro 2011).

The project uses architecture to tell new stories in the landscape. The Norwegian landscape becomes affected by architecture, thus creating new/renewed narratives about the cultural landscape. These narratives rest upon an experience/leisure approach, which marks a change in relation to the past, where man influenced the landscape from a utility perspective. The goal for the Norwegian project is to create experiences and make the already existing landscape experiences more accessible. Furthermore, they stage the landscape experience by framing a certain landscape view and a certain landscape situation. This approach of adding experiences to the landscape challenges the prevailing understanding that the scenic rural landscape is a sufficient experience in itself.

Thus the project becomes an example of what Corner addresses concerning landscape and culture where the National Tourist Routes Project – through deliberate work with the landscape where new meanings and experiences are created – becomes a moulder of modern culture.

The landscape becomes framed and staged in order to enhance the experience of landscape. Looking at the different projects, a question in relation to this could be whether the staging of the landscape becomes more important than the landscape itself (Stenbro 2011). The interventions propose the audience to view the landscape rather than interacting with the landscape, as emphasized by the staging (Stenbro 2011). However, staging and framing are related to the wish to emphasize the landscape and tell new narratives that make the landscape accessible.

The project creates distinction in the landscape and brings a number of landscape sites to the fore. The two examples from the project shown here, Stegastein and Geiranger, emphasize that certain sites become more evident than others and that it is the architectural installation in the landscape that creates this distinction. The two examples presented here become attractors, strengthening the experience of the landscape through the architectural installation.

Stegastein

One of the most frequently discussed and highly-profiled projects is the Stegastein project along the Aurland Road. This prize-winning lookout, including toilet facilities, was completed in 2006 and is located with a scenic view across the Aurland Fjord. This project was created by the two architects, Todd Saunders and Tommie Wilhelmsen, and their goal was to enhance the experience of the incredible panoramic view over the fjord landscape (Innovasjon Norge 2011). The vantage point is built in laminated wood and steel and stretches 30 metres out high above the fjord. It more or less just shoots out from the road and its monumental appearance pays homage to the fjord and the mountains and their diversity (Evensen 2006), (Innovasjon Norge 2011).

Stegastein makes the landscape experience more physical since the experience of the dramatic topography and natural forces are reinforced by the experience of standing over the cliff. It thus exploits the potential of the site: the topography, the materials and the view to create this vantage point. And as with Zumthor's Thermal Bath in Vals, the project of Stegastein becomes a brand, giving the site a specific character in relation to other similar places with its monumental structure and unique cliffhanger experience.

Geiranger

Another route is Geiranger-Trollstigen. This route is due to be approved in 2012. Within this route, architects 3RW arkitekter and landscape architects Smedsvig landskapsarkitekter have designed a variety of vantage points, paths, items of outdoor furniture and an information building along the road around the Geiranger Fjord (Kraul 2008). The landscape here has been recognised by UNESCO as a world heritage site, and within this unique landscape 3RW arkitekter and Smedsvig Landskapsarkitekter will be creating the spectacular lookout of Ørnesvingen (Kraul 2008). Ørnesvingen is a lookout point nearly 600 vertical metres above the Geiranger Fjord, and 'the project consists of three concrete slabs mounted on top of one another that hang over the edge of the steep mountainside' (Kraul 2008: 98). Furthermore, a river runs through the site and forms a waterfall on the edge of the lookout (Kraul 2008). The lookout hangs out of the cliff and the plateau is graduated towards the edge. The architects thereby deliberately work with the vertical and horizontal lines of the landscape, using the existing verticality of the mountain and adding a horizontal level through the concrete slabs in order to emphasize the landscape experience.

Another hotspot on the same route by the same architects and landscape architects is Flydalsjuvet. This area consists of a vantage point over the Geiranger Fjord, parking spaces and service buildings constructed along the road and connected by means of a pavement (Kraul 2008). Here, old abandoned farmhouses were used as the framework for the development of information stands and public toilets – "the timber modules are mounted on a 2-inch thick structural glass base, which allows light to enter under the wooden walls" (Kraul 2008: 98). The design is custom-made: railings, concrete benches and innovative yellow waste bins have been designed as contrasts to the landscape (Kraul 2008). Thus the history of the site is exploited by transforming a structure used in the past (the farmhouses) into new experiences for leisure.

Architecture + Landscape – Concluding Remarks

The Norwegian National Tourist Routes Project has a sensitive approach to landscape, whereby interesting hotspots are created within the country's grand landscapes. Architectonic installations in the landscape create distinction, and by combining landscape with architecture, unique landscape experiences are created and accessibility to the landscape is enhanced. The important factor in the National Tourist Routes Project is that the experience of the unique Norwegian landscapes is related to architecture, and the meeting between architecture and landscape enhances the experience of landscape. This can be related to the work of Frank Lloyd Wright, who deliberately worked with the building as an adaptor to the landscape, but also as an enricher to the landscape. Thus the architectonic structures can influence the landscape and create new experiences/sites.

The National Tourist Routes Project uses the landscape as a decisive factor in the development of Norwegian rural landscapes. The approach is to combine landscape and architecture in the construction of bridges, parking spaces, picnic areas, vantage points, etc., within the Norwegian landscape, and many of the projects acquire an almost artistic element. However, it is not the objects of art, but the combination of architecture and landscape that provides an artistic element by using architecture to stage the landscape.

> "Installation in nature is characterized by two things: its form and its relationship with the surrounding terrain. A sculpture will probably first and foremost attract attention to its own form. The installations along the National Tourist Routes, however, are lookouts, rest areas, car parks, ferry berths or benches. They all involve some kind of human activity; in other words, they have exceeded their form as their final goal in some way or other. Or have they? The interesting thing about the installations along the National Tourist Routes is that they take great liberties with respect to their own form. They also take great liberties with respect to the views." (Evensen 2006: 45)

These architectural interventions have an experience and tourism objective, and a goal has been to make the interventions as accessible as possible, making it easy for visitors to experience the landscape. Furthermore, the landscape is staged and framed through the creation of the different spots in the landscape. This staging and framing is created by combining landscape and architecture.

However, the project is not only an artistic and architectonic project: the project also has a regional political objective. The routes are placed in the peripheral regions of Norway – regions that are suffering a decline in economy and population, and here the objective of the project is to increase tourism and to make these areas more attractive and more socially sustainable (Stenbro 2011). Here the site-specific potentials of the landscape are used to create surplus economic value in the region by using landscape and architecture to promote an increase in tourism.

The National Tourist Project is in my view trying to address these issues by working with the greatest asset present in these Norwegian rural areas – the landscape – and thus from a tourism perspective trying to attract more visitors. However, it is important to keep in mind that although the Norwegian project enhances the experience of being in the landscape – adding a

5: TOILET FACILITIES AT GEIRANGER-TROLLSTIGEN, GEIRANGER FJORD, NORWAY © 3RW ARCHITECTS

surplus value – the question of whether the project will also be a success in terms of enhancing the economy of a given area is highly dependent upon the number of extra tourists and whether the installations are used. The effect of the investment is not yet measurable, however, although there are some indications that the project is a success. An example of this is the fact that the hotel in Vardø, which is located near one of the projects designed by Peter Zumthor and Louise Bourgeois, has reported an increase in the number of visitors, as has the museum in the area (Jan Andresen project manager, interviewed in Stenbro 2011: 59).

The strength of the project is, however, the sensitive way in which it creates hotspots in the landscape and thereby uses architecture to enhance the experience of landscape, as well as the strategy whereby the landscape is seen as a valuable asset that could be used proactively in these shrinking peripheral areas where the landscape becomes a planning instrument that can improve the living environment architecturally, socially and structurally due to its inherent ability to connect, structure and bind (Laursen and Andersson 2011).

Looking at the project in relation to Denmark, the situation in the peripheral regions of Denmark is very similar to Norway, and the Norwegian project is interesting to look at in connection with Danish rural areas in at least two ways: Firstly, because Denmark, like Norway, has scenic landscapes that are today very attractive in the context of tourism and which could definitely be exploited better; and secondly, because the peripheral areas in Norway, like those in Denmark, are facing difficulties in terms of declining economy and population.

Thus the project indicates that there is a dynamic relationship between landscape and architecture that can enhance the site and the experience of site. This is in line with the theoretical findings of this paper which emphasize the importance of combining landscape and architecture. In this process, architecture can contribute to emphasizing the landscape: staging the landscape and making the landscape more accessible. Moreover, however, the combination of landscape and architecture can contribute to narrating new stories in the landscape and enhancing the landscape at a given place.

References

Corner, J. (1999) *Recovering Landscape*. New York: Princeton Architectural Press

Council of Europe (2000) *The European Landscape Convention, Florence*. Available at: http://www.coe.int/t/dg4/ (Accessed 18 November 2012).

Council of Europe (2011) *Culture, Heritage and Diversity*. Available at http://www.coe.int/t/dg4/cultureheritage/heritage/landscape/default_en.asp (Accessed 31 January 2011).

Danish Forest and Nature Agency (2008) *Miljøministeriet. Naturstyrelsen*. Available at: www.skovognatur.dk (Accessed 18 November 2012).

Evensen, H. B. (2006) ´Homage to Unspoilt Scenery`. In: *Topos – European Landscape Magazine*. Lindau 57: 45-55.

Holden, R. (2006) ´Mapping an identity`. In: The Landscape Architecture Europe Foundation (Ed.) *Fieldwork*. Basel: Birkhäuser.

Hauxner, M. (2011) *Supernatur*. Risskov: Ikaros Press.

Hauxner, M. (2003) *Open to the Sky*. Copenhagen: The Danish Architectural Press.

Høyer, S. A.B. (1999) ´Things Take Time and Time Takes Things: The Danish Landscape`. In Corner,

J. (Ed.) *Recovering Landscapes*. New York: Princeton Architectural Press.

Kraul, J. (2008) *Landscape Design Promenades*. Barcelona: Carles Broto I Comerma.

Innovasjon Norge (2011) ´Norge – tæt på store oplevelser´. In: *Jyllands Posten, visitnorway* (tourist brochure as a supplement to the newpaper Jyllands Posten).

Langkilde, H. E. (1959) ´Frank Lloyd Wright`. In: *Arkitektens Månedshefte*. 10: 203-204.

Larsen, J. R. K. and Laursen, L. H. (2012) ´Family Place Experience and the Making of Places in Holiday Home Destinations – a Danish case study`. In: Sharpley, R. and Stone, P. (Eds.) *Contemporary Tourist Experience: Concepts and Consequences*. Abington, Oxon: Routledge.

Laursen, L. (2009) *Shrinking Cities or Urban Transformation!* PhD Thesis. Department of Architecture and Design, Doctoral School of Planning and Development, Faculties of Engineering, Science and Medicine, Aalborg University.

Laursen, L. (2011) *Stedsspecifikke potentialer i fremtidens feriehus og feriehusområde*. Aalborg: Aalborg University.

Laursen, L. and Andersson, L. (2011) ´Differentiated decline in Danish outskirt areas – Spatial restructuring and citizen-based development in the village of Klokkerholm`. In: *Danish journal of Geoinformatics and Land Management*, 46 (1): 96-113.

Koolhaas, R. (1994) *Delirious New York*. New York: The Monacelli Press.

Marot, S. (1999) ´The Reclaiming of Sites`. In: Corner, J. (Ed.) *Recovering Landscapes*. New York: Princeton Architectural Press.

Realdania (2012) *Stedet Tæller*. Available at: http://www.stedet-taeller.dk/ (Accessed 12 October 2012).

Solá-Morales, I. (1997) *Differences – topographies if contemporary architecture*. Cambridge: MIT Press.

Stenbro, R. (2011) *Hvorfor er der medvind på de norske Nationale Turistveje?* In: Arkitekten 113 (11), Copenhagen: The Danish Architectural Press. pp. 57-61.

Stenbro, R. and Christoffersen, L. (2008) ´Stedets ånd – eller steder der ånder? Arkitektoniske arbejdsmetoder og deres mellemværende med steder`. In: *Proceedings of Architectural Inquiries*, Göteborg.

Tietjen, A. and Laursen, L. (2008) ´Urbanity without growth - Planning and urban design principles`. In: *Shrinking Danish territories*. Unpublished working paper.

Thompson, C. and Herlin, I. (2004) ´The European Landscape Convention`. In: *Topos*, 47. München: Callwey. pp.44-53.

Zumthor, P. (1997) *Peter Zumthor. three concepts*. Basel: Birkhäuser.

A Case Study of Urban Transformation Projects
Anne Juel Andersen

Introduction

Many former industrial cities in the West have undergone an exhaustive transformation during the last 20 years in a shift towards knowledge-based and cultural cities. This article focuses on how urban transformation interventions in dense city centres are part of shifting discourses and rationales. The question of professional practice with place as an integrated part of dealing with urban transformation is an important element of urban design practice.

The article looks in particular at one specific urban regeneration project in Aalborg: a terminal building and shopping centre called 'The Kennedy Arcade', planned and built in the period 2000-2004. Two other projects will be treated in less depth: an urban ecology project concerning urban renewal in an inner city neighbourhood, planned and realised in the period 1994-1998; and a cultural hub in a converted industrial building called Nordkraft, planned and realised in the period 2005-2011. The basis for the article is an ongoing industrial PhD, which represents a collaboration between the City of Aalborg municipal authority and Aalborg University. In the PhD project the three case studies of urban regeneration projects in Aalborg are conducted in a theoretical framework of place, discourse and planning, with the aim of acquiring a better understanding of the shifting rationales, concepts of place, strategies and urban discourses which have been at stake. An investigation is made into the ways in which the projects have changed the places concerned – linguistically/figuratively, physically and socially. The motivation for the study has grown from the author's first-hand experience of planning and regeneration practice in the City of Aalborg, in particular an interest in and awareness of how shifting narratives and rationales play important roles in the planning processes of urban transformation and in drawing perspectives for future urban policy to improve qualities of place and thereby strengthen the role of cities as generators for growth in society.

The analysis investigates how the representation, power and narratives interact in the field between place, discourse and planning. A hypothesis of the study is that there are three main rationales for urban regeneration, fluctuating back and forth throughout history: namely mobility, neighbourhood planning and creation of cultural beacons.

Some of the questions are: How can place be understood as the link between discourse and planning in urban transformation? How is meaning negotiated, and how are places affected by the projects? The article presents the analytical framework, an analytical model and some preliminary results from the case studies. The sources for these are registrations and observations at the places, interviews with involved partners, press coverage and municipal and other kinds of documents about the cases.

The Analytical Framework between Place, Discourse and Planning

The theoretical framework for the PhD and the case study is place, discourse and planning. In the analysis of cases, each of these fields of theory and the relations between them will place certain concepts and perspectives in the foreground and others in the background.

'Place' has become the object for greater theoretical cross-disciplinary interest, referred to by Fabian (2010), among others, as the 'spatial turn', which means that theorists from a broader field of disciplines and research areas are engaged in researching the consequences of the fact that human life and social practice are spatially situated. The reason for applying theoretical focus on 'place' is an interest in analysing how projects affect places and the city, so to say, linguistically/figuratively, as well as physically and socially.

Analysing place will consist of looking at the concepts of place used as integrated parts of planning and whether identities of place are being changed as a result of the projects. The concept of place can differ from Heidegger-inspired phenomenological concepts such as Norberg-Schulz' concept of Genius Loci:

> "The existential purpose of building (architecture) is (therefore) to make a site become a place, that is, to uncover the meanings potentially present in the given environment." (Norberg-Schultz 1976: 132)

where place is understood to have an essence in itself and to give a common identity to a group of people and thereby draw people closer together, as opposed to more pragmatic understandings of 'the generic city' in the globalised world, as expressed by Rem Koolhaas et al.:

> "The generic city is the city liberated from the captivity of centre, from the straitjacket of identity… It is the city without history. It is big enough for everybody. It

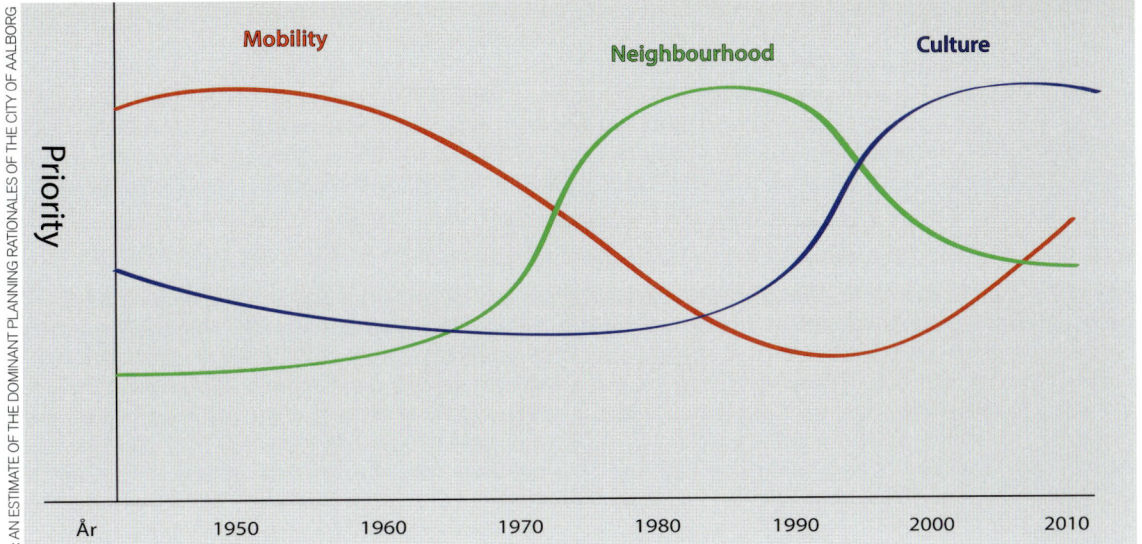

1: AN ESTIMATE OF THE DOMINANT PLANNING RATIONALES OF THE CITY OF AALBORG

is easy. It does not need maintenance. If it gets too small it just expands. If it gets old it just self-destructs and renews." (Koolhaas et al. 2002:1249-50)

These two extremes allow several other concepts to be incorporated in between, and the development of concepts of place is strongly related to societal development. Planners' understanding of a place can easily be different from the understanding and experience of inhabitants and users, and is sometimes more one-dimensional. Dorreen Massey (1997) advocates a relational understanding of place. She sees place as dynamic and heterogeneous and argues for a progressive sense of place and for multiple and 'glocal' place identity. She sees places as bound together and developed and constantly changed through negotiation and rethinking. She writes in her essay, 'A global sense of place', that many identities can be attached to a place at the same time, using an example from Kilburn in London, where she lives:

"Kilburn is a place for which I have a great affection; I have lived there many years. It certainly has 'a character of its own'... it is absolutely not a seamless, coherent identity, a single sense of place which everyone shares. It could hardly be less so. People's routes through the place, their favourite haunts within it, the connections they make (physically, or by phone or post, or in memory and imagination) between here and the rest of the world vary enormously. If it is now recognized that people have multiple identities then the same point can be made in relation to places. Moreover, such multiple identities can either be a source of richness or a source of conflict, or both." (Massey 2010: 141-142)

Jensen (2012) argues for a relational and mobility-oriented concept of place:

"My basic analytical viewpoint is one of acknowledging how all sites, places, buildings, and cities are what they are as a consequence of the extent to which they afford, encourage, and host networked flows of people, goods, capital, and information." (Jensen 2012: 62)

When it comes to discourse analysis in the studies of urban regeneration projects, Dovey (2008) is a source of inspiration. He uses discourse analysis of built form as a key method in his case studies looking at how discourses are materialised in architecture and built form. He argues that all projects are expressions of a discourse to which those involved can act more or less consciously. The discourse expresses itself everywhere, such as in the architecture, the strategy, the plan, etc., and discourse analysis of projects is used to understand representations as built form in relation to power.

"Architecture and urban design 'frames' space, both literally and discursively. In the literal sense everyday life 'takes place' within the clusters of rooms, buildings, streets and cities we inhabit. Action is structured and shaped by streets, walls, doors and windows; it is framed by the decisions of designers. As a form of discourse, built form constructs and frames meanings. Places tell us stories; we read them as spatial text." (Dovey 2008: 1)

Analysing the images and representations of places incorporates the study of spatial conflicts, strategies and branding connected to the specific places, as well as the meaning of socio-spatial practices. Metaphors play an important role in this analysis, and again Dovey says it well:

"A metaphor is a figure of discourse where one thing is represented as if it is, and yet simultaneously is not, another." (Dovey 2008: 15)

The relationship between planning and discourse is analysed by studying the dominant planning rationales and discourses: the values, power and decisions that are made through the planning processes, in which points of view have also been excluded. Narratives and storytelling about places are very often an important part of the planning process. Metaphors and narratives are closely connected, they are competing but also complementary modes of knowing, as Czarniawska (2004), who is engaged with metaphors and storytelling in her research about narratives in social science, points out. The importance of stories and storytelling in planning is emphasised by Sandercock, who argues that a better understanding of the work that stories do can make us better planners. For Sandercock "planning is performed through story, in a myriad of ways" and the narratives have great influence on the urban reality:

"In order to imagine the ultimately unrepresentable space, life and languages of the city, to make them legible, we translate them into narratives. The way we narrate the city becomes constitutive of urban reality, affecting the choices we make, the ways we then might act." (Sandercock 2003:12)

The Case Studies

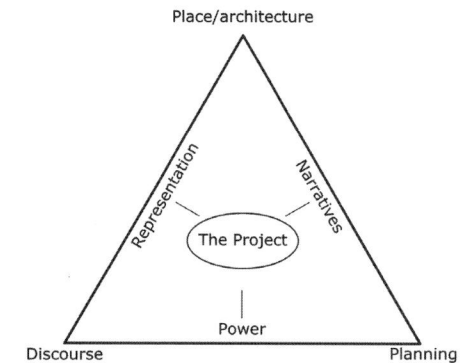

2: ANALYTICAL MODEL FOR THE CASE STUDIES

The aim of the case study in the PhD is to learn about the different rationales and their connection to place concepts and discourses and how they change places. The analytical model is constructed as a triangle between the theoretical fields, and the practice of urban regeneration is illustrated in a way such that the sides of the triangle are designated by representation of discourse at a place, by narratives as an element of planning processes and by *power* respectively.

The three urban regeneration projects in Aalborg have been carried out during the last 20 years as elements in an overall effort to improve and transform the city from an industrial city into a knowledge-based city. The cases above are all chosen as representatives for the dominant rationales in urban regeneration, but they also represent different planning discourses, place concepts and types of place operations. All of them have been the object of intense public debate and have driven the development of planning and urban regeneration into new phases. They can be designated as critical cases.

The *Kennedy Arcade project* was planned as a compact terminal for public transport, driven by the mobility rationale and at the same time fulfilling other planning goals in the city. It is situated as a hinge between the railway station, the freight train area and the inner city of Aalborg. Planning was carried out in cooperation between the municipal authority and a private developer and investor. The project accommodated several aims and consisted of a compact terminal for public transport and a cinema, a shopping centre, offices and a multi-storey car park. The municipal authority wanted to create and strengthen an existing shopping axis by placing the Kennedy Arcade at the outer end and wanted to strengthen the whole area as a nerve centre for public transport. A new road connection was built aimed at relieving bus traffic in the inner city

Mobility was the main driving force for the project. The partners saw a potential in the flow of people generated from the compact terminal, which could be used for attractive public life and trade in the area. This expressed a new and more pragmatic view of place in relation to the former neighbourhood planning tradition illustrated by urban renewal; see the urban ecology project below. However, architecturally the project is in conflict with itself. Aesthetically, the mobility plant is an almost brutally dynamic traffic machine, built on the same principles that were used in road planning from the 1960s, with ramps running above areas used for other purposes providing access to the overall road network outside the inner city and thereby creating a city in several layers. However, what has awakened public and political anger is not the mobility element of the project, but rather the front part of the project that faces onto the city. An urban character and closed spaces were what was wanted, but the new building turned out to be a disproportionate (compared to the neighbourhood), voluminous and architecturally dull building with only sparse details.

Represented in the project as built environment are discourses about mobility, activity and public life, as well as architecture and urban spaces. All the discourses are identified at the place today. After many years of dispute and discussion amongst partners, politicians and citizens, there was a wish to move the central bus terminal to the area beside the railway station, thus creating a hub for all modes of public transport connected to a new multi-storey car park with direct access to and from the overall road network in the city. Metaphors like 'nerve centre', 'link' and 'machine' were used to express this discourse. The wish for more activity and city life was significant amongst politicians, planners and the chamber of commerce after many years of debate about 'better city', but stagnation in private investment and activities. The notion of 'attractive shopping area' was used extensively about the commercial axis, which it was hoped would be improved by the project. The metaphor 'huge' was used several times in the local newspaper to express enthusiasm concerning the big, expensive project. It was an overall planning goal that the project should visualise and strengthen a green connection between the inner city and the valley through which a stream ran to the south, but this wish was not given priority in the final project, and it ended up simply as a path on a ramp beside the bus ramp leading to the main road outside the inner city. The wish to 'build something' at the end of the commercial axis expressed a desire to strengthen the urban space architectonically by ensuring a clear demarcation of the space in front of the railway station and a wish to have a centre which could generate some active public life in the area. Metaphors like 'hinge' and 'classical urban space' have been used as arguments for a big building here, as well as the word 'blurred' as characteristic of the place as it was originally. The metaphors used in this discourse were aesthetic – as indeed was the majority of the subsequent criticism.

The planning discourse of the Kennedy Arcade was clear. Prior to the planning process, agreements were reached between the developer and the mayor concerning the project, so what was practised was top-down planning without much professional dialogue. The local planning procedure was a complex puzzle in which many conflicting interests with different political support bases had to be met at the same time. The project was mostly given beforehand, and it represented a type of planning where developers and their economic interests played the dominant roles in the processes.

The Kennedy Arcade project has changed the structure of this part of the city and turned an open urban space with connection to the stream to the south into a more closed urban space. The architectural adaptation to the city consisted of a limitation of the height of the building to the highest of the adjacent buildings, although the new building has a flat roof and the old ones have steep pitches, and the new building is much broader and deeper than the others. The volume of the new building has a dominant appearance from all sides. As such, the structure of the place has been changed fundamentally by the project. Furthermore, social life in the neighbourhood has been affected by the mobility hub, the small shopping centre and the offices, and by the fact that the new urban space has become a transit space criss-crossed by travellers. The quality of social life is dependent on the degree of open-mindedness in the public space, and this is somewhat limited. Immediately following the opening of the centre, a number of serious social clashes occurred. A large group of so-called 'anti-social youngsters', some of them violent, hung around the centre, creating a sense of insecurity amongst users. This problem was met by the introduction of security guards and video

surveillance in the centre. Today the shopping centre is not seen and understood by the citizens as being part of the central shopping area in the city, but as a place mostly aimed at bus passengers, who are not regarded as a high-status segment in Aalborg. This has, among other things, caused difficulties for the owners in terms of renting out shop space, but they hope that the development of the adjacent freight train area will change the situation. The topicality of all the discourses mentioned – mobility, activity and public life, as well as architecture and urban spaces – has been renewed in relation to the ongoing regeneration of the freight train area immediately adjacent to Kennedy Arcade. The place has acquired a new meaning because of a changed connection to an area outside the place – in accordance with a relational and mobility-oriented concept of place.

The *Aalborg Urban Ecology Project* was an integrated part of a neighbourhood-oriented urban renewal project in the southern part of the inner-city of Aalborg in the 1990s. It was an extensive demonstration project executed jointly by the City of Aalborg, a private consultant and the Ministry of Housing and Building in the period 1994-1998. The project was the first of its kind in Denmark to integrate ecological solutions into urban renewal on a large scale. Four blocks and a public space, 'Louise Plads', in the neighbourhood were included. There was comprehensive economic support from a national programme for pilot projects, and at the same time a lot of public resources were available for urban renewal, in addition to which there was a political consensus between the state and the municipal authority concerning goals and means. The main driving force for urban renewal was the improvement of housing and sanitary conditions, as well as the recreational areas in the neighbourhood. The concept of place is phenomenological in the sense that the project sought to strengthen a historical and inherent identity and quality of place, and the neighbourhood is seen as a community in which people's lives are played out. The driving force for the ecology element was an effort to modernise the concept of ecology and make it urban, and it very much involved development and testing of high technology to reduce the consumption of water and energy. The Urban Ecology Project represents a kind of place intervention where the project adapts to the existing structure in a homogeneous area

The metaphor 'display window' concerning Louise Plads has been used by the project managers to stress its intended role as a landmark and symbol for the ecology project, and to emphasise the urban focus. Other urban metaphors were 'information shop', 'stage' and 'amphitheatre'. The word 'green' confused and disappointed some of the local citizens when they realised that some of the 'green' morphed into pavements and solar cells. The project represents a kind of planning where the planners govern the course of the project to a high degree. The financial support from the state had a significant influence on the planning and the processes. The municipal authority completed the planning in a rational and quick way in order to make full use of the money from the state, and the owners and most of the inhabitants said 'yes thank you' to the projects – they were given new solutions in their buildings and apartments at no extra cost. In fact, there was less participation from the inhabitants in this project than in earlier urban renewal projects in the city, despite the fact that the Urban Ecology Project was articulated to have a high degree of participation.

Looking at the area today, the altered public space, Louise Plads, is the most visible result of the project. It was totally reconstructed into a square with uniform surfacing from building to building and a range of significant items of urban furniture. With a 'square', the ground is now prepared as a place to make a stop and take a break, as opposed to its function prior to reconstruction. The new design put demands on use and life, which have not been fulfilled. The Urban Ecology Project did not have much impact on the place in terms of meaning and social life in the neighbourhood. The status of a 'sleepy' neighbourhood on the outskirts of the city centre has not changed.

The cultural project *Nordkraft* has been developed as a hybrid cultural facility converted from a former heat and power station at the waterfront in Aalborg. Nordkraft has become a centre for a wide range of different kinds of cultural activities, including restaurants, music and sports facilities, theatres, art school and exhibitions, music school, youth club, cinema and education and offices related to culture and sport. More than 25 partners occupy approximately 30,000 m2. The driving force for the project was the idea of a cultural beacon, where synergy from many different partners could be generated, and that this would strengthen the cultural life in the city. The conversion of the industrial plant has contributed to the very strong narrative of a new power plant – for culture – and it has become a symbol of the transformation of the city from industrial city into a knowledge-based experience city. This means that Nordkraft has become a strong brand for Aalborg. Nordkraft is situated at the central harbourfront, immediately adjacent to the site of a new concert hall, the House of Music. Together, Nordkraft and the House of Music express a comprehensive focus by the city on creating a cultural hub. The idea has been to support connections and synergy between these two projects in terms of function and specific cooperation, as well as in terms of architectural scale. The whole area is a transition zone between the old inner city and the industrial harbour with a totally different structure and much bigger volumes, and the powerful transformation has a significant impact on the skyline. The concept of place in the project is relational – the whole correlation in the area is what is interesting. The place is understood as a hinge between the medieval city and the harbour industry.

4: KENNEDY ARKADEN

5: LOUISE PLADS IN THE DANMARKSGADE NEIGHBOURHOOD

A Case Study of Urban Transformation Projects
Transformation

Preservation and reuse of industrial heritage is a discourse that is strongly represented. The building and the surrounding urban spaces are treated in a rather pragmatic way: elements which had a useful value have been reused, and new elements appear in contrast to the old. New added elements harmonise the functionalistic industrial architecture with huge concrete constructions from the 1950s and clean brick surfaces from the 1940s, and are illuminated from below. Raw materials such as steel sheathing with functional industrial spots are added to the building, and concrete blocks salvaged from the bottom of the fjord mixed with plant pots made of rusty steel are scattered across one of the urban spaces – the industrial aesthetics are apparent. The names of the different parts of Nordkraft, referring to the time when it was a combined heat and power plant, emphasise the focus on industrial heritage.

The strong focus on public urban spaces in the experience city is very different from the perceptions of place used in the urban ecology project and the Kennedy Arcade. The Nordkraft project represents a type of planning involving complex cooperation between many parties, cross-disciplinary in nature within the administration as well as between a lot of partners, stakeholders and advisers, and characterised by extensive political involvement and ownership. The planning discourse has been dominated by a project-oriented focus on possibilities and network cooperation, where enthusiasm, persistence and the search for support of many kinds have been crucial. The conversion of Nordkraft and transformation of the whole context area is a physical example of the ongoing development from that of an industrial city into a knowledge-based city with major focus on culture, knowledge and experiences. The industrial cultural heritage has been used to create a new identity for the neighbourhood, and a certain gentrification has already taken place. Nordkraft has become a strong node and landmark in the city, and the case analysis will examine whether it has affected the area and the identity of the city to a further extent.

Conclusions

The case studies illustrate how shifting rationales and narratives, in close relation to development in society, play important roles in urban transformation. The societal discourses meet the planning processes by means of architecture at the places concerned, which thereby become the central link between discourse and planning. The study shows that the focus on 'place' varies strongly at different times and in different projects, and the role of place has undergone considerable development. The theoretical framework and the analytical model, which looks at the projects from three sides – place, discourse and planning – have proven to be rewarding as the approaches employed in the case studies. Often there is a tension between the project's focus on place and the strategic and more general goals. Furthermore, the tensions between planning and the representation as architecture at a place are frequent. Narratives and discourses relate to each other in the sense that the narratives in the planning processes depend on the prevailing discourse and its aspects: meaning, power and practice – and looking at the narratives in planning processes can help identify the discourses.

The different concepts of place identified in the projects have followed theoretical developments and also the shifting rationales of urban regeneration. The three cases represent different dominating concepts of place, with a phenomenological focus on neighbourhood planning in the urban ecology project, a focus on flow and mobility in the Kennedy Arcade project and a great focus on public spaces in the Nordkraft project. Hopefully, the framework developed here can inspire both more studies and experimental practice. New knowledge and understanding are needed to bring perspectives for development of new strategies, perhaps a new discourse, in urban transformation in the future, and for exploration of how urban interventions as part of urban policy can create new inspiring stories about places in the city and thereby lead to more inspiring cities and better planning practice.

References

Czarniawska, B. (2004) *Narratives in Social Science Research*. London: Sage.

Dovey, K. (2008) *Framing Places: Mediating Power in Built Form*. London: Routledge.

Fabian, L. (2010) ´Spatiale forklaringer, Da den geografiske tænkning kom på den humanvidenskabelige dagsorden`. In: *Slagmark, tidsskrift for idehistorie*, 57.

Jensen, O. (2012) ´If only it could speak: Narrative Explorations of Mobility and Place in Seattle´. In: Vannini, P. et al. (Eds.) *Technologies of Mobility in the Americas*. New York: Peter Lang.

Koolhaas, R. et al. (2002) *S M L XL*. New York: Monacelli Press.

Massey, D. (2010) ´En global fornemmelse for sted`. In: Mai, A. and Ringgaard, D. (Eds.) *Sted. Moderne Litteraturteori*. Aarhus: Aarhus Universitetsforlag.

Norberg-Schulz, C. (1976) ´The Phenomenon of Place`. In: *Architectural Association Quarterly*, 8 (4): 3-10

Sandercock, L. (2003) ´Out of The Closet: The Importance of Stories and Storytelling in Planning Practice´. In: *Planning Theory & Practice*, 4 (1): 11-28

6: NEWLY REFURBISHED NORDKRAFT CULTURAL HUB IN AALBORG

7: URBAN SPACE OUTSIDE NORDKRAFT

A Case Study of Urban Transformation Projects
Transformation

Urban Design and Spatial Equity: The Favela-Bairro Programme Experience in Rio de Janeiro, Brazil

Victor Andrade

Introduction

Many of the significant urban transformations of the new century are taking place in the developing world, and the relationship between formal and informal settlements has been the subject of renewed attention in recent years, with an increase of interest in upgrading programmes from architects and urban designers.

The Harvard Design Magazine published a special issue in 2008 presenting this challenge: "Can designers improve life in non-formal cities?" This provocative question highlighted one of the main challenges facing most of the cities in the developing world, and the editor of the issue – William Saunders – suggested that the topic reflected a refreshed social and environmental activism by architects and urban designers (Saunders 2008).

The socio-economic and environmental inequalities in Brazil are well publicized and one can state that spatial segregation has been a defining factor in its urbanization. Brazilian cities, such as Rio de Janeiro, are increasingly characterized by the presence of very wealthy neighbourhoods provided with top quality services lying adjacent to poor communities with extremely limited infrastructure (Abreu 1987; Andrade and Ribeiro 2006). Rio de Janeiro`s urban fabric is critically divided between formality and informality, extreme richness and severe urban poverty.

In that context, there are several definitions of informal settlements and most of them are context-specific. However, the United Nations Habitat has probably the most widely applicable definition. According to the United Nations Habitat, informal settlements can be defined as (i) areas where a group of housing units has been constructed on land to which the occupants have no legal claim, or which they occupy illegally, and/or (ii) unplanned areas where housing is not in compliance with current planning and building regulations (unauthorized housing).

Informal settlements have different denominations throughout the world – slums, barrios, squatters settlements, marginal settlements, temporary settlements, etc. – and in the case of Brazil such a settlement is known as a favela. The Brazilian metropolis comprises two realities – the formal city and the favelas. Unlike in the favelas, the government has historically provided excellent infrastructure in the formal city.

During the last two decades Brazilian municipal authorities have launched several policies and urban interventions in an attempt to minimize urban inequality (Britto 2003). In this context, the Favela-Bairro Programme, launched by the Rio de Janeiro municipal authority in the 1990s, is one of the most successful urban upgrading and poverty alleviation projects developed in Brazil. Considering that Bairro has the meaning of a conventional quarter in the formal city, the name of the programme – Favela-Bairro – reveals its main purpose of giving the favelas the same status as conventional city neighbourhoods (bairros) and consequently integrating favelas and the formal city.

To date, Favela-Bairro is the largest-scale informal settlement – favela – upgrading programme implemented in Latin America. It aims to upgrade favelas and to bridge the gap between them and the formal city (IPLANRIO 1993).

The aim of this paper is to account for practices of the Favela-Bairro Programme and its background and context, as well as to answer to what extent the Favela-Bairro Programme has contributed to integrating the favela and the formal city. Aiming not only to deepen current understandings of the programme itself, this research adds to the international debate on upgrading policies, using the example of Favela-Bairro to reveal some of the challenges and contradictions which surround the implementation of large-scale upgrading programmes.

In order to do this, the paper looks at the Favela-Bairro interventions in Borel and the impacts of the programme on the relationship between Borel (favela) and the district of Tijuca (part of the formal city). Tijuca is a wealthy city district where most of the residents have a Portuguese background and Borel is a low-income squatter where most of the residents are Afro-Americans.

Research based on a case study is a viable strategy for investigating the government`s strategic use of urban design. Methods for data collection were mainly questionnaires, mapping and document retrieval and analysis.

Informal Settlements

Informal settlements range from high density, squalid central city tenements to spontaneous squatter settlements without legal recognition or rights. Currently, informal settlement dwellers make up one third of the world`s urban population, accounting for a total of

1: DENSE TYPOLOGY AND COMPACT SPATIAL FLOW © SENAD GVOZDEN

Urban Design and Spatial Equity: The Favela-Bairro Programme Experience in Rio de Janeiro, Brazil
Transformation

more than one billion people. 32% of urban dwellers live in slums, often living no better – and often worse – than people in rural areas (UNDP 2005; Davis 2006).

In accordance with the definition of the United Nations Habitat, the World Bank describes informal settlements as neglected parts of cities where housing and living conditions are inadequate, appallingly deprived and often hazardous, exposed to a number of health and environmental risks, precarious accessibility and mobility, spatially segregated from the formal city, and where basic services are lacking and there is limited access to income and formal employment.

Latin America is the most urbanized part of the underdeveloped world. In 1950, only 42 percent of Latin Americans were city dwellers; today almost 73 % live in cities, according to the United Nations. This compares with 34% in Africa and 33% in Asia.

In Brazil, estimates indicate that 36.6% of urban dwellers live in informal settlements – the so-called favelas – which corresponds to 51.7 million inhabitants (UN-Habitat, 2003). The Brazilian urban poor are at a critical disadvantage in comparison to the wealthy population living in the formal city. Favelas are often located in environmentally fragile areas – such as steep hills and riverbanks – environmentally unsafe areas – such as polluted sites near solid waste dumps, open drains and sewers – near pollutant industries, previously closed polluted sites, etc. Usually these are the only available urban land areas where the poor can settle.

With Rio de Janeiro as an example, large cities have become centres where vast numbers of people compete for the most basic elements of life: for a room with an affordable rent within reach of employment, or vacant land on which a shelter can be erected without fear of eviction; for places in schools; for medical treatment for health problems or injuries, or a bed in a hospital; for access to clean drinking water; for a place on a bus or train; and for a corner on a pavement or square to sell some goods – quite apart from the enormous competition for jobs. In the majority of cases, governments have the power and resources to increase the supply and reduce the cost of many of these (Hardoy 1995).

Rio de Janeiro's Favelas

Regarded as the second largest city in Brazil, Rio de Janeiro had a population of approximately six million people in the year 2000 when the last Brazilian census was conducted (Britto 2003). Approximately 25% of its population live in favelas, which means a total of 1.5 million inhabitants living in inadequate conditions. Favela is not a singular phenomenon from Rio de Janeiro, but it has very specific characteristics. Unlike most of the favelas sprawling at the edge of the cities, the Rio de Janeiro landscape is composed of favelas situated on steep hillsides offering panoramic views of the city and the ocean, while the affluent neighbourhoods are located at the bottom of the hills.

The reason is that in the early days of settlement, wealthy inhabitants laid claim to sites near the harbour, leaving the steep, inaccessible hillsides to the poor. Many of these communities command spectacular views of the ocean and the city below and such famous Rio landmarks as the Sugarloaf and the mountaintop statue of Christ.

The favelas' establishment on public land represented a failure of property rights. Lacking the appropriate price incentives, the pattern of informal urbanization holds little relation to the negative externalities imposed by their expansion, both in terms of environmental and health hazards, and in terms of a sub-optimal utilization of public land. On the other hand, the absence of the presence of the state in the favelas and the uncertainty in tenure of informal settlements – particularly prior to the 1980s – has obvious welfare consequences with regard to the inhabitants of favelas.

Although there have been initiatives at community level to fill the vacuum produced by the absence of the state, such as the establishment of neighbourhood associations, most public utilities, such as water, sewerage, electricity and security, have remained underprovided. The consequences of this are evident in the high rates of vector-transmitted disease in informal settlements, the high incidence of geological disasters (mudslides, etc.), and the relatively low quality of housing. In the case of security, the absence of the state has opened up voids that are filled by illicit entities, mostly related to drug trafficking, that take up functions related to policing and enforcement of norms.

Favela-Bairro Programme

Rio de Janeiro's urban development is undergoing contradictory transformations that point in opposite directions. While several gated communities – designed for privileged groups – have been constructed by the private sector, the local government has been struggling to physically and socially connect favelas and the formal city.

Launched in 1993 by the Rio de Janeiro Municipal Government, the Favela-Bairro programme aimed to improve physical conditions that would enable favelas to be seen as part of the formal city – tackling poverty, lack of infrastructure and spatial segregation (SMH 1995). The Favela-Bairro Programme was conceived by the municipal authority in Rio de Janeiro as a tool to promote urban and social integration between the favelas and the formal city through design. With carefully planned and reparative interventions, the favelas are upgraded and connected to the city. Unlike past urban planning initiatives in Rio de Janeiro, the Favela-

Bairro programme represents a practice of mending the city fabric (Rio de Janeiro City Government 1996)

The first phase of the programme (1993-2000) comprised 90 favelas totalling about 316,000 residents and had a budget of US$ 860.5 million. This was made up of a combination of loans by the Inter-American Development Bank (US$ 350 million) and Japan's International Cooperation Agency (US$ 236.7 million), as well as funds from the Rio de Janeiro municipal authority (US$ 273.80 million) (IDB 1997). Rio de Janeiro's municipal government administrated the programme, architecture offices worked as lead consultants of multi-disciplinary teams and local community associations were engaged as main project partners.

Promoting Integration through Design

In order to achieve a more socially integrated city, urban design strategies were developed to integrate the urban fabric of the favela and the formal city. Therefore Favela-Bairro is regarded as an inflection in Rio de Janeiro's urban policy. Previously, Favela-Bairro interventions were limited to provide basic infrastructure or resettlement. Therefore the gap between the quality of public spaces in the favela and the formal city has been growing over time.

In order to integrate favelas into the urban fabric of the formal city, the programme has a number of strategic actions: (a) completing or constructing key urban infrastructure; (b) providing environmental changes that make the favelas look like a "normal" city quarter; (c) introducing visual symbols of the formal city as a sign of identification as a neighbourhood: paved streets, plazas, urban furniture and public services; (d) consolidating the insertion of the favelas into the planning process of the city; (e) implementing activities of a social nature, such as setting up day-care centres for children, income generation projects, training programmes, and sports, cultural and leisure activities; (f) promoting the legalization of land subdivision and providing individual land titles and (g) building up a street network interrelated to the formal city.

The design of public spaces was a major element in the favelas' physical and social change. Public space became a strategic element in the projects, based on the fact that spaces bring different people together, emphasizing how important public spaces are for social integration. Paved roads, squares and facilities were designed to improve accessibility and break down boundaries that had divided the favelas from the planned city.

2: ENERGY SUPPLY PROVIDED BY THE FAVELA-BAIRRO PROGRAMME

3: TIJUCA NEIGHBORHOOD AND BOREL NEIGHBORHOOD IN THE BACKGROUND

Borel and Tijuca. Favela and Formal City

Tijuca is a traditional neighbourhood in the northern area of Rio de Janeiro, and is a traditional and affluent city quarter from the formal city. According to the 2000 Census, Tijuca has 180,992 inhabitants. It is primarily an upper middle class district. Tijuca is located in a valley and is surrounded by favelas on the hillsides; and one of these favelas is Borel. Like many of Rio de Janeiro's favelas, Borel is located on a dangerously eroded steep hillside. According to the 2000 Census the district has 10,228 inhabitants. Borel is at a critical disadvantage in comparison to the wealthy population living in Tijuca. It is located in an environmentally fragile area – a steep hillside which was the only available land where the poor could settle in proximity to job opportunities in Tijuca and other central neighbourhoods.

In terms of income and racial background, there is a clear spatial segregation and social polarization between Tijuca and Borel. While the average monthly income of a family resident in Tijuca is US$ 1,092.22, a family living in Borel has an average monthly income of only US$ 131.64. Moreover, most Tijuca residents have a European background, while the majority of Borel residents are African and American native descendants (IBGE/Censo 2000)

People Flows between Formal and Informal City

The analysis presented in this section is based on the data collected on a field study – including questionnaires, mapping and observation – carried out by the author in June 2009. Its main goals were to identify to what extent the Favela-Bairro Programme contributed to the integration of Borel (favela) and Tijuca (formal city), as well as the awareness of dwellers in the formal city and favela about the programme. The questionnaire was a strategic source of data that helped to achieve the above goals and highlight the current relationship between Borel and Tijuca.

The questionnaire has 3 main themes that are described and analyzed in this section: (i) the engagement and awareness of the dwellers from the formal and informal city with regard to the Favela-Bairro programme; (ii) the opinion of the dwellers from the formal and informal city about the status of Borel after the Favela-Bairro intervention and (iii) the flux of people between Borel and Tijuca/Tijuca and Borel before and after the Favela-Bairro intervention.

Questionnaires were submitted to 200 residents in Borel (1.95% of the population of Borel). In the case of Tijuca, questionnaires were submitted to residents living adjacent to Borel – representing a population of

4: TIJUCA NEIGHBORHOOD. THE FORMAL CITY IN THE VALLEY AND THE TIJUCA HILLS IN THE BACKGROUND.

around 34,000. 200 residents in Tijuca responded to questionnaires (0.6% of Tijuca dwellers living adjacent to Borel and 0.11% of the total population of Tijuca).

Favela-Bairro projects were designed through a participatory process where community participation included involvement in the decision-making and design process. In order to make feasible the participation in large-scale communities, local organizations were formalized and used as interlocutors between the local authority, the architecture office and the local community.

While 22% of Borel respondents were engaged in the Favela-Bairro Programme, only 0.3% of Tijuca respondents have a role in the proposal developed for Borel. In its aim to integrate Borel and Tijuca, the Favela-Bairro cannot succeed without participation by the residents of Tijuca.

In Borel the questionnaires highlighted different scenarios. 83% of Borel respondents knew about the Favela-Bairro. Respondents made comments about the positive impact of the programme in terms of quality of life in the neighbourhood, providing basic infrastructure and leisure facilities and improving accessibility between the favela and the formal city. On the other hand, only 46.20% of Tijuca respondents knew about the programme.

Despite large investments in infrastructure, urban renewal and improvement of public spaces, public officers, urban designers and local residents are sceptical about the main goal of Favela-Bairro – integration between the favelas and the formal city.

Data from interviews carried out with local residents highlighted that the socio-economic circumstances of the respondents play an important role in their perception of the relationship between Borel and Tijuca. Successful physical integration is not enough to promote social integration between dwellers from Borel and Tijuca. Physical changes can occur within a short period, but it takes a long time for the identity and image of a place to change.

After Favela-Bairro interventions, Borel and Tijuca are physically more integrated. Roads and paths in Borel are connected to the formal city network and nodes were created at the boundary between Borel and Tijuca.

Respondents were asked which term would better define Borel: bairro (a regular city quarter) or favela (a squatter). The respondents did not receive any definition of favela and bairro – they used their own understanding of these terms.

The questionnaire was also used to obtain information regarding the perception of Borel amongst respondents. Results highlighted a critical gap between Tijuca and Borel respondents. Despite infrastructure investments and improvement of public spaces, 96.9% of Tijuca respondents still consider Borel to be a favela. In the case of Borel respondents, 40.5% of them perceive Borel as a bairro, but the majority (47.5%) still consider it to be a favela.

Finally, respondents indicated how many trips per week they make between the two areas. Results show that the number of trips between Borel and Tijuca increased among Borel respondents. All Borel respondents go to Tijuca every week and 89.3% of them do so at least 5 times per week.

On the other hand, 90.4% of Tijuca respondents never go to Borel. More worrying than this, however, is the fact that among Tijuca respondents the number of trips to Borel fell in comparison with the period before the Favela-Bairro intervention.

The results indicate a critical social polarization between Borel and Tijuca. The relationship between Borel and the affluent Tijuca is almost symbiotic because the latter has an enormous need for cheap services and helpers. Dependant on the formal city in which they have their jobs, large numbers of Borel dwellers commute to Tijuca and other neighbourhoods in the formal city every day.

On the other hand, most Tijuca dwellers have never set foot in Borel. Besides the lack of economic and leisure options, most of the Tijuca respondents are afraid to go to Borel, which is considered a dangerous area where rival drug gangs (Comando Vermelho and Terceiro Comando) are constantly fighting for territorial control.

Moreover, it is important to take into consideration the emblematic distinction between the spatial typologies of the formal and informal city. This distinction has a critical role in Rio de Janeiro`s landscape and it has strong consequences for spatial and social relations in the city. Whilst the precarious brick houses on the steep hills of Rio de Janeiro promote a spectacular and colourful landscape, they are also stigmatized as the space of poverty.

Conclusion

Favela-Bairro is a ground-breaking project in a Brazilian context, teaching important lessons and pointing to new directions for Brazilian urban designers, such as (i) favela upgrading instead of resettlement, (ii) approaching public space as a place for social integration and interaction, (iii) participatory process and (iv) redirection of public investments in order to minimize social inequalities and spatial segregation.

Favela-Bairro brings an innovative approach to the Brazilian scene, whereby urban designers, city planners and grassroots movements were invited to coordinate the programme, assigning value to the importance of the quality of urban space, participation and social equality.

Favela-Bairro relies on the role that public space can play in bringing people together, emphasizing how important this is for social integration. Quality of public spaces and services are critical issues for ameliorating the gap between rich and poor. Having said that, results indicate that physical interventions are not enough to integrate, but are a step in that process. Social policies are critical in terms of enhancing a more equal society where urban spaces are less polarized and spatially segregated.

The case of the Favela-Bairro Programme is advanced by a better economic situation and the reduction of both poverty and violence, and will thus have a better chance of drawing a larger number of favelas out of their isolation and integrating them into the formal city.

Nonetheless, it is necessary to point out that bridging the gap between the informal and formal city requires comprehensive policies aimed at transforming favelas into regular neighbourhoods by providing infrastructure, land tenure, public facilities, environmental amenities and quality public spaces.

Despite the fact that the Favela-Bairro Programme aims to break down the boundaries between the formal city and the favela, it is important to respect the spatial and social qualities of the favela. Therefore the main challenge is to search for a city that is tolerant, multiple and diverse. In order to do that, it is important that architects and urban designers find ways of upgrading the favelas without becoming formal neighbourhoods with their traditional typology, public spaces and urban life.

References

Abreu, M. (1997) *Evolução Urbana de Rio de Janeiro*. Rio de Janeiro: Prefeitura de Cidade do Rio de Janeiro, Secretaria Municipal de Urbanismo, Iplan-Rio.

Andrade, V. and Ribeiro, G. (2006) ´Spatial Analysis of the Rio de Janeiro Metropolitan Area and Social and Environmental Management Issues`. In: Tenedório, J. and Julião, R. (Eds.) *Proceedings of the 14th European Colloquium on Theoretical and Quantitative Geography*. CD-ROM. Lisbon: Universidade Nova de Lisboa.

Britto, A. (2003) ´Implantação de Infra-estrutura de Saneamento na Região Metropolitana do Rio de Janeiro`. In: *Revista Brasileira de Estudos Urbanos e Regionais*, 5 (1): pp.63-77.

Davis, M. (2006) *Planet of Slums*. New York: Verso.

Hardoy, J. and Satterthwaite, D. (1995) *Squatter Citizen – Life in the Urban Third World*. London: Earthscan.

IBGE (1996) *Censo Demografico, 1980, 1991 e Contagem 1996*. Fundação Istituto Brasileiro de Geografia e Estadistica, Rio de Janeiro.

IDB (1997) *A New Future for Rio's Favelas*. IDB Extra, Inter-American Development Bank, Washington.

IPLANRIO (1993) *Statistical Yearbook of the City of Rio de Janeiro, 1992/93*. City of Rio de Janeiro, Brazil.

Rio de Janeiro City Government (1996) *Favela-Bairro Program: Integrating Slums in Rio de Janeiro*. City of Rio de Janeiro, Brazil.

Saunders, W. S. (2008) ´Design politics... and parametrics`. In: *Harvard Design Magazine*, 28 (Spring/Summer).

UNDP (2005) UN *Millennium Project—Investing in Development: A Practical Plan to Achieve the Millennium Development Goals*. London: Earthscan.

UN-HABITAT (2003) *The Challenge of Slums: Global Report on Human Settlement 2003*. Available from: http://www.unchs.org/mediacentre/presskits.asp (accessed on 18 November 2012).

Haderslev Nature School - landscape and architectural interventions in the Haderslev hospital area

Martin Frank Petersen, Senad Gvozden, Siri Laursen & Sofie Brincker

The project proposed a strategy for the transformation of a 26 ha. post-industrial landscape, which used to facilitate the city hospital. The vision was to build upon and promote the city of Haderslev and its natural scenic surroundings, through the creation of a nature school. Experimenting with natural and built spatialities, the programmatic and architectural proposal works with themes as: 'Temporality', 'Motion' and 'Layers'. The focus has been to intertwine fluent and contrasting transitions, the natural and the built, the united and the individual, the desolate and the active, between which the framework for different and varying spatial experiences occurs.

NEW BATHING EDGE CREATES A VISUAL AND PHYSICAL CONNECTION TO HADERSLEV

PROPOSAL WORKS WITH REINTERPRETING THE MIXTURE BETWEEN THE BUILT AND THE NATURAL

VIEWS FROM THE DENSE FORESTS. DESIGNED IN AN ORTHOGONAL GRID, CREATE VARYING RELATIONS BETWEEN ARCHITECTURE AND LANDSCAPE

Selected student project / 6th BSc 2011 / Supervisor: Shelley Smith
Transformation

The New Story of Odense - riding on a roof top, playing on a rail track, living in a fairytale

Jacob Bjerre Mikkelsen, Ida Sofie Gøtzsche Lange, Marion Højris Jensen, Rasmus Davidsen & Stine Ellegaard Jakobsen

WICKED DESERT

Working with concepts related to 'sustainable transportation', 'compact garden city' and 'fairytales', the project aimed at promoting what is unique for the city of Odense. The local context of a main thoroughfare in the city, Thomas B. Thriges Gade, has been taken into account and the area subsequently divided into three subareas: The Wicked Desert, The Enchanted Village and The Vibrant Neverland – each area a combination of its location and the place-specific characteristics, as well as new identities. The urban transformation of Thomas B. Thriges Gade tells a new story of Odense – a positive tale of a city that is true to its own characteristics and confident to tell of them.

SITE PLAN

VIBRANT NEVERLAND

THE ENCHANTED VILLAGE

Selected student projects / 2nd MSc 2011 / Supervisor: Victor Andrade & Shelley Smith
Transformation

Climate Design – working with vulnerable urbanities in Mozambique
Stine Sonne & Anne Lærke Jørgensen

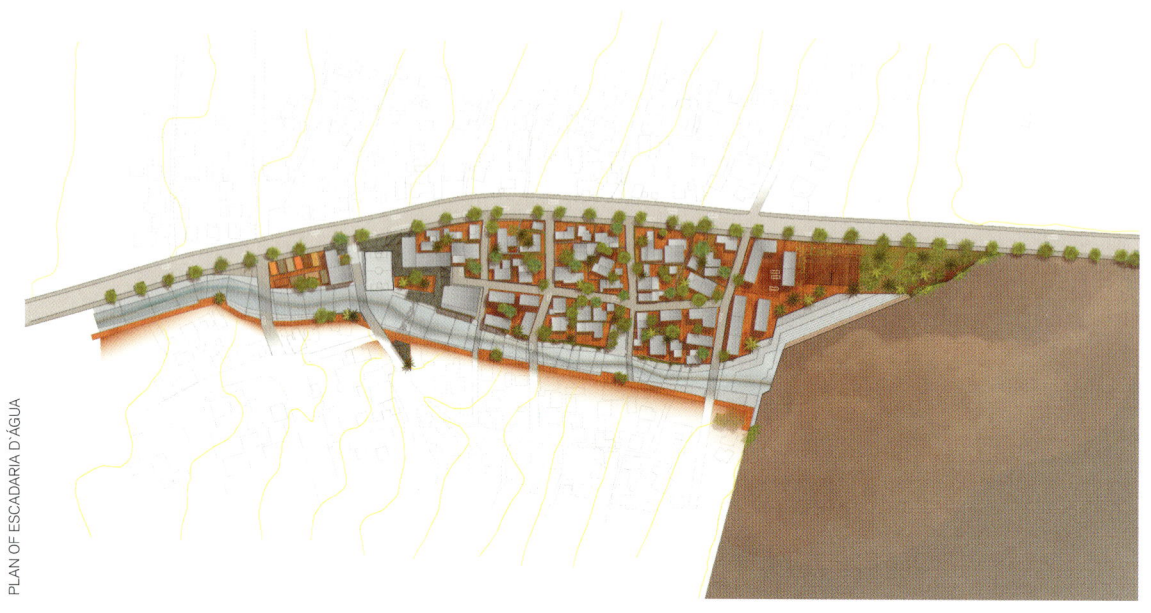

PLAN OF ESCADARIA D'ÁGUA

The project dealt with the challenges of climate change adaptation in vulnerable urban areas in the Northeastern part of Maputo, Mozambique. The location, close to the ocean at a low elevation, makes the area vulnerable to both rising sea-levels and run-off water from the city behind it. At the same time it has of late experienced rapid and uncontrolled urban growth.

The thesis proposed a strategic process and action plan focusing on how uncontrolled development and climate change can become sustainable urban development. Infrastructure, barriers and landscape modification form a flexible solution for how the area, over time, can adapt to its changing surroundings. A detailed design proposal focused on how a new road and a *wadi* can accommodate the local concerns for a stable environment, and become the new urban centre for the neighborhood.

SECTION OF THE NEIGHBORHOOD CENTRE

THE NEIGHBORHOOD CENTRE

STAIRS OF WATER - ESCADARIA D'ÁGUA

Selected student projects / Master Thesis 2010 / Supervisor: Victor Andrade
Transformation

Intensified Concorde Neighborhood

Lucile Hamoignon

The project was a proposal for renewing the Concorde neighborhood, a modernist social housing scheme built in the fifties, in Lille, France. The concept of intensifying was used to produce interest for the neighbourhood, enhance its good qualities, and to activate and strengthen urban life. Through this, the intention was to bring more life into the neighborhood and integrate the neighbourhood with the dynamic of the city. In the project, intensification of the neighborhood was achieved by working with concepts of connection, diversification, densification, polarities and hierarchy.

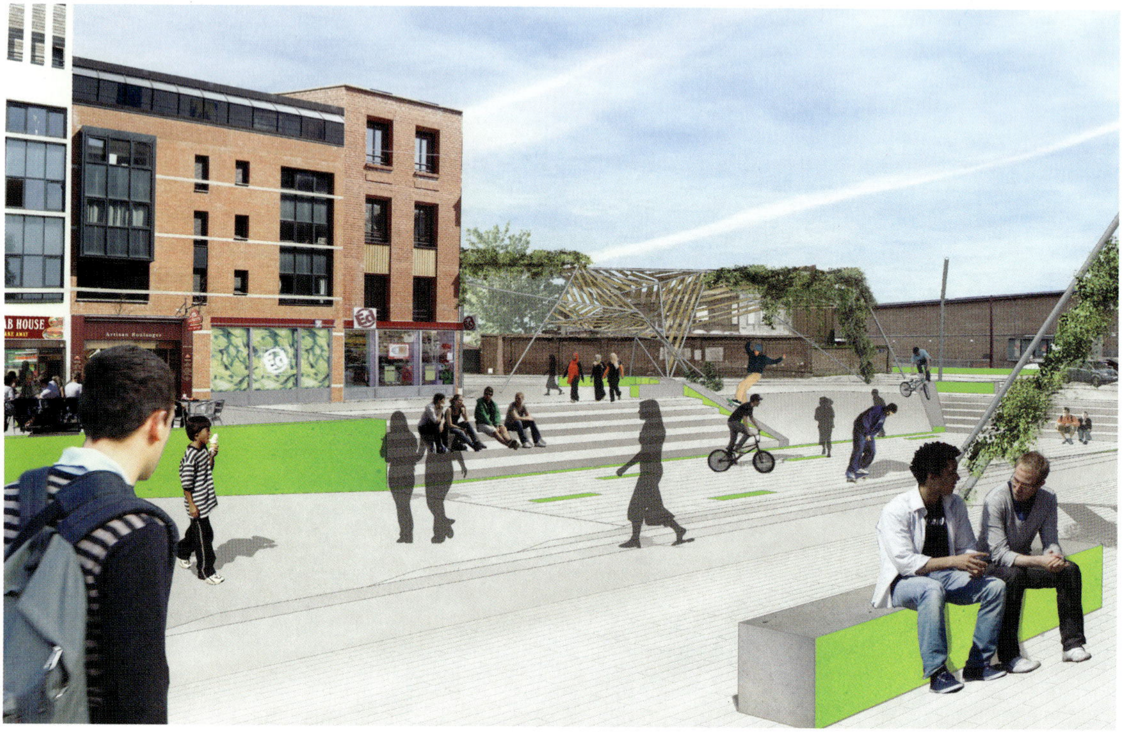

CONCORDE SQUARE

PLAN OF THE INTENSIFIED CONCORDE NEIGHBORHOOD

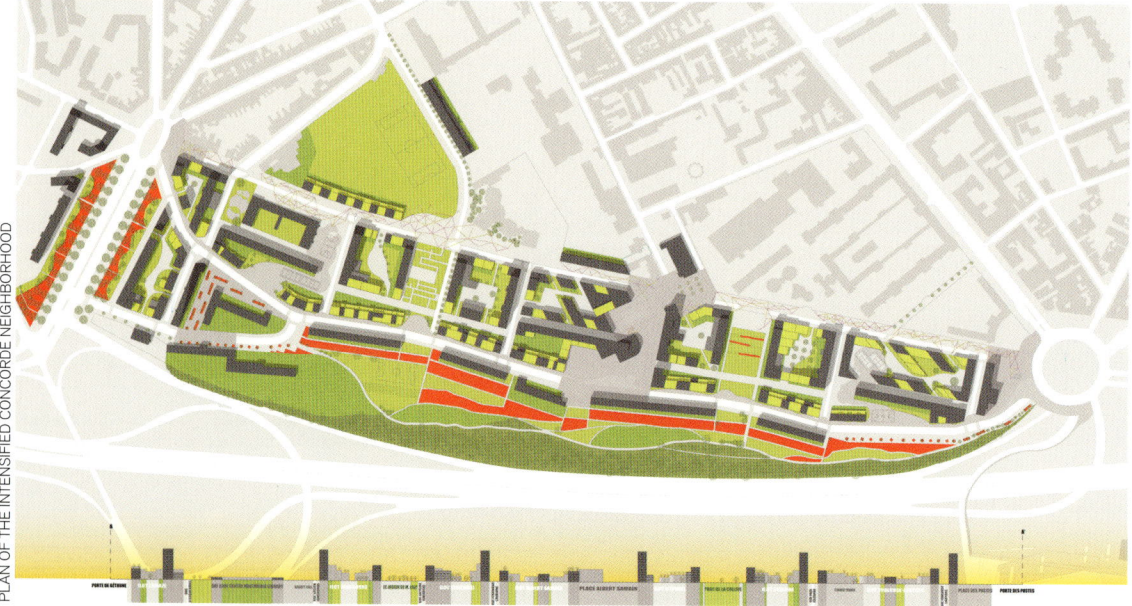

COMMUNAL GARDENS AT CONCORDE

RETROFITTED STREET AT CONCORDE

Selected student projects / Master Thesis 2010 / Supervisor: Victor Andrade
Transformation

135

The New Karolinelund – Aalborg's diverse venue
Jakob Charmoth Nielsen

SPACES AROUND THE NEW CHANNEL IN KAROLINELUND

Karolinelund is the former amusement park of Aalborg, located in the northern part of Jutland, Denmark. The aim of the project was to transform the site into a public park surrounded by various new buildings with hybrid programmes. The project focused on a long-term process where new programmes could be discovered through the temporary use of the spaces so that the possibility for designing useful facilities in the long run would be enhanced. Physical interaction replaced the machine generated attractions – e.g. the bumper cars were replaced with a moon car track. In addition a flower park, concert pavilion, skate park, a new channel etc. create main dynamos in the New Karolinelund.

ALONG THE CHANNEL

THE MOON CAR TRACK AND ITS SURROUNDINGS

RECREATIONAL PROGRAMMES AND A PUBLIC DOMAIN

Selected student projects / Master Thesis 2010 / Supervisor: Lea L H Laursen
Transformation

Meadow Patterns with an Edge - urban development in the northern freight rail area in Aarhus
Rikke Schjødt Brink

THE MUSIC PARK

The project describes a framed cultural production in a folded urban landscape which includes natural habitats as visual windows through which to view and experience an urban metropolis. The idea behind the project was to improve the Municipal Local Plan 886 for the northern freight area in Aarhus. Based on site mapping, theory and analyses identifying and clarifying problems, potentials and possibilities, the project visualised the historical meadow patterns by creating 'water', 'swamp', 'herbal', 'self-grown' and 'concrete' zones, and explored the notion of folding as a technique for developing form.

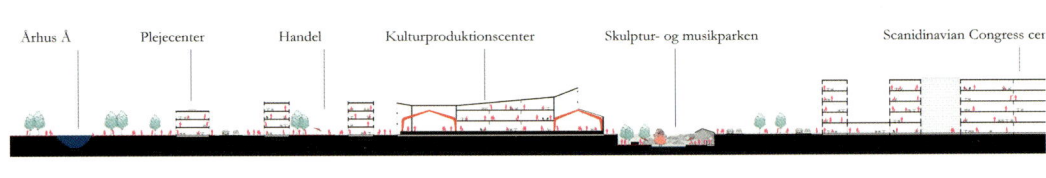

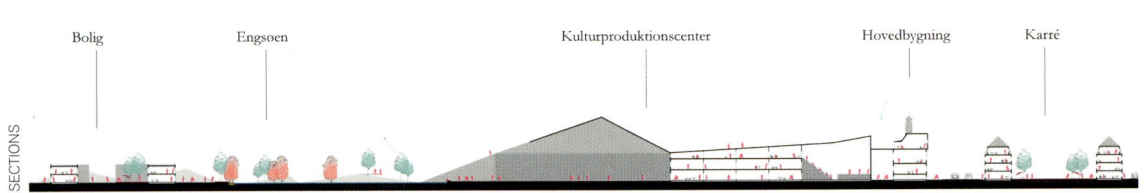

SECTIONS

THE MEADOW POND

MASTERPLAN

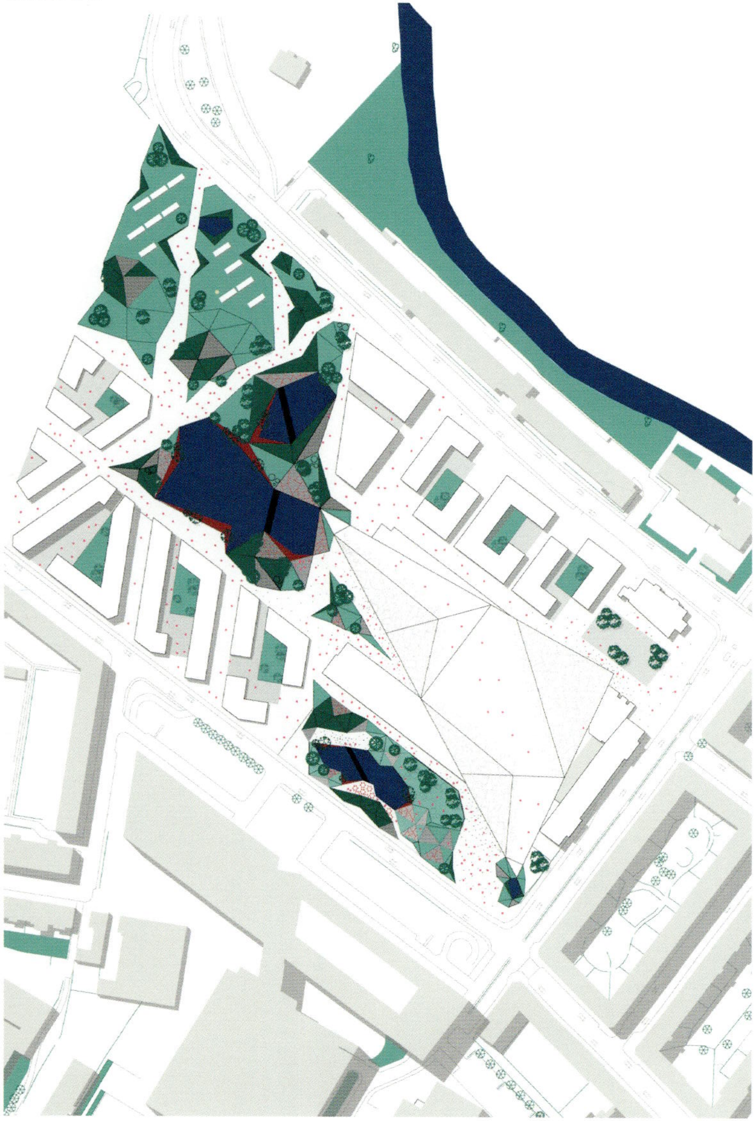

Selected student projects / Master Thesis 2011 / Supervisor: Shelley Smith
Transformation

139

DESIGN AND METHOD

ABSTRAKTISTAN CITY- PURPLE FOAM WORKSHOP 2010, AALBORG UNIVERSITY. © HANS TOFT HORNEMANN

Urban Songlines
– the city experienced by ordinary people
Gitte Marling

This article presents a method called Urban Songlines, which is a kind of 'story-telling – method' that has been developed in order to present urban qualities experienced by ordinary people. It is a tool, which supports researchers and urban designers in removing themselves from the role of expert in order to see the city through the lens of ordinary people.

The aim of the method is to get a better understanding of the way in which people with different cultural backgrounds, ages and genders practice their everyday lives and shape places and give them meaning through actions.
The main question asked for the development of the method has been: How can the experiences of ordinary people be mapped and presented?

The main focus of this article is to present the 'Urban Songlines Method', and give an example of its use. However it starts with a brief introduction of mapping methods used earlier in urban design research, including theories on life style, which are essential for the way 'urban songlines' has been developed and used. The potentials and weaknesses of the method are briefly discussed at the end of the article.

Urban Songlines – A Method Related to the Analysis of City Life and Urban Architecture

In the investigation of city life in the permanent or temporary city, the concept 'urban songlines' is used with a dual meaning - on the one hand it refers to the lines, nodes and landmarks that the individual follows on his or her way through the city. In this sense, an urban songline is the line or the track that each of us follows in our daily movement in the city, from one place of meaning to the next; for example from our homes to work, the bar, the music venue, the school, the local shop etc. On the other hand, urban songlines have to do with mental tracks, places of historical importance or places that you and your group find intriguing. In this sense, urban songlines are tied to our social behaviour and mental memories and connections. (Marling 2003)

The Urban Songlines methodology has been used to combine architectural mapping and the everyday practice of different lifestyle groups. It has been done through interviews, mapping everyday songlines and weekend songlines, sorting pictures, taking photo safaris with the respondents or collecting the results of the respondent's own photo safaris, visiting places of meaning together with the respondents etc.

The urban architecture that has been explored by the respondents has been investigated and analysed. Landmarks and nodes have been mapped, i.e., open urban spaces, parks, harbour fronts, golf courses, leisure parks, voids etc. and indoor meeting places like shopping malls and clubs. Walks with the respondents through their territories have been tools to create 'serial visions', which is a way of relating urban architecture to the body (Cullen 1961). Likes or dislikes along the pathways have been part of the mapping too. On the way – and after the walks – the respondents have talked about their experiences of the city, of the meaning of history, architectural values, taste and contents.

Through storytelling, the respondents have shared their experiences of the part of the city to which they relate themselves. The sense of the whole is a summing up, not only on the mapping the urban architecture in a songline or the territory of the respondent, it is also – and this is important to stress once more - combined to form an understanding of the respondents' lifestyle and values.

The Origins of the 'Songlines' Concept

A source of inspiration for using the method to uncover the connection between an individual person's architectural and socio-cultural preferences comes from Bruce Chatwin's book *The Songlines*, from 1987. Essentially, the book deals with the problems of 'being', of defining oneself and one's territory, and with orientating oneself by means of psychological connections and places of spiritual and mental significance. Bruce Chatwin was interested in nomadic peoples and their ways of navigating the landscape. He studied the Australian aborigines and the cultural phenomenon of 'songlines' or dream tracks containing sacred places and narratives. Among other things, the tracks comprise a kind of atlas or guide. 'Songlines' means much more than this, however.

In his book, Chatwin describes the aborigines' genesis, which defines the songlines that according to legend, weave a web across the entire Australian continent. The creation myths tell of the totem creatures that walked the continent in the time of dreams. They created the world through their song; in a manner of speaking 'they were singing the world into existence'. During their wanderings, they sang the name of everything that crossed their paths, e.g. birds, rocks, cliffs, animals, plants or waterholes. As the ancestors wandered, they witnessed various events taking place by a rock, a stream etc. The locations of these events became sacred to the descendants of the ancestor in

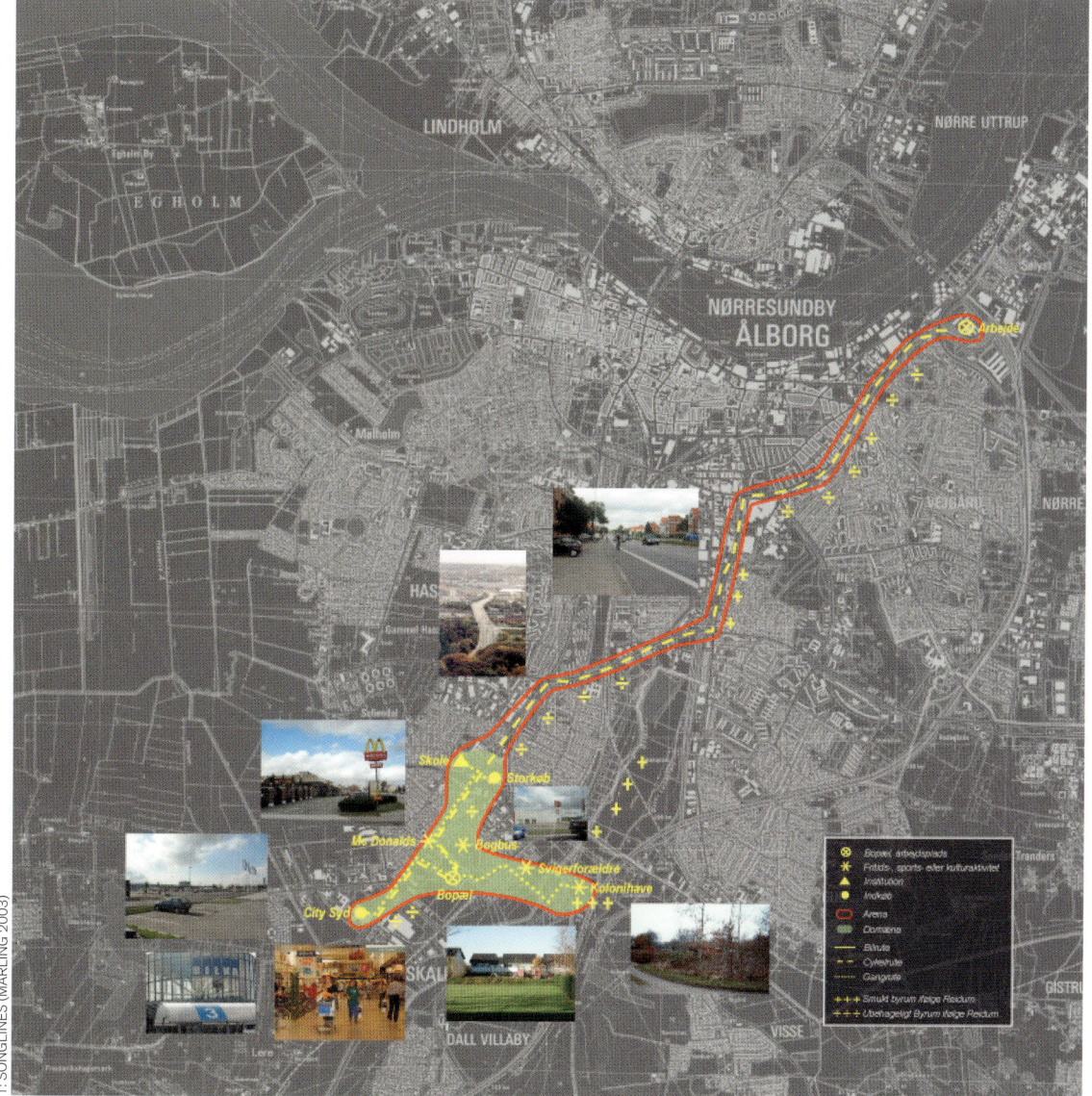

1: SONGLINES (MARLING 2003)

issue – to his clan. These places and the lines between them are songlines. The distance between two such places can be measured as a songline.

Through interviews and historical accounts, Chatwin discovered that Australia could be read as a score, and that there was hardly a cliff or a stream that couldn't be sung. He further stated that every aborigine had two fathers: a biological father and a spiritual ancestor. The ancestor had created a song, which lay in an unbroken chain of couplets along the ground - one couplet for each of the ancestor's footprints. When a pregnant woman going about her daily business stepped on a couplet, the 'spirit child' would enter her body through a fissure in her foot and work its way up to her womb and fertilize the foetus with its song. The foetus' first kick corresponded to the moment of spiritual conception. The mother-to-be marked the location of this event and contacted the village elders, who subsequently determined which ancestor had come this way and thus which stanzas would become the private property of the baby. (Chatwin 1987: 68)

The aborigines thus believe that everything is created and exists as spiritual concepts that have to be sung into being. This means that 'being' is to be 'perceived'. Moreover, the beliefs about 'being' also had to do with belonging to a clan and being spiritually connected to a variety of places along a stretch of land. The domain or the territory is tied to the stretches, the so-called songlines.

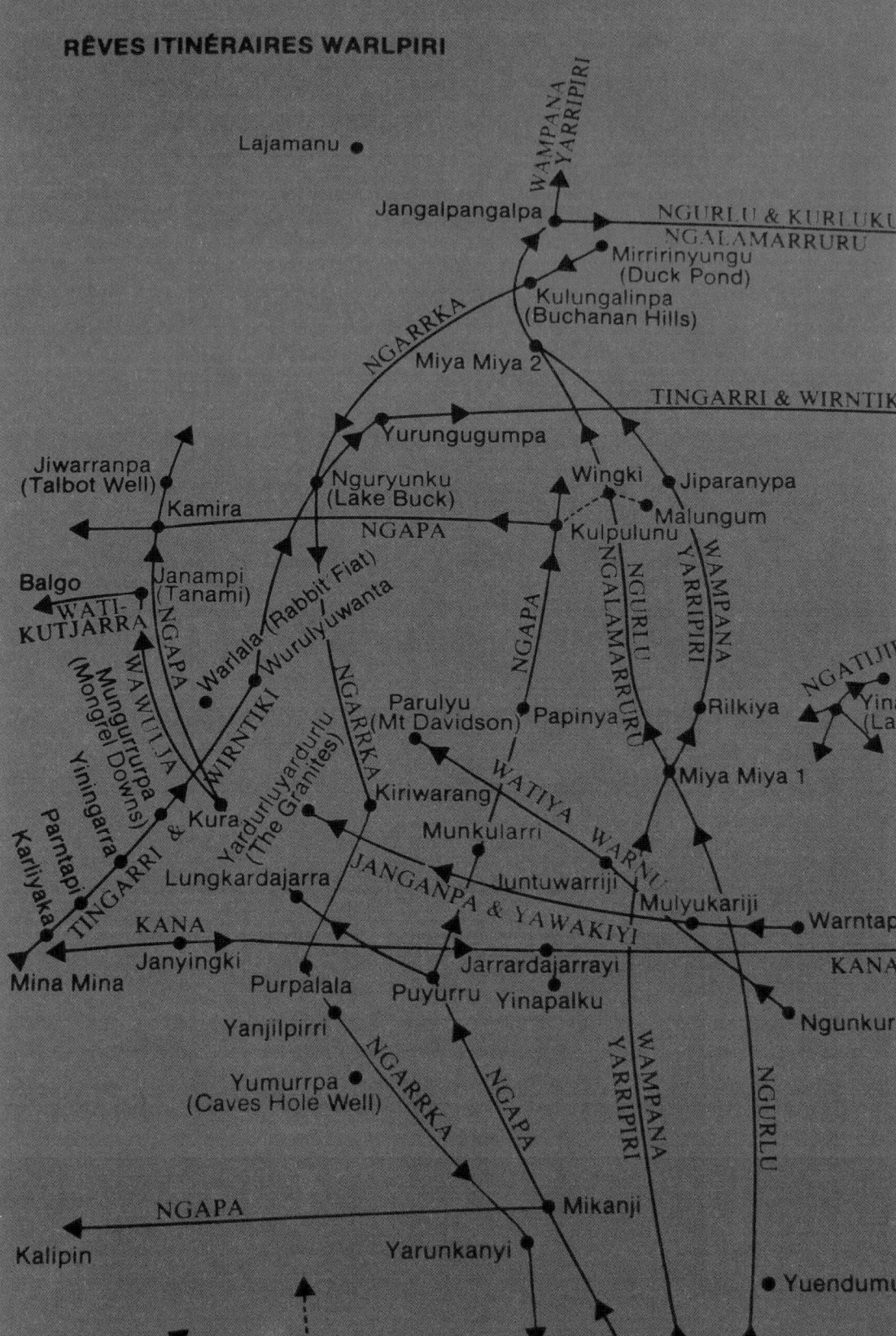

Songlines Related to the Analysis of City Life

One could rightfully wonder what connects the Australian Aborigines and their 'songlines' to the way people find their way through and experience cities today. There is obviously no direct connection between everyday life in the Australian desert and that of a modern city – be it a permanent or a temporary one. The connection is one of association and becomes relevant due to the fact that life in the modern city has changed. Most people no longer live their everyday lives in limited local areas. On the contrary it has become more and more common that they live in a fragmented urban landscape with loosely attached social structures.

So in order to find more specific analytical categories, the Songlines analyses are based on scientific literature about mapping and analysing urban architecture and lifestyle in modern cities.

Previously Developed Mapping Methods in Sociology & Urban Design Research

Many theories on urban life in the metropolis (Baumann 2005), (Sennett 1995), (Waltzer 1995), on behaviour in public places (Simmel 1995), (Goffman, 1966), (De Certeau 1984), and on life form and life style (Douglas 1996), (Højrup 1987) have influenced the development of the method – and different methods of mapping the experiences of urban architecture and the urban landscape (Cullen 1961), (Venturi, Scott Brown and Izenour 1972), (Corner 1999), (Sadler 1999) are part of the common base. However in the following a brief introduction is given of two specific theoretical approaches. Both of them have been particularly essential for the way 'urban songlines' has been developed and used.

Urban Architecture - experiencing the image of the city
Kevin Lynch was a pioneer, who worked with the way human beings explored the city. He stated that: *"Every citizen has had a long association with some parts of his city, and his image is soaked in memories and meaning"* (Lynch 1960: 2)
Lynch's work in the late 1950s concentrated especially on one particular visual quality of the city: the apparent clarity and 'legibility of the city-scape'. By this he meant the ease with which its parts can be organised into a coherent pattern. The result of his studies was that a legible city would be one where the districts, landmarks or pathways of which were easily identifiable and grouped into an overall pattern. If the city is legible, it can be visually grasped as a pattern of recognisable symbols.
You could say that his interest was in city images as communication systems communicating memories, history and identity.

What Lynch did in three different cases (Boston, Los Angeles and New Jersey) was to talk to the inhabitants in order to develop and test his idea of imageability, and to compare images with reality in order to learn which forms made for strong images. Together with a group of his students, he interviewed local people in the three cities. He asked the respondents to answer questions about what symbolises the word 'Boston', or 'Los Angeles' or 'New Jersey' to them. He asked them to draw a city map on a blank piece of paper. He asked them to draw their route from home to job and describe the sequences. He asked them what they saw, heard, smelled etc. He asked about their feelings.

Some of the respondents were invited to participate in walks in which they were asked to lead the interviewer from one point in the city to another, and to explain the route. Photos were taken, and the respondents were asked to comment on the important elements, which he or she found along the way. The interesting part for Lynch was to combine the elements and extract the relationship between them. Kevin Lynch names it 'the sense of the whole'. It is by putting all the elements together in a pattern that the sense of a city's image springs to life.

The songline method is more inspired by Kevin Lynch's research approach than by his maps and categories. It is obvious that the way he involved the citizens in registering their own city raises an interesting discussion of storytelling related to architecture and space. His work is inspiring and gives examples of how the experiences of ordinary people can be mapped and presented. However, there is a lack of social and cultural dimensions. Lynch had his focus on common experiences and images, rather than on diversity.

A life style approach to mapping
In the development of the urban songlines method a strong focus on the experiences of different cultural groups has been added. An important research question in developing the methods has been: How do elements such as gender, age and culture influence the urban experiences of ordinary people? Theories, derived from sociology and anthropology, have been used as 'stepping stones' in conjunction with the research of architects and urban designer. Mapping the city inside out is about combining a lifestyle approach with an approach related to storytelling.

One of the leading theorists in that respect is the French sociologist, Pierre Bourdieu. He has had a major international influence on contemporary research in lifestyle, taste, values and everyday praxis related to the 'habitus' of the individuals and the culture of lifestyle domains. He operated with three important terms in lifestyles: 'capital', 'field' and 'habitus'. The term 'capital' means both economic and symbolic capital. It is the capital a person gathers in the form of passed examinations, prizes or artistic performances etc. The term, 'field' refers to the space where individuals find similarly disposed people. It is a space where certain values and norms are constituted. 'Habitus' is a form of 'modus operandi'. It is an abstract term, which in a very basic way structures our social orientation. Habitus contains social elements and our individual values, and it sets a framework for people's opinion, standards, interpretations and actions. Furthermore habitus contains the objective conditions, that have left their marks on us during childhood and youth, and which we meet again as adults. But habitus also contains the way we as individuals use objective conditions. In this way, habitus is a dialectic term; it is a term for both the conditions that structures the way we live our daily lives; and it is a term for structuring, as long as we as actors actively influence the conditions (Bourdieu 1984).

The 'songline method' draws upon the key concepts utilized by Pierre Bourdieu in his theory of practice – especially the concept of 'habitus'. The motivation for this lifestyle approach is to gain new knowledge of how different groups of ordinary people experience their city; what they like or dislike; where and with whom they feel at home, and with which terms they explain their feelings.

Psycho-Geographical Mapping and Representation

An important part of the Songline Method is the presentation of the narratives where statements and maps supplement each other. The mapping representation has developed over time from mapping along linear city structures to using the more creative layered or 'rhizome' approaches inspired by James Corner (Corner 1999). The presented map fig. 6 is graphically and representationally inspired by the psycho-geographical maps of 'The Situationists'. The Situationist Maps were created by Guy Debord and Asger Jorn in the late 1950s project "The Naked City" (Sadler 1999). (See figure 3)

The Use of the Method

The concept of 'urban songlines' refers to the way people live in and move through a contemporary urban landscape, which can often feel like an infinitely large space with only a few landmarks. In this urban field, tracks are made and traced. With a point of departure in the above theoretical concepts, the object of study is how connections are created. Furthermore the aim is to investigate what makes sense and forms the identity of urban man today. Urban Songlines trace and emphasise diversity in cities, but at the same time places in the city, which are significant are pointed out.

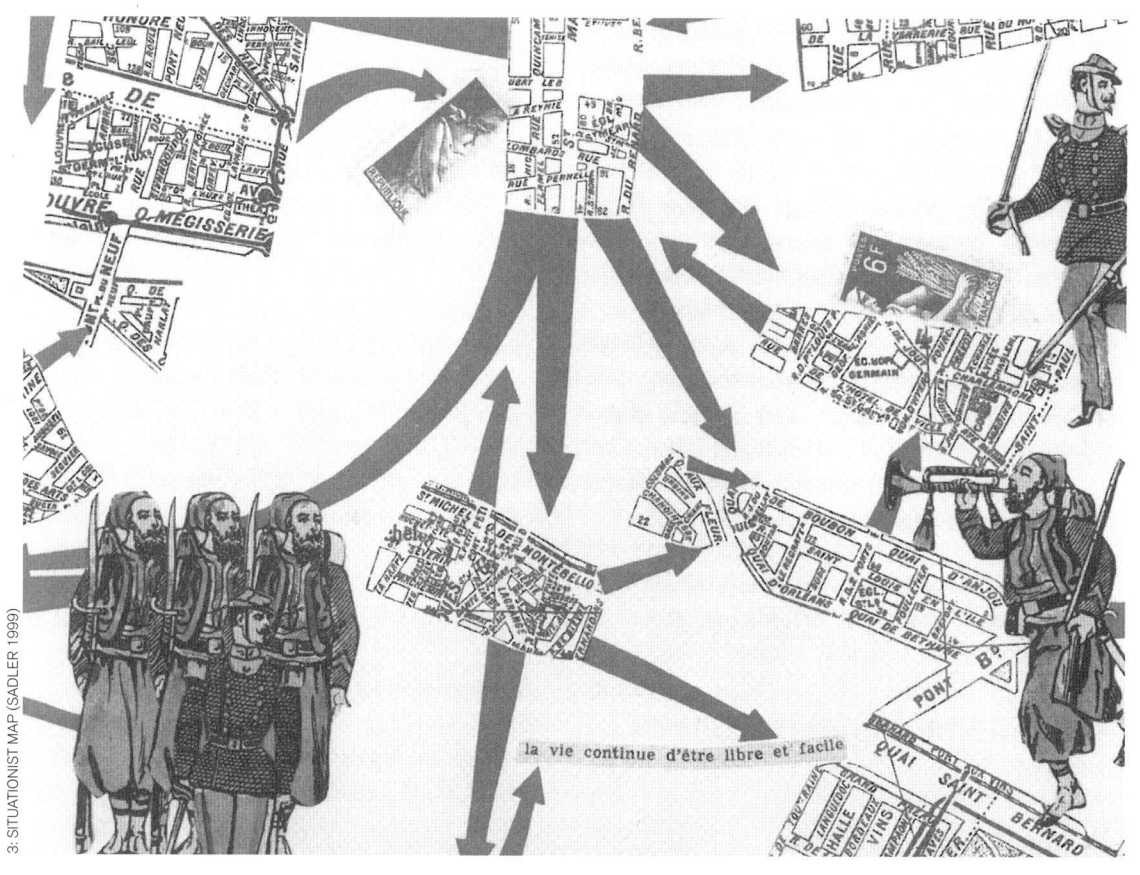

3: SITUATIONIST MAP (SADLER 1999)

The method has been used and developed through research and studies with students in different urban cultural contexts. As mentioned above the first study was in the city region of Aalborg, Denmark in 2003 - 2004. A year later in 2005 an urban studio was set up in Bangkok with 34 urban design students mapping Bangkok Songlines, and in 2007 a similar workshop was set up in Hong Kong & Bangkok (Marling 2005), (Marling 2007).

Recently, planning praxis has adopted the method. In Malmø, Sweden, the planning office has ordered a 'Songline Mapping' in order to investigate in which way different cultural groups use the open spaces in the city. It was also asked if it was possible to make the songlines of different cultural groups meet. On this basis, the goal had been to design new meeting places, new public domains (Hajer and Reijndorp 2001), where social and cultural exchange can take place. (Malmø Stadsbyggnadskontor 2006).

Urban Songline Mapping of City Life at Instant City- Roskilde Festival

In 2011 the method was used in a research project about architecture and urban life in an instant city context. A case from this work will be presented in the following as an example of the method in use. The following is an edited section from the book 'Instant City@Roskilde Festival' (Marling and Kiib 2011).

The Roskilde Festival area is planned and built like a city, with a city centre, local centres and living areas. The temporary city (1-2 weeks) has a series of urban places, urban parks, and a wide range of paths, landmarks and a multitude of boundaries dividing the city into different neighbourhoods.

The instant architecture and art installations can be described as relative and form a performative urban scenography. In this context a diverse city life takes place. Urban Songlines has been used as one of several methods to analyze everyday life in this the temporary city. (Marling and Kiib 2011)

A journey of exploration at Instant City – Roskilde Festival

In the songline analysis of Roskilde Festival the inhabitants are given a voice. In 12 short narratives, they present their everyday habits and their experience of the community, music, art and architecture during the festival. The narrators link the way they experience moods, parties, concerts and everyday life at the festival to the spatial organization of the temporary city. They draw maps of their routes, and they point out, photograph and comment on the particular places and events where they either feel at home or are intrigued. They, so to speak, pin down their territories and points of interest. It is essential for the Urban Songlines method to connect the narrator's aesthetic experiences with his or her cultural preferences. (Marling 2003), (Marling 2004)

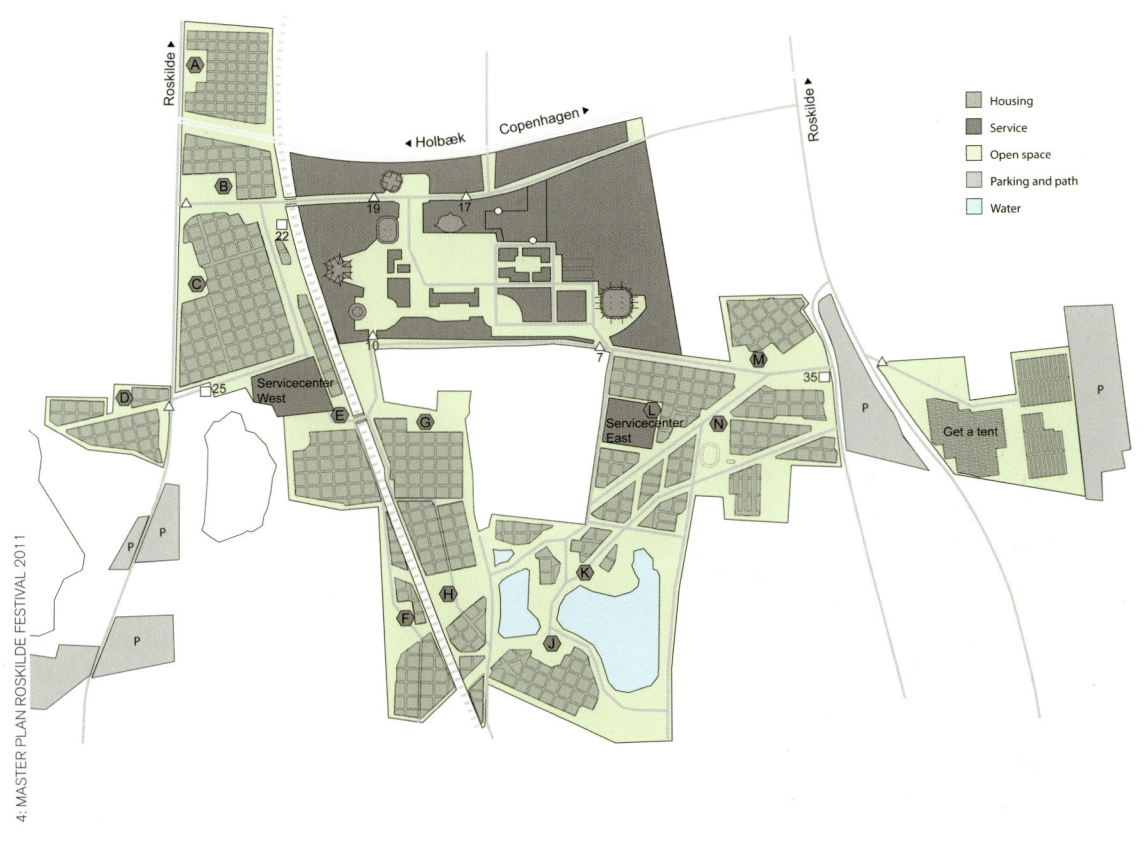

One of the respondents was Pernille Krogh Nielsen, a 19-year-old student. She is, in her own words, curious and wants to experience as much as possible, and this takes her far and wide. She plays music (the piano) in her spare time and is in a couple of bands. She has come to Roskilde Festival to listen to music; familiar and unfamiliar bands alike.

This is Pernille's third Roskilde Festival and a number of her friends are there:

"Many people drop by the camp for a beer or to chat – I think that is really nice. A lot of different people drop by… also strangers who sit down because they think it looks nice. It's cool that they have the nerve!"

There are some things that Pernille feels she 'has to' participate in because they are important to her overall experience.

"I always catch the last concert on Orange Stage with the fireworks… and I have helped topple the fence every year; have queued up and been here for the ENTIRE festival."

Drifting through the city
Pernille gets about a lot.

"It's best with a balance between being in the camp and in the festival area. In the camp, we chat, and play games… and I wouldn't want to do without… (But) you miss out on a big part of Roskilde (Festival) if all you do is hang around the camp! There is music in the festival area and a lot of things to do. It is a really big part of it…
I don't think I follow a certain pattern when I move around. I keep an open mind and take in whatever I feel like… there's nothing you have to do – just be here and have a good time!"

Thursday, Pernille woke up early (1). It was hot, and she could not sleep any longer. She went to the staff tent, Hall 4, for breakfast (2).

"After breakfast, we (five people from the camp) took our sleeping bags and slept for an hour and a half in the shadow of the trees to the left of Orange Stage (3). Some others had been there yesterday and said it was really, really nice. We listened to music as we slept under the trees. They were sound testing on Orange Stage while we lay there – so we heard some blues…
We went back to the camp (1) for some lunch. We usually have black bread with liver pâté, mackerel etc. for lunch, but I didn't really feel like it, so I went back to 'Bolleboden' (4) with Nikolaj."

5: PERNILLE IN HER CAMP IN THE SUBURBAN AREA. THE CAMP CONSIST OF SIX BOYS AND THIRTEEN GIRLS

6: PERNILLE WORKS AT 'BOLLEBODE'. 24 HOURS OF WORK GIVES HER A FREE FESTIVAL TICKET AND FREE SANDWICHES

7: PERNILLE'S SONGLINE MAP – REPRESENTED AS A 'SITUATIONIST MAP'.

"Cosmopol er en af de bedste scener"

8 COSMOPOL

3 AFSLAPNING

9 ORANGE SCENE

2 HAL4

"Det er fedt med overdækkede steder"

6 BAD

7 PAVILLION

10 PARISERHJUL

4 BOLLEBODEN

"Der kommer mange forbi lejren. De vil lige drikke en øl eller sidde og snakke - det synes jeg er vildt hyggeligt"

1 PERNILLES LEJR

"Det er ligesom at ligge på stranden"

5 BADESØEN

Urban Songlines - the city experienced by ordinary people
Design and Method

149

After lunch they wanted to go for a swim in the lake, so they went back to the camp to change into their bathing suits. On their way back they noticed a lot of booths and art installations.

"We actually spent quite some time looking at stalls yesterday," says Pernille. "There are some really cool girls' clothing shops, vintage clothes, scarves… and when we left the Arena Stage, we walked along the fence looking at the graffiti."

Pernille likes the area by the lake (5). It's a nice place to be cooled down.

"It's a bit like being on the beach, when you lay there in the sand wearing a bikini… it's really nice. And you also get to meet other people."

She thinks the lake is very nice once you get in, but yesterday there were simply too many people.

"It was just too gross, and we'd also forgotten our towels," she says and continues, "So we went home to get our towels and then to the cold showers by City Centre West (6)."

It was now 4.30 p.m., and Pernille spent the next 30 minutes in the camp (1). She made herself comfortable with some candy and beer bowling.

The concerts started at 5 p.m. She had decided to hear either Lucy Love at Cosmopol (7) or Katzenjammer at Pavilion (8).

"But we walked past Cosmopol because it was too crowded, so we went back to Pavilion and listened to Katzenjammer Rock. It was actually a very good concert," she says.

They also had dinner at Bolleboden (4).

"Apart from that we just strolled around in the festival area looking at stalls and the small shops and spent some time in the shade under the awnings looking at people etc."

Later in the evening (10 p.m.), she returned to Orange Stage (8) where she attended a Kanye West concert with her friends. That particular concert was a bit of a 'must' and they were right in the middle, says Pernille.

"We were between the two speakers… We'll gladly queue for an hour and a half to get into the pit if it's a concert we really want to see and have been looking forward to. It is a completely different experience. Everybody else is as much into it as you are. If you are down in the back, it is to enjoy the concert and have a good view."

They left the area in front of Orange Stage before the concert was over and headed to the big Tuborg Ferris Wheel (9).

"You have to pedal for three minutes to ride the wheel. Everybody's pedalling, and if anyone stops and gets off, you can feel it getting heavier… You get an egg timer… We pedalled for three minutes

8: THE INSTANT CITY FROM THE FERRIS WHEEL, FIRST PERNILLE HAS TO PRODUCE THE ENERGY FOR THE WHEEL HERSELF

and then saw the last three numbers from the Ferris wheel. It was cool seeing the area and the lights from above."

Pernille had planned to see Sunday Shop afterwards, "but we didn't feel like it. We bought some rice-stuff and a burger by the Ferris wheel. Then we went back to the camp to hang out for a while before we went to bed (at 1.30 a.m.). We go to bed late every day and get up early when it's hot, so it was really nice to get some sleep yesterday!"

Cosmopol is my favourite place

Cosmopol, and its surroundings, is one of Pernille's favourite parts of the festival area.

"Cosmopol is one of the best stages. It offers a lot of different things: world music, brass bands and a lot of hip-hop – a really, really cool stage with some really cool performances. You just have to go into the tent to participate ... I also like the area and the clothes shops here. It's one of the places I go to, if I can't think of anything to do... The seating arrangements here by Cosmopol are good, and there are interesting things to look at!"

Pernille has spent quite a while examining the festival area. She likes the art installations and graffiti art. She has also used the hammocks by Pavilion quite a bit.

"I guess I'm a bit curious," says Pernille. "I want to see it all. So I went into the yellow pavilion just to see what it was. It's a bit weird. It has this mirror that makes it look like there are four exits, but there are only two. Last year, there was this art installation that spewed flames/fire – it was so cool. You don't really get the point, but it's cool that it's there... It's really interesting when you get to be a part of it, get to experience it yourself by participating. I like the fact that Roskilde is doing so much to make the audience feel they're a part of this place. There are so many graffiti artists decorating everything, and there are so many fun installations ... There's also the 'Human Car Wash'! (11) There's so much to do. We just go for anything that looks exciting!"

Pernille drifts through the temporary city. With an open mind, she lets herself be swept away by the fun and preferably peculiar experiences that the temporary city has to offer. She finds it positive that there is such a big supply of art and playful things. When it comes to music, she takes a somewhat different approach. She is very conscious about what to hear. Music is a big part of her life, and her experience of the city. Therefore, the place where she is most comfortable is connected to music. She declares that Cosmopol is the best stage with the most interesting music. To her, the culture, city life and art by Cosmopol are in coherence with the music, which is why it is her favourite place at Roskilde Festival. This is where she goes if she has an idle moment. (Marling and Kiib 2011)

9: "COSMOPOL IS IN A LEAGUE OF ITS OWN", PERNILLE

Strengths and Weaknesses - Concluding Remarks

The Songline method takes time. It takes time to interview the respondents twice; to walk through the city with them; to discuss their photos and to produce the maps.
This is the weakness of all qualitative methods – including the 'Urban Songlines Method'.

Some planners see the method as too explorative and open because it seldom seeks information about common interests, but presents the pluralistic. If you have an exact planning task it seems very time consuming and disturbing with this magnitude of varied information.

On the other hand it is important to remember, that the goal has been to develop a method which gives a better *understanding* of the way in which people with different cultural backgrounds, ages and genders practice their everyday lives, and shape and give places meaning through actions. The method is *explorative*, and as such the strengths of the method are, that the storytelling about urban experience is linked to everyday practices and the physical territories of the city. It is possible to work with very different impressions linked to for instance, architecture, social environments and elements like atmosphere (smell, sound etc.) – e.g., in the case of Roskilde Festival some of the respondents talked about atmosphere as 'the orange feeling' and how this feeling was connected to the culture of laughter, to music, to urban architecture, to city life and to the feeling of being free. These elements are connected to maps and photos/films. This will be developed further in future research.

The maps give important information for urban planners, architects and urban designers, because they combine these very different and often immaterial conditions with something physical. The maps are illustrative ways of presenting the findings and the given information is important in forming an overall approach to city planning, urban transformation, urban renewal etc.

References

Bourdieu, P. (1984) *Distinction. A social Critique of the Judgement of Taste*. Cambridge: Polity Press.

Careri, F. (2002) *Walkscape – Walking as an Aesthetic Practice*. New York: GG Land & Scape Series.

Chatwin, B. (1987) *The Songlines*. London: Jonathan Cape.

Corner, J. (1999) ´The Agency of Mapping´. In: Cosgrove, D. (Ed.) *Mapping*. London: Reaktion Books.

Cosgrove, D. (Ed.) *Mapping*. London: Reaktion Books.

Cullen, G. (1961) *The Concise Townscape*. Essex: Architectural Press.

De Certeau, M. (1984) *The practice of everyday life*. Los Angeles: Berkeley.

Douglas, M. (1996) *Taught styles: Critical essays on good taste*. New York: Sage Publisher.

Goffman, E. (1966) *Behaviour in Public Places: Notes on the Social Organisation of Gatherings*. New York: The Free Press.

Hajer, M. and Reijndorp A. (2001) *In Search of New Public Domains*. Rotterdam: NAI Publishers.

Højrup, T. (1987) *Det glemte Folk*. Copenhagen: Museum Tusculamuns Forlag.

Malmö Stadsbyggnadskontor (2006) *Mötas i Malmö*. Malmö: Gidlunds Förlag.

Marling, G.(2003) *Urban Songlines*. Aalborg: Aalborg Universitetsforlag.

Marling, G. et al. (2004) *Urban Lifescapes*. Aalborg: Aalborg University Press.

Marling, G. (2005) *Bangkok Songlines*. Aalborg: Department of Architecture & Design. Aalborg University.

Marling, G. (2007) Nordark #307: *Bangkok, Hong Kong & Pearl River Delta*: Mapping outside in/ inside out. Aalborg: Department of Architecture & Design. Aalborg University.

Marling, G. and Kiib, H. (2011) *Instant City@Roskilde Festival*. Aalborg: Aalborg University Press.

Sadler, S. (1999) *The Situationist City*. Boston: Massachusetts Institute of Technology.

Simmel, G. (1995) ´Metropolis and Mental Life´. In: Kasinitz, P. (Ed.) *Metropolis: Centre and Symbol of our Times*. New York: New York University Press.

Sennett, R. (1995) ´Community becomes Uncivilized´. In: Kasinitz, P. (Ed.) *Metropolis: Centre and Symbol of our Times*. New York: New York University Press.

Designing Concepts and Strategies
Hans Kiib

In urban transformation some of the most interesting and complex design challenges are related to the redevelopment of waterfronts and former industrial sites. Here the conflicts between 'the old' and 'the new' are greatest and the potential for mistakes is at a critical level. One of the problems is that new developments often employ very modest research on the subject and often very little has been done in order to challenge traditional concepts for redevelopment.

In order to avoid mistakes in urban redevelopment, we need to learn from research and evaluation of the best planning practice, which can give us a comprehensive understanding of our complex cities. However, what might be just as important is to learn from innovative concept development practice, which would promote development of unique possibilities related to the location of the site. This article focuses on the design-based methods in concept development, which can be tested with the purpose of developing new design concepts and generating easily grasped images of a coherent transformation. The article argues that the combination of design-based development and research can provide us with a range of conceptual models for qualitative development of different valuable parts of the city. The strategic development of city life has to build on lessons learned from the dullness of the single-minded spaces of many new developments, although new concepts and strategies have to be designed in a site-specific way in which local resources and global possibilities have to be combined. New innovative design concepts can challenge the scale and the unique qualities of the architectural typologies, thus providing these sites with a range of interesting performative architecture enhancing the mental link between the past and the future.

The examples in the article are taken from the development of the waterfront in Aalborg, where a series of architecture and building workshops have been conducted. The methodology is described in relation to four workshops from 2005 and 2008 challenging different aspects of site-specific developments here. The design concepts and strategies are described and the impact on city planning is evaluated.

Aalborg Waterfront Development Revised

Aalborg is a twin city located on the banks of the Limfjord, Denmark. It has 170,000 inhabitants, and for many years large-scale industry within cement, food and shipbuilding occupied the waterfront on both sides. The experience gained from the initial transformation in the 1990s from industry to a mixed residential and office area on the Aalborg side gave cause for concern. The new developments were based on a tall and dense block structure, and, in spite of vocal and forceful criticism from local citizens, the block structure excluded public functions. The building projects here could be termed project-initiated development with fragmented programming and a frail architectural idea. Finally, the projects were not linked in a distinct urban space policy or an inclusive preservation policy. One might speak of a boomerang effect, as these buildings brush aside the bustle and atmosphere that make up the attraction of the harbour.

In the wake of the heavily criticized projects from the 1990s, the City of Aalborg municipal authority brought the harbour into focus for the first time as a renewed opportunity for urban regeneration. However, the question was, "How?" By adding more city to the pre-existing city core, or were there other ways of achieving urban regeneration? The continuation of short-sighted development would have a great negative impact on the relation between the city and the fjord, which, in turn, would be in danger of becoming just another suburban neighbourhood with mono-functional structures devoid of any noticeable excitement or activity.

Organizing Research and Design-Based Methodology in Concept Development

The City of Aalborg initiated a new effort to create a general foundation for the regeneration of the harbour, and the "Fjord Catalogue" (City of Aalborg 1999) put a range of new principles on the agenda: Preservation of industrial heritage, public squares, diversity of functions and new cultural projects. On the basis of this, a series of different workshops were organized in 2005 and 2008, conducted by the Department of Architecture and Design at Aalborg University in close cooperation with the City of Aalborg municipal authority. The "Harbourscape" project (Kiib 2007) hosted the workshops in which 45 architects, engineers and planners from Denmark, Norway, the Netherlands, the United Kingdom and the USA took part. The aim was to develop visionary design concepts emphasising the development and regeneration of the waterfront in Aalborg.

In 2005 the workshops also involved a full-scale dialogue on concepts and architectural quality in the waterfront development amongst stakeholders in this process. It became an inspiring source for the development of new architectural typologies in different post-industrial sites and for the redesign of the public spaces along the waterfront on both sides of the twin city, Aalborg - Nørresundby.

In 2008 a new series of workshops was held, focusing on themes related to performative architecture, learning environments and temporary use. These workshops focused on how we could add new performative elements to existing building structures, how we could add a new layer of learning to the existing urban fabric, and how we could use large abandoned areas for a period, since redevelopment was scheduled to take very long time (Kiib 2009).

The two events were based on a number of general principles:

- A close cooperation between the City of Aalborg, invited teams of architects, and researchers from Aalborg University. This cooperation was responsible for the preparation of the workshops, clarifying the themes for the developments and providing a common ground for suggested methodologies.
- Open lectures by internationally acknowledged researchers and architects that theoretically and empirically illuminated the subject by way of international examples and the results of their own research.
- A five-day workshop led by three teams of esteemed architects.
- Public hearings. Presentations were held highlighting the results of the workshop (intermediate results and finished products), and a panel of local representatives within building and planning answered questions regarding the future expansion of the harbour, the quality of the construction, etc.

The workshops were inspired by the Hamburg "Bauforum", which in many ways has served as the breeding ground for design-based development strategies in urban transformations. Bauforum 2003, "Sprung über de Elbe", comprised 15 groups, each with 10-12 architects, landscape architects, planners, urban builders, university personnel and students (Freien und Hansestadt Hamburg 2003). Five themes, each with a specific geographical focal point in the area between Hamburg and Harburg, were propounded. Carved into the Isle of Elbe, this large harbour area mainly constitutes a deserted industrial zone with undreamt-of potential for urban and landscape development. Expe

1: DESIGN-BASED METHODOLOGY IN CONCEPT DEVELOPMENT - COLLAGE BY JENS RIX

rience from Hamburg indicated that a design-based development strategy affords a great graphical and procedural bank of ideas for general planning work, and, subsequent to the workshop, the planning authorities in the region and in Hamburg spent the better part of a year collecting material and incorporating it into the strategic plan.

Another inspirational example was the so-called Oslo-Charrette development, in which various design strategies for transforming the boundary zone between city and fjord were proposed (Fjordbykontoret 2004a, 2004b, 2005). Oslo City Council had assembled teams to work with three different scenarios: 'Oslo Large', 'Oslo Park' and 'Oslo Network'. Each team provided an overall assessment of the possibilities for expanding the city's harbour area. In Denmark inspiration was drawn from the large-scale *"Copenhagen X"* project, which commenced in 2002, and from the Harbour Workshop, which was carried out by the Danish Arts Foundation in 2002-2003.

Experience from Hamburg and Oslo demonstrated that architectural workshops have great potential in *the development of new concepts and strategies in urban design*. However, dialogue sessions and development projects will be unsuccessful unless they are based upon solid professional and methodological preparation. It is important that a thorough analysis of policies and practices to date is in place, and that solid empirical research on a number of international cases and theoretical knowledge concerning the driving forces of waterfront development are available.

Themes and Methods

On the basis of learning from failures in waterfront developments, the researchers and the municipal authority presented four central themes summarising the challenges that face the twin-city waterfront development. They were to serve as the primary starting point for the five-day-long professional workshop on concept development in 2005:

1. The first theme was "multifunctional programming". Complex programming has the advantage of allowing space for programmes that assign priority to activities such as existing industrial and artisan areas, as well as harbour-related cultural landscapes and event spaces, but also spaces for working and living. There must be room for functions that make a positive contribution to the new economy of the experience industry. Finally, by reserving some areas for temporary activities, this type of programming can benefit life at and around the harbour, thus keeping the harbour area open for future initiatives and ensuring that different lifestyle groups have cause to use the area.

2. The second theme was called "The Harbour as the Core Urban Space". This theme involved the overall physical design of the urban harbour space, including connections and movement along the waterfronts and across the fjord, and how to build in a manner that avoids turning the fjord into an obstacle, but instead establishes it as a large connecting urban space in the core of the twin city.

3. The third theme was labelled "The Harbour as a Big Stage and a Public Domain of the Fjord-Side Town". It focused on the programming of spaces for different lifestyle groups at the harbour. It aimed at ensuring a variety of activities and cultural exchanges between different communities. This accommodated minorities and ethnic sections of the population, whilst simultaneously taking into consideration senior citizens and young people. This theme had the purpose of investigating which spatiality should be brought into play and given life.

4. "Designing Ten Public Domains along the Edge of the Fjord" was the title of the fourth theme. It comprised the physical design of locations and harbour spaces, passages along the quay progressing coherently with the harbour promenade, the bridges and surplus landscapes. The theme marked an attempt to find means of ascertaining the variation of open as well as closed urban spaces and landscape spaces that could be established along the fjord.

In 2008 the researchers presented two new important themes related to the current recession:

5. "The City as a Learning Lab". This theme employed a range of scenarios, whereby the city could extend the use of resources present in the city and combine these in new ways. The idea was to combine 'the major engine of the region' – the University – with cultural institutions and businesses in the city centre, and how this concept could be developed and how the city and University could work together in attracting new activities.

6. "Urban Catalysts - the potentials of temporary use in urban transformation." This theme had a strong focus on how city planners and developers could cope with the economic recession in the redevelopment of former industrial zones in core areas of the city. To what extent would it be possible to employ new economic and social resources that could work as catalysts for a long-term transformation?

Different methods were employed with a point of departure in the aforementioned themes. Each of the team leaders was responsible for a unique methodological approach to the work, and the outcome was to be oriented towards strategies and concepts, and new urban proposals had to be quickly designed and implemented in sketches and physical models.

Programming City Life Before Architecture – The Spine Workshop (2005)

The intention of the Spine workshop conducted by the Gehl Team (Gehl Architects, Copenhagen) was to create the harbour as a pleasant place teeming with activity. In all its simplicity, the method reverses the traditional focus on architecture – approaching firstly *urban life*, secondly *urban space*, and finally *the edge* and *buildings* (Kiib 2007).

In general, the buildings along the waterfront were not treated as building-volumes, but as edges and frames for the public space. Thus focus was first and foremost on the spaces between the buildings, the transparency between the interior and the exterior at ground level, and the function and activity of a given building rather than its form. This method had four steps:

- Life: the definition of functions and activities
- Space: the design of the qualities of the urban space
- Edge: the facades and the related interfaces between space and buildings, and
- Buildings: design of building volumes and architectural qualities.

Being very critical towards traditional urban planning and towards the strong focus on architectural form and volumes in architectural practice, the team suggests an upside-down approach to planning. When developing a successful city area – whether it is a new or existing city area - life needs to be in focus from the beginning of the design process. By turning the traditional methodology on its head, people and city users would become more visible in the planning process. People, life and vitality are, and always will be, the biggest attractions in a city, they argued.

The impact of the workshop
This concept has had a huge impact on the development strategies along the waterfront in Aalborg in subsequent years. The biggest impact came from the increased awareness of the potential of the water as 'the big common space linking the two shores of the city' - and not as a dividing element splintering the city into two separate parts. A lot of new public space developments along the fjord have been developed since 2005 strengthening the focus on regaining the connection between the city and the water and on accessibility for all user groups in the city.

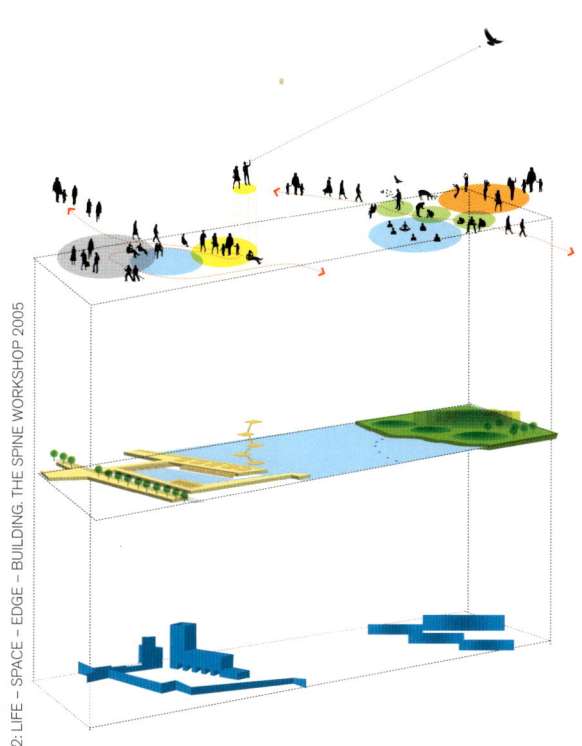

2: LIFE – SPACE – EDGE – BUILDING. THE SPINE WORKSHOP 2005

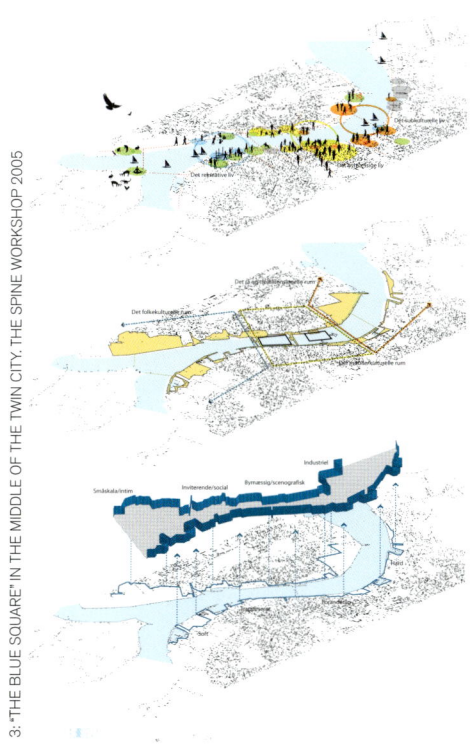

3: 'THE BLUE SQUARE' IN THE MIDDLE OF THE TWIN CITY. THE SPINE WORKSHOP 2005

New Architectural Prototypes - Bridging Aalborg Workshop (2005)

The workshop by the BIG team (Bjarke Ingels Group) in 2005 took as its starting point the physical and mental connection of the twin cities with bridges as architectural projects (Kiib 2007). Four new prototypes of hybrid bridge were proposed to connect the two sides of the harbour, thereby laying the foundation for a new perception of the harbour as the common space of the city. A new elevated bridge to the east, the 'Residential Viaduct', was remarkable as a new and innovative design. It consists of a number of residential towers with an urban park and low-speed traffic and pedestrians on top, and a parking deck below the urban park. It contains a total of 1000 dwellings and 1000 parking spaces.

All the bridges were to be financed through double programming, and the 'Residential Viaduct', for example, was to be financed through the residential project.

The 1.5-km-long residential bridge was designed to connect Aalborg and Nørresundby by way of a vacant industrial area to the north. The idea was to utilize private willingness to invest and to exploit the historically high value of building dwellings in order to create something extraordinary for the public. Primarily, it was a permanent traffic connection, which Aalborg sorely needs. Secondly, it links two historical areas that contain a vast potential. If they were gradually developed into two different cultural parks in two urban surplus areas, each with its own specificities and identity, they would comprise two fantastic poles for the bridge to connect.

The dwellings would be located in the piers, and on top of them would be a parking deck. Cars and pedestrians could cross the bridge, and there would be access to the parking zone below the decks, from where the apartments could be accessed by elevator. Here, people would be able to sit on their terraces and enjoy the view of the industrial areas, the fjord landscape or the city.

The hybrid bridge is a metaphor for the neo-pragmatic way of thinking in urban design (Ingels 2009). 'Hybrid economy' and 'hybrid space' can be understood as linking 'a traditional economy' to a new 'experience economy', and merging 'traditional private urban spaces' with 'new types of public domains'. This coupling is the point of departure for the mental shift from an industrial mindset towards a new pragmatic philosophy in the development of our cities based on knowledge and culture. The term 'Hybrid urban domain' breaks down the traditional division between public and private and seeks to choreograph the city as the space of experience, which serves both as a framework for traditional functions, whilst simultaneously taking on new roles, new meanings and new narratives.

The impact of the workshop

So far, the impact of this concept in city planning has been minor. The 'Residential Bridge' attracted a great deal of attention at its presentation – partly due to the scale and design, and partly due to its composition of dwellings and its importance in terms of traffic. However, the discussion related to how to link the two shores of the twin city has been overtaken by familiar concepts of mobility focusing on accessibility by car. In spite of the discussions on sustainable transport, politicians are still in favour of a traditional motorway to the west of the city, which gives little hope for smaller bridges which could serve a more vibrant development of a new urbanity with the fjord as the connecting element. Furthermore, the hybrid programming of complex building typologies has not been a stronghold for new developments along the fjord. Most projects are still mono-functional housing or office projects, thus leaving very little space for a more vibrant development of urban architectural typologies in the area.

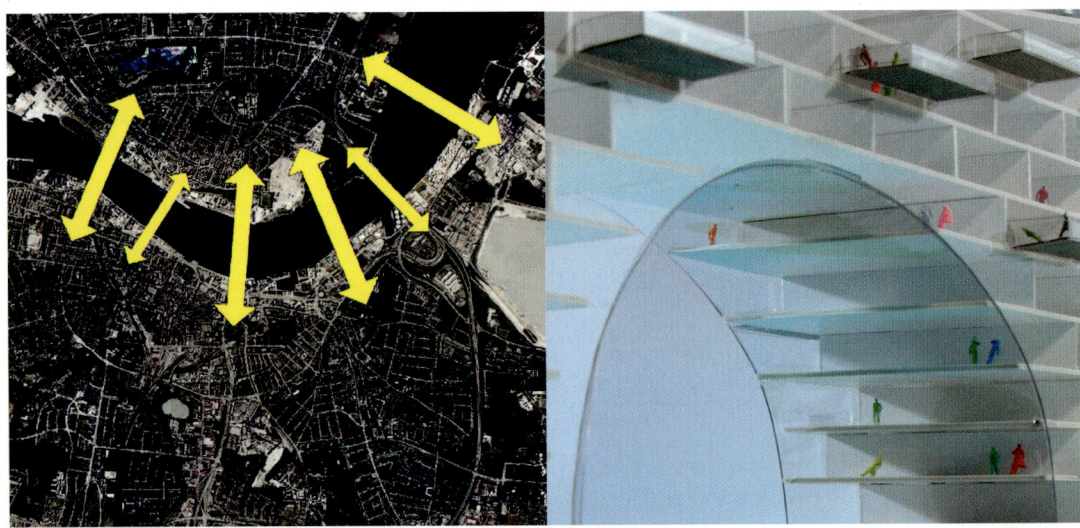

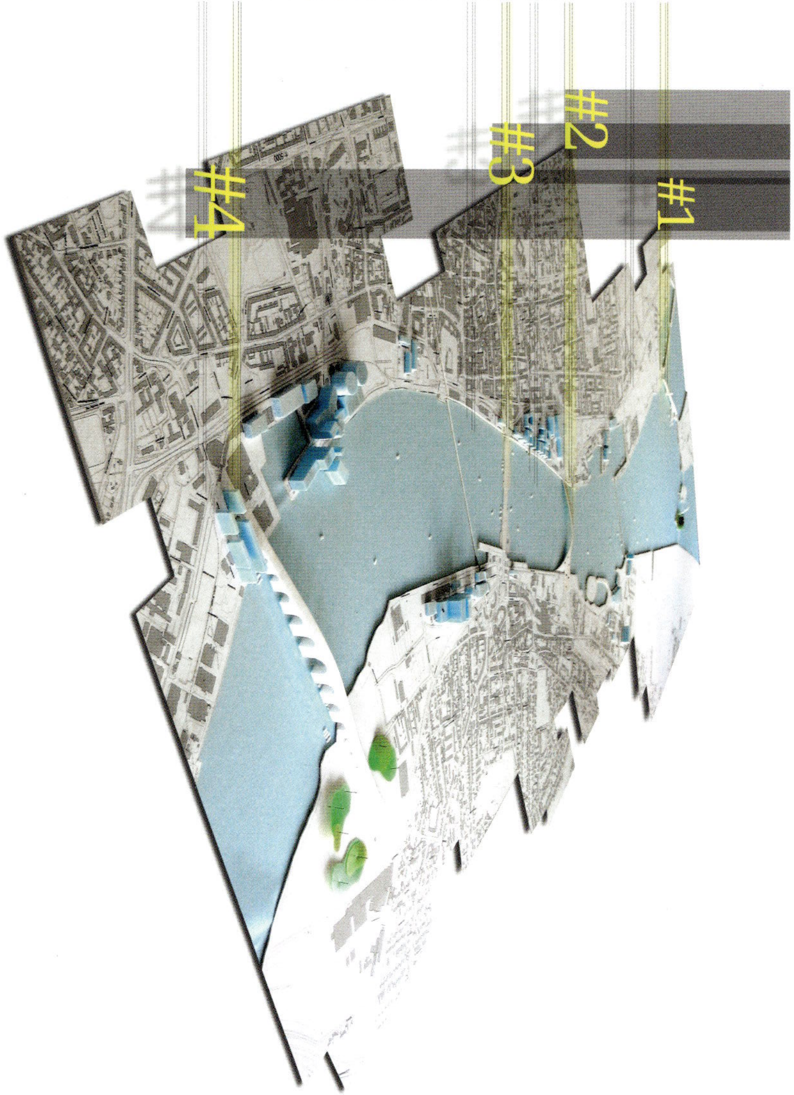

6: VIADUCT FEATURING APARTMENTS, PARKING SPACES AND A PEDESTRIAN PARK ON THE TOP. BRIDGING AALBORG WORKSHOP 2005

7: FOUR HYBRID BRIDGES IN THE LIMFJORD. BRIDGING AALBORG WORKSHOP 2005

Designing Concepts and Strategies
Design and Method

New Urban Layer of Learning - The Learning Lab Workshop (2008)

The concept from the HAO+WE team (Holm Architectural Office, NY, and WE Architects, Copenhagen) in 2008 took as its starting point the question of how we can design playful urban environments that will enhance learning and cultural exchange. "In spite of the crisis, they argued, Aalborg is in unique position to re-invent itself. By simply enhancing its existing resources it could successfully become a new and vibrant urban entity. The economic and physical growth of any given city is defined by its ability to evolve; if a city fails to engage on a variety of levels, it will become obsolete" (Kiib 2009: 189).

The team focused on the role of universities as urban generators. Like industries of the past, an economy of knowledge is growing, transforming universities from passive institutions into defining attractors. The strategic tool should be a deliberate move towards merging City and University, which could define Aalborg as a global institution with the ability to attract global talent. It would engage its inhabitants on new levels of expertise and exploration. It would constitute 'a new economy of knowledge' (Kiib 2009: 190).

The HAO+WE team suggested a scenario where all programmes of study at Aalborg University were to be moved from the campus, 7 km to the east, into the city centre. In order to integrate city and university seamlessly, great importance was placed on identifying existing areas of the city which could be utilized with minimal interference to the existing city fabric. The team identified a number of areas, which were divided into three distinct site typologies throughout the city: Existing vacant city plots, open areas and existing buildings with unused space.

The university programme was broken down into two overall categories. The *first* category contained the programme elements which uniquely serve the university: Areas such as classrooms, study halls, offices, group rooms, etc., were extracted in order to establish the part of the university that serves as the academic core of each faculty and institute. The second category of programme comprised elements that essentially function as shared spaces within the university. Programme elements such as auditoriums, labs, administration, café, library and sports facilities were identified and extracted to create a new programme that could be maximized in use and serve both the city and the university - a series of incubators which would actively engage all inhabitants of the city.

The impact of the workshop
The concept of moving the university to the city centre will of course not be realised in practice. However, the workshop has had a major impact on how the City and the University are working together on a new campus development at the waterfront. In 2010 Aalborg University decided to develop a new City Campus with more than 3000 students and 400 employees related to creative programmes of education at the waterfront. These programmes will be closely integrated with cultural institutions in the area, and the idea is that the different institutions will share a number of facilities and develop joint projects. The goal is for these joint efforts to develop a vibrant environment for cultural production, as well as spaces in which all citizens can have fun or participate in cultural projects.

8: 10MIN. CIRCLE OF FACULTIES. LEARNING LAB 2008

9: CIRCLE OF FACULTIES & INCUBATORS. LEARNING LAB 2008

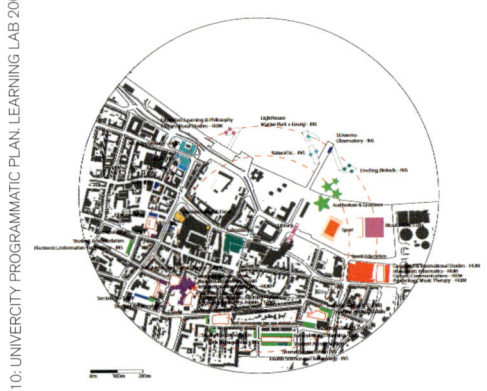

10: UNIVERCITY PROGRAMMATIC PLAN. LEARNING LAB 2008

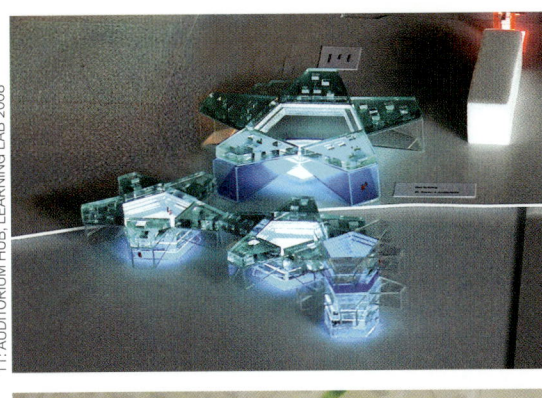

11: AUDITORIUM HUB, LEARNING LAB 2008

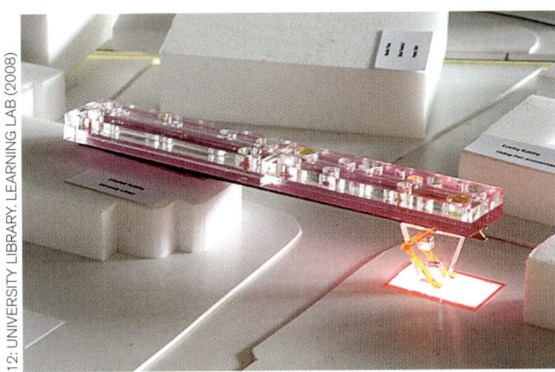

12: UNIVERSITY LIBRARY, LEARNING LAB (2008)

13: WORKSHOP PARTICIPANTS AROUND THE 10MIN. UNIVERCITY, LEARNING LAB 2008

14: CIRCLE OF FACULTIES BECOMES VISIBLE, FACULTIES HAVE A 'TOWER', LEARNING LAB 2008

Designing Concepts and Strategies
Design and Method

Master Plan for Temporary Use – The Urban Catalyst Workshop (2008)

The concept from the Urban Catalyst team (Raumlabor Berlin and Studio UC, Berlin) in 2008 took as its starting point the question of how we can activate urban development by means of 'soft planning strategies' related to temporary use, events and art in the city (Kiib 2009: 363). During the five-day workshop this team employed more than 20 architects, students and artists in the development of a range of urban installations that could be metaphors for a temporary use of urban space in slow transition from empty industrial land into vibrant urban mixed-used areas. The metaphors were related to urban farming, to leisure and sports, and to low-cost housing programmes. The team also developed a site-specific 'Master plan for temporary use', exploring the potentials of a slow process of urban transformation, where the resources and ideas of the citizens could act as a catalyst for transition from wasteland to new and permanent urban structures.

The master plan should represent dynamic planning, unlike traditional planning, aimed at a gradual densification of activities, programmes and networks, which are also becoming structural elements in future design processes. As with soundtrack sampling in music, it is necessary to enlarge the areas of action in city planning, to connect short-term as well as long-term planning and to combine hard and soft tools in planning strategies. Calls for projects on pioneering uses, cultural activity in public spaces, the manipulation of accessibility, reprogramming of existing structures or the networking of operators are a complement to a number of facilities: the local public infrastructures, open spaces, structural activities.

Despite her training, the planner herself is in danger of losing the reference of the object in the working process. Through the construction of 1:1 objects she can avoid this danger. At the same time, it is important not only to negotiate the right subject, but also to act independently on the spot.

The impact of the workshop
The focus of the workshop on 'Urban Catalysts' in relation to temporary use on urban redevelopment has had significant impact on the planning discussion amongst planners in the city. After the workshop took place, the municipal authority and the developer of the harbour at Østre Havn came up with some preliminary suggestions for temporary use of the buildings here. However, it has been difficult to identify enough resources and intellectual talent to come up with good suggestions for 'urban innovators' that could form the basis of a slow but innovative development of the site. However, the discussion about 'urban catalysts' and 'temporary use' is now on the agenda as a new inspiring strategy in many municipal authorities today where a lot of development has been put on hold. The first 'master plan' for temporary use approved in a municipal context has yet to see the light of day, but many development corporations are working with this type of planning in relation to major waterfront developments in Denmark today, e.g. Carlsberg (Copenhagen), Nordhavnen (Copenhagen), Køge Kyst (Køge) and FredereciaC (Frederecia).

In review, the following aspects seem to be essential for a new type of 'Master plan for temporary use':

MANIFESTO

1. Identify waiting spaces, timegaps and potential activist networks.

2. Make a strategic plan prioritizing focal areas for different temporary use typoligies.

3. Open up timegap-spaces for spontaneous use.

4. Initiate public life at non-public place.

5. Re-use existing spatial structures.

6. Allow direct implementation.

7. Get key-agents involved supporting informal networks and strategic coalitions.

8. Make as many actors as possible become part of the process.

9. Create a negotiation platform to combine formal and informal development strategies.

10. Follow flexible strategies: Allow temporary activities to become permanent as well as closing them down if necessary.

Conclusion

The workshops show an impressive range of new concept designs – a 'goldmine of advanced concepts and ideas' for future developments. New concepts on hybrid urban spaces and new architectural prototypes are revealed, and new process thinking and the employment of 'temporary use' in long-term transformation processes are put on the agenda. Thus, when evaluated in relation to a methodological point of view, the workshops have been a great success.

The workshops in Aalborg in 2005 and 2008 have provided detailed methodological knowledge of the combination of research and design-based development. By promoting different set-ups, a variety of context-related designs have emerged, and, in terms of approach, strengths as well as weaknesses can be compared. However, comparable methodological achievements require a consistent line in the professional approach of the team leaders. The teams must be composed of people with different competences. Design-based development can make an independent contribution to the visioning process and new architectural discourses can be developed, but this has to be

16: UNDER THE TABLE NEGOTIATIONS, URBAN CATALYST WORKSHOP 2008

17: MASTER PLAN FOR TEMPORARY USE, URBAN CATALYST WORKSHOP 2008

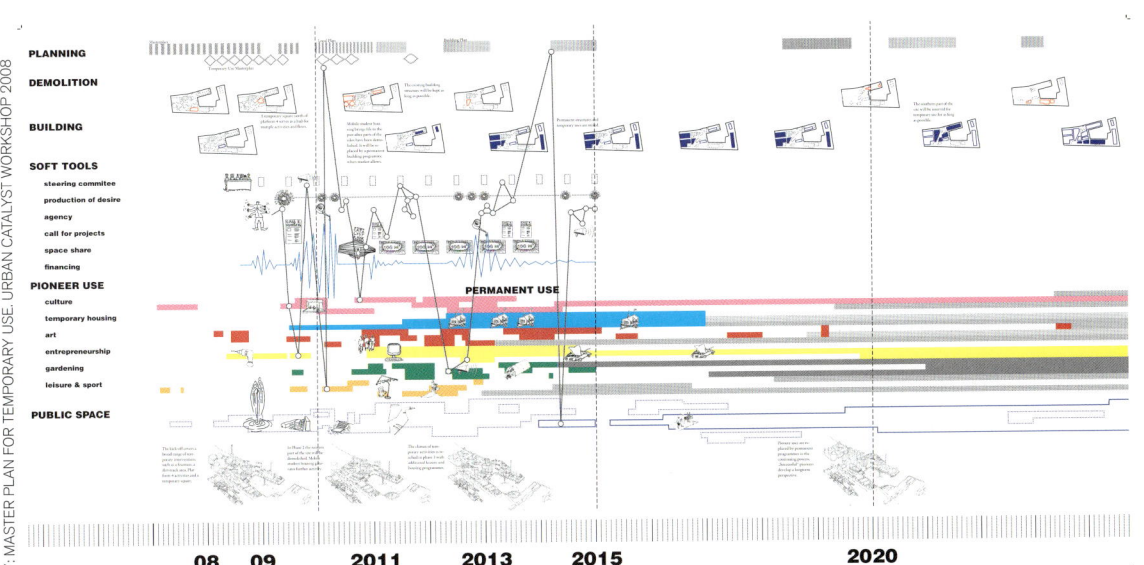

Designing Concepts and Strategies
Design and Method

based on a 'non-dogmatic' approach in the architectural development of prototypes and urban space design.

Measured in terms of their impact on municipal planning in Aalborg, the workshops in 2005 and 2008 have had some impact in relation to a more focused agenda for future waterfront development amongst city planners and some politicians. However, in relation to implementation, it is too early to judge the success of the methods. From a practical planning point of view, some of the developed concepts from the workshops have had a substantial impact on the planning process and the decisions in the city, and some of the ideas are now being implemented as architectural projects. Other ideas have not been successful. This could be due to the fact that the dialogue concerning the ideas behind the concepts has not always been good. One big challenge here is the transition from concept into realistic projects – not only in terms of architecture, but also in terms of economically and socially sustainable development of the city.

On the basis of this evaluation, it can be concluded that architectural workshops can be a useful tool in the development of new strategies and concepts in political organisations. However, dialogue sessions and planning will be unsuccessful unless they are based upon solid professional and managerial preparation. In the implementation of the concepts in planning documents and in site-specific projects it is important that a thorough analysis of policies and practices to date is in place, and that solid empirical research on a number of international cases as well as theoretical knowledge about the driving forces of waterfront development are available.

18: BIRD'S NEST. IT SERVED AS A METAPHOR FOR URBAN FARMING AS TEMPORARY USE IN DEVELOPMENT AREAS. URBAN CATALYST WORKSHOP 2008

References

Aalborg Kommune (1999) *Fjordkataloget – Aalborg Kommunes Fjordkyster*. Available at: http://www.aalborgkommune.dk/images/teknisk/B&M/PDF/PlanVis/stadark/fjord.kat/Fjordk99.pdf. (Accessed 18 November 2012).

Aalborg Kommune (2004) *Visioner for Aalborg Havnefront*. Aalborg.

Aalborg Kommune (2005) *Forslag til Hovedstruktur*. Aalborg.

Andersson, L. and Kiib, H. (2007) ´Multifaceted Programming and Hybrid Urban Domain`. In: Kiib, H. (Ed.) *Harbourscape*. Aalborg: Aalborg University Press.

Ingels, B. (2009) *Yes is More: An Archicomic on Architectural Evolution*. Köln: Taschen.

City of Oslo (2003) *Bærekraft i Bjørvika – designhåndbok*. Oslo.

Danish Arts Foundation Architecture Committee (2004) *Workshop*. Copenhagen.

Fjordbykontoret (2004a) *Oslo Sjøfront 2030 – program for 3 fremtidsbilder – Oslo-Charrette 1-5*. Oslo.

Fjordbykontoret (2004b) *Oslo Sjøfront 2030, Program for 3 fremtidsbilder*. Oslo.

Fjordbykontoret (2005) *3X Fjordbyen - fremtidsbilder – steder – team – en utstilling med resultaterne fra Charette om Oslo Sjøfront 2030*. Oslo.

Freien und Hansestadt Hamburg (2003) ´Sprung über die Elbe/Leap Across the Elbe`. In: *Documentation of the International Design Workshop*. Hamburg.

Kiib, H. (2007) *Harbourscape*. Aalborg: Aalborg University Press.

Kiib, H. (Ed.) (2009) *Architecture and Stages in the Experience City*. Skriftserien, 30. Department of Architecture and Design. Aalborg: Aalborg University.

Unfolding Architecture – workshop events retold
Shelley Smith

"I am forever unfolding between two folds, and if to perceive means to unfold, then I am forever perceiving within the folds." (Deleuze 1993: 93)

Prelude

In the spring of 2011, as part of the 6th semester bachelor project, *Buildings in Landscapes*, for students of Urban Design at Aalborg University, a workshop was organised with the intention of exploring the possibilities of integrating built structures and landscape – or alternatively put, exploring spatial generation and the interaction possible when working with built structures and their sites. Concurrently a 10th semester Urban Design student doing her master thesis, an urban transformation project on a post-industrial site, conducted a mini workshop in order to investigate the potential connections of her site to the existing city context and its landscape history, as well as to conceptually and spatially develop her project. In the wings, behind both of these workshops, the desire for new methodologies to address contemporary urban problems, coupled with the need for tools with which to facilitate this, were motivating factors. The technique of folding was identified as such a tool – one that could generate spatial ideas – both *space*, and *idea*, being the key words here – in the complex and large-scale urban contexts that formed the framework of the projects. What follows is a retelling of these workshops and an extrapolation of the events that took place within them. By setting the workshops within the framework of folding as a theoretically founded act, the intention of this article is to explore the methodology of folding as a tool that not only generates space, but also as a tool that has the potential to foster spatial understanding a priori scale or context. In short, this article will unfold folding as an architectural and theoretical method in the making of space.

Folds in Stuff

As your eyes get opened to this folding universe, it becomes apparent that you are not alone in thinking there could be some potential here – this is not new – and folding can be found everywhere; in fashion, in architecture, in furniture, in jewellery. In the physical manifestations of 'folded works', folding is the end result, the product – it has become an aesthetic expression. However, folding utilised as method is quite another thing. As method, the focus is on the process

2: DANISH PAVILION, SHANGHAI, BIG 2010 © WILLIAM

3: WOODEN TEXTILES, ELISA STROZYK 2011 © NEEB

4: EDUCATORIUM, UTRECHT, OMA 1997 © HYDE

5: ROM, D. LIBESKIND 2007 © JARAMILLO

6: ACCORDIAN CABINET, STROZYK & NEEB 2011 © NEEB

7: VILLA VPRO, HILVERSUM, MVRDV 1997 © HYDE

8: ICA, BOSTON, DILLER & SCOFIDIO + RENFRO 2006 © TRAN

9: OPERA HOUSE, OSLO, SNØHETTA 2007 © VISITOSLO

Unfolding Architecture – workshop events retold
Design and Method

– on the *becoming* – rather than on an end result and in this regard, the method of folding is linked to a philosophical concept, in the work of the French philosopher, Gilles Deleuze. In particular and most directly in *The Fold – Leibniz and the Baroque*, but as well, in Deleuze's work with Félix Guattari in e.g., *A Thousand Plateaus* - particularly regarding the notion of the 'abstract machine'. For Deleuze, the concept of *becoming* is a generative process and this leads directly into the use of folding as a methodology in the context of the workshops. In *The Fold*, Deleuze uses one of the main characteristics of The Baroque, the fold, and the theories of the 17th century philosopher and mathematician, Gottfried Wilhelm Leibniz as models through which to view time, space, movement and aesthetics. "The experience of the Baroque entails that of the fold. Leibniz is the first great philosopher and mathematician of the pleat, of curves, of twisting surfaces." (Deleuze 2004: xi) The fold represents a key notion of the Baroque – a figure that is found in many ways and in many places – it is a figure that speaks of multiplicity, complexity and of infinite possibilities. The Baroque produced huge amounts of folds and although the fold is a recognizable feature of the Baroque, the fold was not a Baroque invention, nor was it its' essence. Rather it was 'an operative function'. (Deleuze 1993) "Yet the Baroque trait twists and turns it folds, pushing them to infinity, fold over fold, one upon the other. The Baroque fold unfurls all the way to infinity.'"(Deleuze 1993: 3) In the context of the workshops, the notion of the infinite is tied to the process of folding itself which is concerned with the becoming. The 'operative function' of folding is then concerned with opening, with exploring, with developing - and ultimately with articulating.

"Opening a fold in a surface creates spaces, which in our minds are filled with volumes. Thus the technique of folding makes it possible to reappraise every step. Each step is laden with potential." (Vyzoviti 2004: 6)

Sofie Vyzoviti, an architect who has worked with folding in workshops in The Faculty of Architecture at Delft University of Technology, indicates that folding is akin to language; producing a 'language of architecture' through initial folds like 'sounds' that only 'much later becomes words' (Vyzoviti 2003: 7). The development of an architectural spatial vocabulary through folding goes beyond the linguistic association though. Here it is not only the amount of 'words' in the vocabulary, but the precision of their meaning in use that is of importance in grasping how folding can be used as an architectural tool and in the act of generating space. Folding is more closely linked to spatial *understanding*, in that the focus is on the process and the 'infinite' generation of spaces where folding becomes a *means* to expression, rather than being the expression itself.

The Tool Outside of the Box – and Inside the Workshop

The intent of the workshops was in part to utilise methods that provided an approach that could respond to the spatial and temporal challenges facing the urban design practice, not least of all those regarding increased scale and complexity in the urban context. It is imperative to initiate new tools and methodologies in order to fully understand these new contextual realities as also being spatial and experiential.

In the 2 workshops chronicled in this article, folding has been used as a tool to get at results that could contribute to spatial understanding without dictating 'absolute results'. In the act of folding, unfolding and refolding a myriad of possibilities are created and as Vyzoviti notes, choosing from among them is a necessary part of the process (Vyzoviti 2004: 6). The process then is an extended period of exploration and in this sense, the act of folding can be seen as an educational act articulating through choice and informing the design process. Unfolding is not seen as the opposite action of folding – but is a part of the process and one that also leads to new things. "Fold over folds: such is the status of the two modes of perception, or of microscopic and macroscopic processes. That is why the unfolded surface is never the opposite of the fold, but rather the movement that goes from some to the others. Unfolding sometimes means that I am developing – that I am undoing." (Deleuze 1993: 93)

Folding - and implicitly unfolding - is an efficient tool. The easiest materials to fold are cheap and readily available, it's an easy method to work with and it doesn't take forever to create models that in their readiness to be analysed, surprise and spark further ideas. As a generative tool it is genius. Because there isn't an enormous expenditure of either time or money, the creation of models tend to foster a 'learn as you go by making another model' attitude, which in turn makes for an incredibly dynamic process in which the fear of 'mucking up the model' is completely taken out of the equation.

The created models are not representations of previously created spaces – they are space in the making and they allow – no, demand, - an exploration – a delving in, an envisioning and a further development. Folding is a scale-less tool. The models created could be jewellery or furniture just as well as they could be a building or a landscape. As such folding focuses on space that has no context and this allows for an openness in the process. Although this may initially seem counterproductive in the quest to find new tools and methods relating to new scales in the contemporary urban context, it is in fact in this way that scalar jumps can be made – jumps affording interpretation at many different scales and with the potential to address spatiality as both large scale context and tactile, bodily-

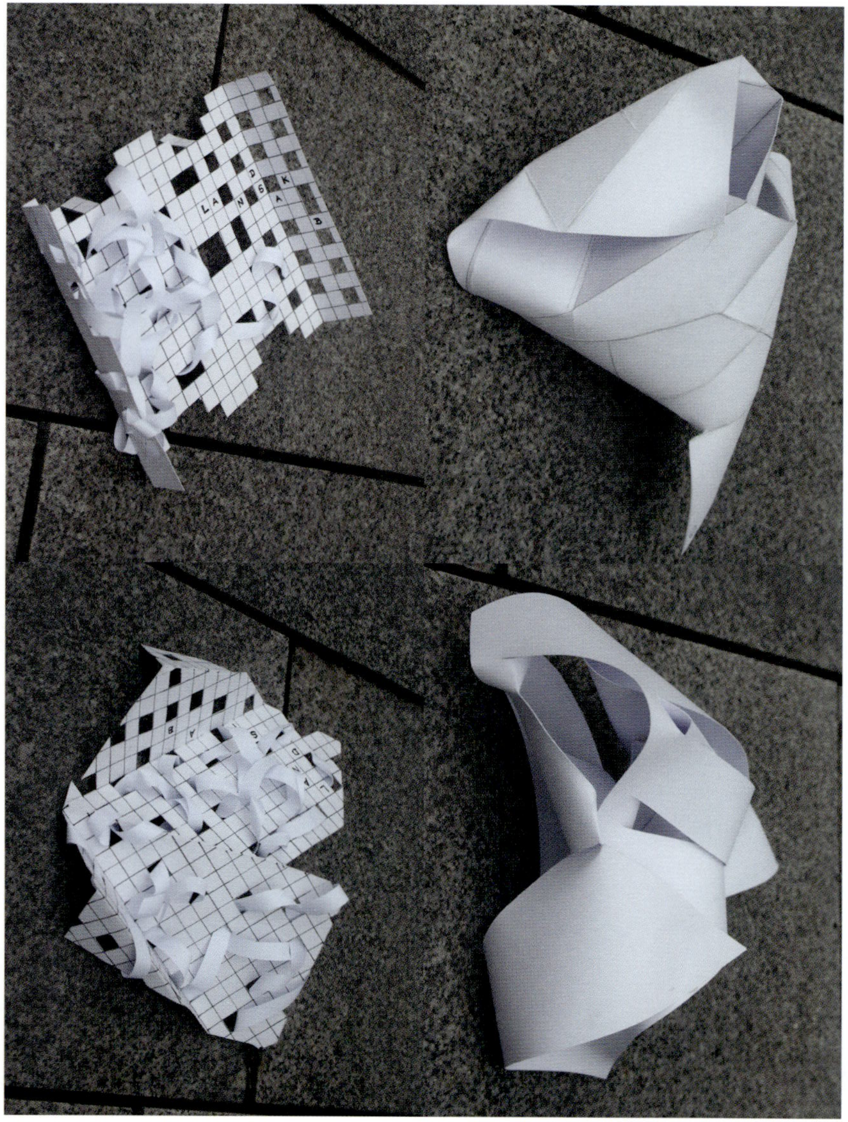

10: THE FOLDS IN THE SURFACE

11: MULTIPLICITY

Unfolding Architecture – workshop events retold
Design and Method

experienced space simultaneously promoting a spatial understanding – a kind of living-in/body-present perception awareness that can be so difficult to instil in large scale.

The models have no intended purpose, no programme to fulfil. However, it is important to note that despite the fact that the models can be perceived from a number of scalar positions the notion of subject/object is not part of this perceiving. This can be linked to the way in which Deleuze sees the Leibniz's theoretical models. For Deleuze, "Leibniz's theories are not specifically 'objects' but in Deleuze's lexicon, Baroque territories." (Deleuze 1993: xvii) This can also be applied to models created in the folding workshops – they are not objects to be viewed with distance from a subject/object perspective – they are territories, one can immerse oneself in, spaces for flights of the imagination, they are landscapes begging to be explored.

Unfolding Workshop Methodologies

In the workshops folding has been used as 'an operation' and seemingly arbitrary actions have been used as a way of, from outside of the process, directing the process, but not defining the results. In the 6th semester workshop, the first introductory exercise in the workshop was based on getting to know the material of just plane ordinary paper and to investigate its capabilities. To facilitate this and to make possible

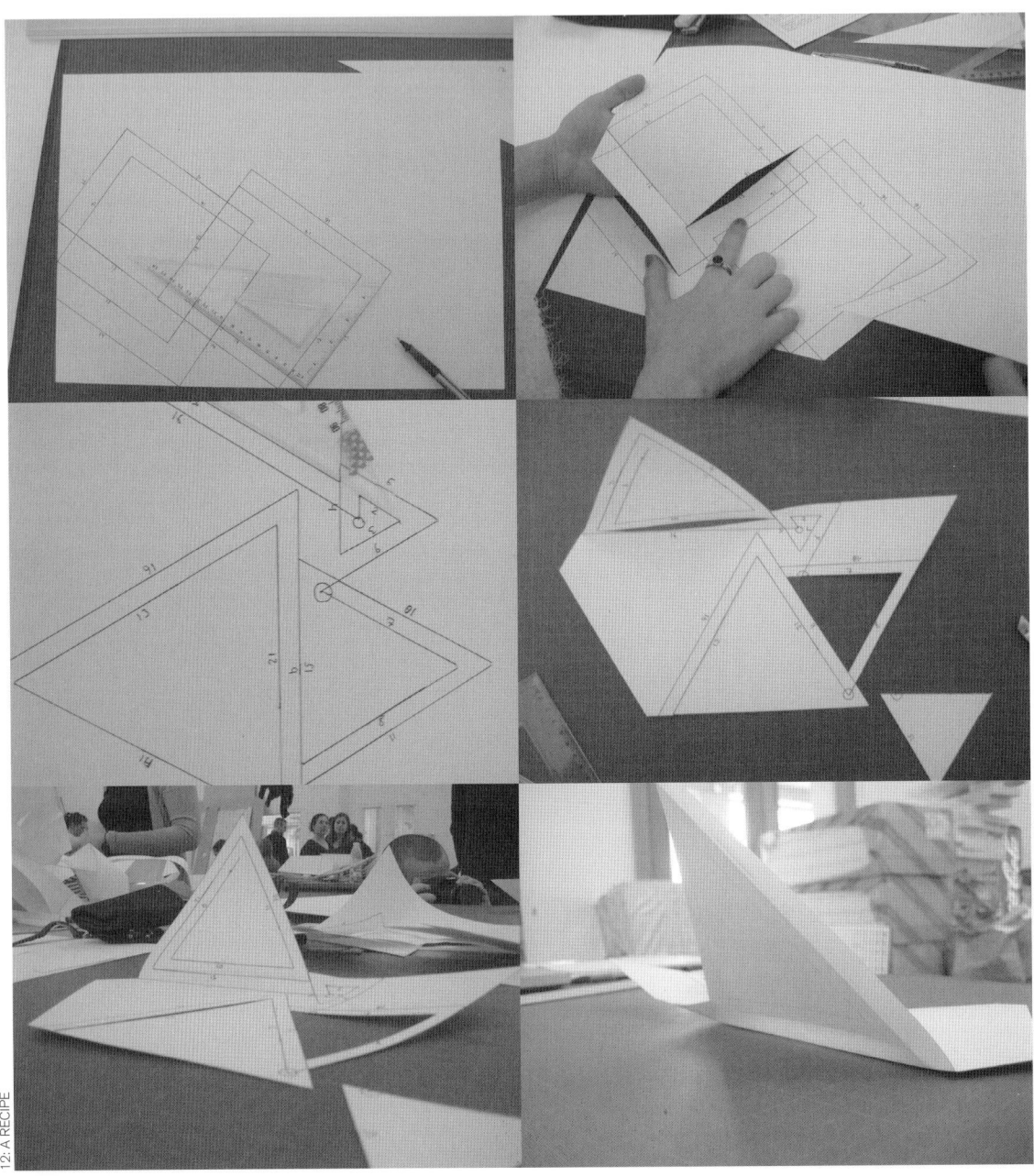

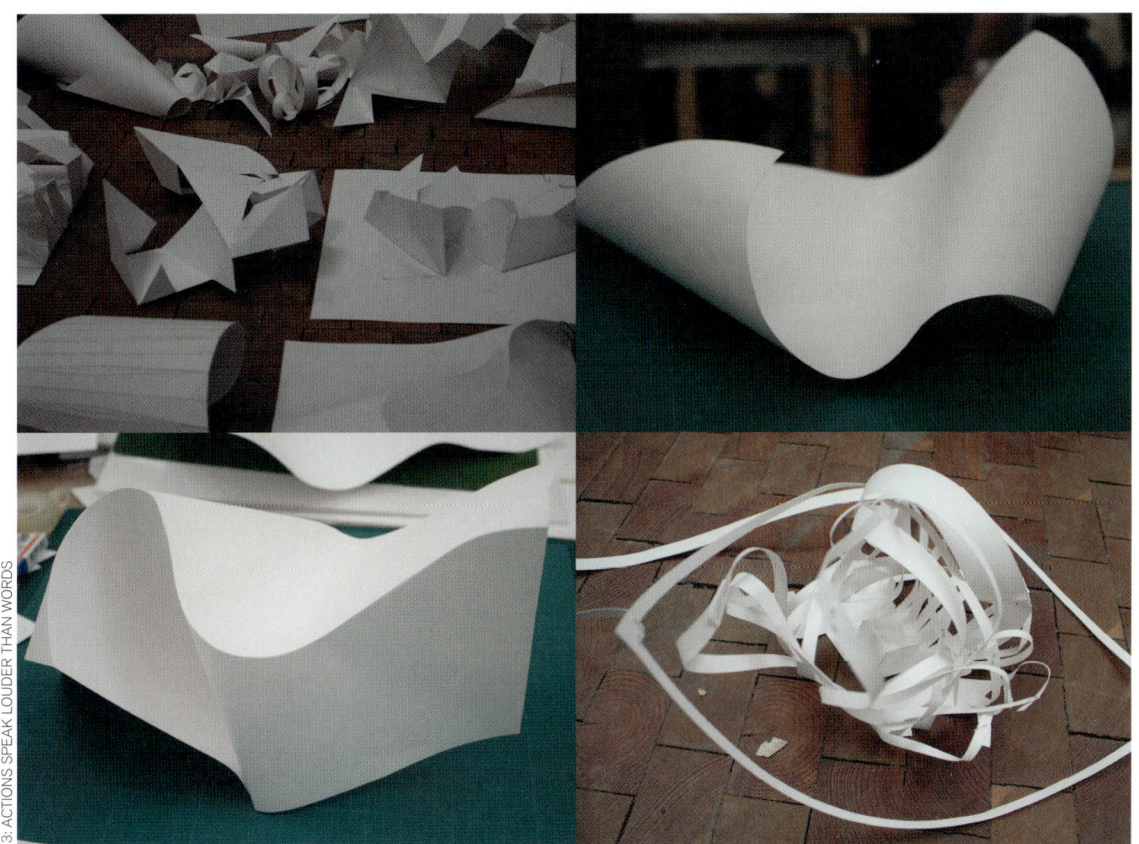

an illustration of the range of possibilities – a generic 'geometrical recipe' was utilized:

Take a 150 g piece of paper. Draw 20 lines. Cut along 3 of them and fold along 17 of them - remove between 2 and 4. Glue as necessary.

The second exercise, took cues from the experiences documented by Sophia Vyzoviti in her case studies of workshops taught at Delft (Vyzoviti 2004) and presented a set of verbs from which the undertaken actions stemmed. The verbs *fold, pleat, crease, score, cut, rotate, twist, turn, wrap, enfold, pierce, hinge, knot, weave, compress, balance and unfold* were introduced as a catalogue of activities from which to choose different combinations.

The third exercise, in two parts, employed a 'Chinese menu' technique utilizing choices from *Category 1* and *Category 2*. This part of the workshop also got 'more real' in the sense that physical materiality was introduced through additions to the materials that could be used to make the models – these now included different weights, colours and textures – and the insertion of the element of water in different forms as a parameter. Here, the introduction of the notion that the models could be something – i.e. a shift from 'becoming' to 'being', from matter to substance, and from function to form.

The first 2 exercises opened and the final exercise specified – at no point however did the exercises conclude. A final exercise comprised a photo documentation of the process – and was not a result – but served to further illustrate the multiplicity of creation in the workshop – both as regards the individual student's models, but also as regards the tremendous variation in models all created from exactly the same material and instructions.

Postscript

And so at the end of this extrapolation, rather than concluding, I would like to point out that, what could outwardly appear restrictive and limiting, e.g. as a recipe to follow or a set of prescribed actions to adhere to, was in fact a key to unlocking creativity. And regarding the creative process - it is worthy to note that the same set of instructions in the hands of individuals never produced the same things.

In addition to using folding as a method rooted in a deeper philosophical tradition, the workshops also accessed Deleuze and Guattari's notion of the abstract machine – defined by them as a moment at which nothing but functions and matters remain. (Deleuze 1987) As such, the abstract machine is not informed by, or concerned with, form and substance – but operates through matter and function. Seen in this way

15: BECOMING - DETAIL

the models created by the folding of paper (matter) according to an express series of actions (functions) can be seen as abstract machines. Rather than being 'models' they then become diagrams - since Deleuze and Guattari define the diagrammatic as an intrinsic aspect of abstract machines. "The diagrammatic or abstract machine does not function to represent, even something real, but rather constructs a real that is yet to come, a new type of reality." (Deleuze 1987:142) This is an extremely important consideration in terms of the folding methodology as it relates to new thinking and spatial understanding of complex contemporary urban contexts, as this distinction perpetuates the explorative and the searching. Rather than attempting to answer and conclude, the attempt is at finding an appropriate tool to address and understand space outside of scale and context. There is no question to answer, no style to follow, no form to trace. Through an adherence to matter and function, a process of becoming was instilled in which the focus was on the diagrammatic rather than representative. The workshops created a forum for 'perceiving within the folds' – emphasizing a process which honed spatial awareness and created a myriad of spaces that could simultaneously be imagined as traversable planes, inhabitable voids, and containers that cradle.

References

Deleuze, G. (1993) *The Fold – Leibniz and the Baroque*. Minneapolis: University of Minnesota Press.

Deleuze, G. and Guattari, F. (1987) *A Thousand Plateaus: Capitalism and Schizophrenia*. Minneapolis: University of Minnesota Press.

Vyzoviti, S. (2003) *Folding Architecture – Spatial, Structural and Organizational Diagrams*. Amsterdam: BIS Publishers.

Acknowledgements

I would like to thank the students that participated in the workshops – Siri, Sofie, Senad, Martin, Thomas L., Thomas M., Elfriede, Ralph, Kenneth, Lise and Rikke - for their energy and the learning that they have instilled, and for the gracious use of their photos. In addition I would like to thank my colleague Lea Louise Holst Laursen for inspiring discussion and planning. There would have been no becoming without them.

WE LOVE THE CITY
- a pragmatic approach to urban design
Lasse Andersson

Introduction

This article will address a key issue within the urban design discipline in which architecture becomes secondary to activities in the city supporting the 'good urban life' due to urban designers trying so hard to do good (Kvorning in Vindum and Weiss 2012: 280). To some extent, one can argue that the success of the grand old man of urban design, Jan Gehl, is responsible for this over-exposure of urban life(style) within the urban design discipline in Denmark due to his mantra of 'life between buildings'. This is not an explicit critique of Jan Gehl's work starting with his first book in 1971 (Gehl 2011). Rather, it is a critique of the rest of 'us' who work with or teach urban design, and of the lack of interest in architecture that, to a certain extent, has evolved as a result of it being replaced by a focus on activities and users in urban space. When urban design initially started in the 1960s and 1970s, it was a reaction to the rigid and undifferentiated cities that followed modernism. Urban Design was a critical approach toward the development of the city that had lost track of the daily life in the city (Jacobs 1961), (Gehl 2011). Somehow, especially in a Nordic context, we now need to take a critical look at our praxis of creating 'the good urban life' as the primary focus. 'The good urban life' cannot be omnipresent; there is simply neither enough energy nor people in the average Nordic city. The main argument in this article is therefore that there is a need within urban design, especially in a Danish context, to develop both praxis and urban design curricula towards focusing on space and form, which, to a certain degree entails having to forget about 'the good urban life' and good activities for a while.

There is a need for future urban designers to understand architecture and urban space design more profoundly. There are two reasons for this. First of all, they are the ones that will be hired by municipalities, state administrations and engineering companies to create the future schemes and plans for architecture. Secondly, most bachelor students of architecture or architectural engineering tend to go for the architectural scale in Denmark. At the schools in Aalborg and Aarhus, only approximately 10 percent of the students attending one of the master's programs choose to study urban design (Bro, Laursen and Andersson 2010). This is a problem in itself as there will be a demand for good urban designers in the near future.
With a point of departure in, amongst others, the Danish office of ADEPT's approach, 'the city in the building and the building in the city' (ADEPT 2012), it is consequently the aim of this article to show how workshops can help shape and develop a spatial and architectural approach to form finding in the urban design scale.

1: ABSTRAKTISTAN MODEL IN THE WE LOVE THE CITY EXHIBITION AT THE UTZON CENTER, APRIL 2011

Secondly, the article also intends to show students that working with urban design on a large scale, is also about designing. Thus, urban design is perceived as a discipline bridging the scales from building over urban space to urban planning. The author of this article sees this as a key challenge if urban design is to avoid becoming stuck within a paradigm of designing urban life(styles). A place to seek help in a turn towards a more architecturally agile version of urban design could be in the new pragmatic turn among young Danish architectural firms, here exemplified by the office of ADEPT.

The Pragmatic Turn in Danish Architecture

The most pragmatic solution is to look nearby for a more design orientated approach linked to one of the most influential trends in architecture and planning for the last ten years – the pragmatic turn in Danish architecture. The Pragmatic Turn, or the New Wave (Vindum and Weiss 2012), has flooded the thinking of young Danish architectural firms for the last decade with offices like PLOT, BIG, EFFEKT, TRANSFORM, COBE and ADEPT, to mention a few, at the forefront. It is founded in a wish to engage the world as it is and not as an academic, aesthetic discipline as it was seen in the Postmodern or Deconstructive period. This new wave has its roots in the second Dutch modernism, spearheaded by OMA and Koolhaas, in the 1990s and into the 00s (Koolhaas and Mau 1995), (Mass, van Rijs, de Vriess 1998).

> "Architecture is now also assessed on the contributions it makes to community, its problem-solving capacity and the analyses and improvements it represents. Buildings and urban planning offer added value as an expressive medium for insights that are generated by analyses of societal challenges."
> (Vindum and Weiss 2012: 384)

One characteristic of the new wave is an interest in the fifth facade of architecture, creating new public spaces on buildings, which, again, is linked to ideals of creating strong synergy between the plot and the surrounding city. One of the firms in the new wave that insists most strongly on a connection between the architectural scale and the urban planning scale is ADEPT. Their projects are created between architecture and urban development. Their statement, 'the city in the building and the building in the city' (ADEPT 2012), can be found in all their projects as a constant attempt to overwrite the dichotomy between building plot/architecture and the city.

The question then is, what is the role of urban design if it is linked to this new wave, and how can we approach it in the context of teaching in Denmark? The following section will, firstly, outline the intentions of the workshop series and hence the workshop in relation to a more architectural approach to urban design.

> "Urban designers have to work with form, space and design, they are 'Space Shapers' that is their core competence." (Jacob van Rijs 2010, own notes from a lecture held at Utzon Center, DK)

Secondly, it also contains a discussion of how urban design can be a part of reinstating a critical approach in this new pragmatic wave in Danish architecture. Critics claim that the New Pragmatic Wave is perhaps too focused on creating added value, and that there is a consequent tendency to become uncritical and overly positive towards a developer focus. In the book *The New Wave in Danish Architecture*, Keld Vindum states that he does not see the inherent existential issue between architecture and the world in projects by architects in the new wave (Vindum and Weiss 2012: 376).

To some extent, the new Danish wave lacks the agitation, restlessness and critique that Rem Koolhaas brought forth in the 1990s, and which he still does (Koolhaas and Mau 1995). So, at this point it is safe to state that there is a need for a more architectural approach in urban design teaching, and, at the same time, there is a need for a more critical approach within the New Wave in Danish architecture if it is to keep its momentum and develop further. Jens Thomas Arnfred from the architectural office of Vandkunsten also sees a risk of architecture in the new wave becoming too mainstream and too focused on pleasing its clients by creating conceptual concepts that can be exported anywhere. Architecture needs to be formed by the conditions of place and with a point of departure in a critical dialogue.

> "From my point of view, it is still a care for the social space, the human scale, the poetic intervals, the precisely refined, the knife-edge modesty that should be considered when the world is built….'To venture into the world' is also a question on how one sets foot on the door frame."
> (Jens T. Arnfred in Vindum and Weiss 2012: 205)

It is in the doorway between building and city, to continue Jens Thomas Arnfred's metaphor that the potential for finding a more architectural approach within urban design can be found, particularly when it is linked to the working methods and architectural approach in the new wave. It is also on that doorstep, however, that urban design can discuss a more grounded understanding of place towards the working methods and ideals in the New Danish Pragmatic Wave. The following section of this article will unfold how working with 'endless' numbers of foam models can create a more architectural approach to urban design teaching. It is a workshop process in which discussions about the good urban life are forgotten and replaced by a strict focus on the spatial properties of forming the city.

ABSTRAKTISTAN 2008-2011

In the ABSTRAKTISTAN 2008-2011 workshops held at the Utzon Center in Aalborg, Denmark, the ambition has been to introduce 4th semester students to a laboratory that studies urban form in the XL scale. This is done by introducing them to intensive foam modeling studies and the use of physical models in urban design, just as ADEPT practices it in their office in Copenhagen.

In the workshops, the basic elements of the city are reduced to the interplay between positive and negative forms and spaces represented in simple building typologies and grids. The students' formal investigations and research are kept at an abstract level and conducted on the basis of paradigmatic topics within urban morphology. The Abstraktistan workshops have been developed over the past four years with the purpose of enhancing the students' initial awareness of the design of urban voids, and of introducing them to the method of the workshop, which can be described as 'foaming', combining a neo-pragmatic approach to design with a playful and intuitive approach when producing models in foam. This method with comprehensive blueprint models in foam forms the core of the design practice that Martin Krogh and Martin Laursen work with on a daily basis at the architectural office of ADEPT.

The aim of the workshop series is, through physical models, to investigate and understand Rem Koolhaas' discussion of Bigness from S, M, L, XL, in which he examines the properties of the link between large-scale architecture and urbanism (Koolhaas and Mau 1995). Where Koolhaas states that Bigness is the only architectural scale that can survive in the global, generic city, ABSTRAKTISTAN encourages the students to discuss this through simple, abstract models over a four-day period.

"Bigness no longer needs the city: it competes with the city; it represents the city; it pre-empts the city; or better still, it is the city. If urbanism generates potential and architecture exploits it, Bigness enlists the generosity of urbanism against the meanness of architecture. From Bigness=urbanism vs. architecture." (Koolhaas and Mau 1995: 515)

ABSTRAKTISTAN – Understanding Urban Morphology, Designing Urban Architecture

For four days, the students work with foam models in the workshop at the Utzon Center. Here they become familiar with Giambattista Nolli's map of 18th century Rome, which portrays the city as a series of interconnected, introvert spaces that, in a manner of speaking, simultaneously have been 'carved out' of, and create a medieval city setting. Giambattista Nolli's urban maps of Medieval Rome are both snapshots of urban complexity and a very simple way of highlighting the distinction between the positive and the negative spaces in the city.

In contrast to this urban paradigm, the students also meet the extrovert spaces of the modernist city in urban paradigms such as Le Corbusier's dream, La Ville Radieuse (The Radiant City) from 1935, or Chandigarh from the 1950s. The open plan and points are examined, compared and contrasted to the mass and the block with a point of departure in two urban paradigms: the medieval city where the city can be seen as being carved out from a mass, and the modernist city defined as points on an infinite plane. The most simplistic version is the transition from solid to void. The two afore mentioned positions can also be seen as the distinction between an urban model which is 'accidental' and a product of a contradictory origin, as in the case of the historical and medieval city, versus a city model based on strict planning, measured according to a certain meaningfulness, functionality and process of composition in the modernist planning paradigm (von Meiss 1991).

As the workshop progresses, the most simplified typologies of the city, the point, the line/slab and the block/courtyard block are introduced. Furthermore, the grid is discussed in the context of being the urban element that creates spatial relations or forces voids into the urban structure and which, in turn, also connects the different city quarters. During the different model studies, the students must discuss dichotomies such as high/low, distributed/collective, open/closed, horizontal/vertical while transforming typologies and grids into coherent spatial aggregations. The scale at this stage is not measurable but a matter of spatial and formal relations in the model.

The investigations are done by mixing analogue and digital models. Each day of the workshop brings the students through abstract model exercises on 30x60 cm plots and ends with form studies that have moved from the medieval city over modernist plans in order to ultimately arrive at an understanding of the city, e.g. central parts of Barcelona mixing old and new, WEST 8's stringent Borneo Sporenborg in Amsterdam working with scaling and contrast, or OMA's plan for the Dutch New Town Almere, which aims at recreating its own context.

All examples are rooted in a planning paradigm with a pragmatic approach to urbanism and architecture (Brorman Jensen 2009), (Vindum and Weiss 2012). An important lesson from the workshop model studies is that urban design is about giving form to space. It is the voids that aggregate urban form and urban architecture, and this comes before urban life and urban activities. This is not to mimic modernist charters (Mumford 2000) but to show the students that they are designers of the built environment before they design urban activities.

2: GIAMBATTISTA NOLLI'S MAP OF 18TH CENTURY ROME

WE LOVE THE CITY - a pragmatic approach to urban design
Design and Method

177

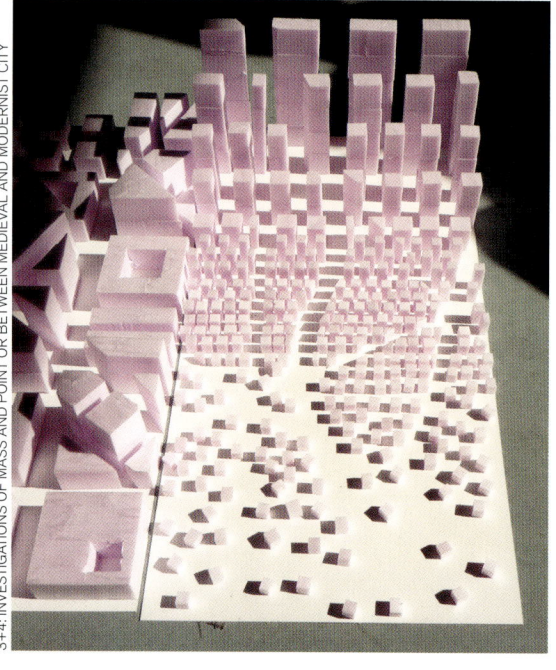

3+4: INVESTIGATIONS OF MASS AND POINT OR BETWEEN MEDIEVAL AND MODERNIST CITY

5+6: BLOCKS, SLABS AND POINTS ARRANGED IN GRID STRUCTURE INVESTIGATING SCALE

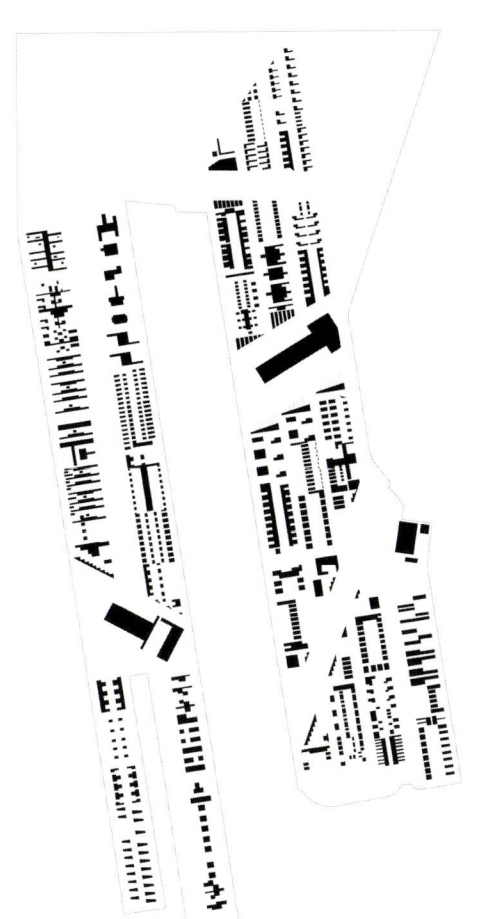

7+8: WEST 8 PROJECT VIEW AT BORNEO SPORENBORG © JEROEN MUSCH

9+10: 30X60 CM MODELS INVESTIGATING FORMAL COMPLEXITIES, SPATIAL RELATIONS AND SCALE

WE LOVE THE CITY - a pragmatic approach to urban design
Design and Method

The numerous model studies at the workshop are concluded by connecting the more than 100 individual experiments on 30x60 cm sheets in a huge city model of more than 25 square meters, thus forming a large, abstract city in foam; a city that queries the boundaries of urban design through stylized urban paradigms. The result is an abstract mega city that to some extent mirrors Rem Koolhaas' discussion of the generic city and the lack, or rather the death of planning (Koolhaas and Mau 1995). At the same time, however, the students get an eye-opening experience and see that the city is actually an aggregation of smaller, distinct models, and that these models are the orchestrated chaos forming the city. The city as such can only be fully controlled in certain parts, functional layers, but it is a spatial system that, in parts, has to be spatially designed – just like the single architectural entity. Urban design is also urban architecture and urban planning.

Perhaps the Abstraktistan model can answer Sam Jacob's question in WORK AC's book, 49 Cities, which examines how urban paradigms and utopian city models in new combinations may rethink the city of the future (WORK AC 2010).

"Could you fuse disparate elements together to create, for example, floating, linear, garden-Ville Radieuse's? Might the non-judgmental re-assessment of the projects allow us to recompose the languages of urban planning outside of the traditional partisan arguments? And in doing this might we forge solutions that addresses present concerns that learn from histories real and fictional, ancient and modern?" (Sam Jacobs in Work AC 2010: 122).

The Abstraktistan workshop 2008-2011 has some similarities to Michael Sorkin's workshop, *The Aarhus Protocols*, from 2005 that examined the city in small models investigating different elements of the city. These models were connected through negotiations between the workshop groups, and a big model was formed (Sørensen 2006). Similarly, Abstraktistan is also comparable to a workshop called *Module 2.0 urban morphology*, which was organized by Thomas Clemmensen and Hans Dahl at the Aarhus School of Architecture in 2010 (Clemmensen and Dahl 2011). In Thomas Clemmensen's workshop, the students study urban morphology from the block towards the urban quarter, which is collected in a big model with overall infrastructural and landscape constraints forming a big coherent city model.

In terms of learning, the aim of the Abstraktistan workshop is to create knowledge of urban morphology, the form of the city, historically as well as theoretically. More importantly, though, the intention is also to qualify the student's ability to shape the city by working with in-depth model studies, and, ultimately, to start developing the competencies required to work with the complexity of the city in terms of scale and an architectural focus in the XL scale. In the workshop, this is done without any preconceived values as the studies are abstract and, as such, are only intended to understand the city as constituted by positive and negative space. Any ideas of urban life, urban activities, social issues etc. are excluded from the studies.

12: SNAPS SHOTS FROM ABSTRAKTISTAN MODEL CAN BE SEEN AS A DISCUSSION OF THE GENERIC CITY

WE LOVE THE CITY - a pragmatic approach to urban design
Design and Method

13: OVERVIEW OF ALL MODELS SEPARATED

The City in the Building, The Building in the City – WE LOVE THE CITY

Following the Abstraktistan workshop in the spring of 2011, the exhibition WE LOVE THE CITY was on display in The Utzon Center, jointly curated by Lasse Vegas, ADEPT and 8 4th and 8th semester urban design students. The exhibition took its point of departure in two central themes, one of which being the process and the working method as perceived by ADEPT. The other theme is closely linked to the first one by opening the doors to a laboratory that is in love with urbanity, and which shows the viewer that the potential for a new generation of city-loving architects is found in the phrase 'The city in the building, the building in the city!'

The duality of the phrase emphasizes the fact that the focal point in urban design will always be the work of architecture, but not the work as a singularity in the city. In ADEPT's approach and in the urban design curriculum, each architectural project is rather a generous addition to the city. ADEPT has an underlying ambition in their projects to transgress the urban intent, or lack thereof, of the individual building program, or perhaps the office perceives the city as an exaggerated interior that connects buildings and users thereby trying to dissolve the classic dichotomy between building plot and urban space, as is seen in much of their recent work (Vindum and Weiss 2012: 172-185).

With the huge 'Abstraktistan City' model from the workshop as its focal point, WE LOVE THE CITY displays ADEPT's approach and method of pursuing a greater degree of urban intention in architecture narrated through the subtitle 'The city in the building, the building in the city'. The close relation and urban intent in each architectural project and an urban claim of co-existence from the city towards the single building is, of course, nothing new, but it is a paradigm that serves as a strong guiding principle in all ADEPT's projects. ADEPT's approach is influenced by the approach of offices like OMA and MVRDV which can also be seen in other young Danish offices like BIG, EFFEKT, COBE (Koolhaas and Mau 1995), (Brorman Jensen 2009), (Vindum and Weiss 2012).

The interrelation between building and city similarly creates urban hybrids that inform both architecture and urban design as discussed by Per, Mozas and Arpa in their book on urban hybrids from 2011.

"The ideal hybrid feeds on the meeting of the private and public spheres. The intimacy of private life and the sociability of public life find anchors of development in the hybrid building."
(Per, Mozas and Arpa 2011: 43)

The urban hybrids serve a broader social intent in the city and focus on forming social life within the building and hence also on establishing a close relation towards the city. The primary intent is therefore urban before architectural, which must not be mistaken for a lack of interest in architecture. The urban is just the starting point for the process of creation, creating an urban architecture that goes beyond the dichotomy of building plot and urban public space (ADEPT 2012).

Among ADEPT's hybrid projects are Skyvillage in Rødovre, which stacks the detached housing district in a vertical city, recombining the detached house into a new skyscraper typology in search of a new urban hybrid.

14: OVERVIEW EXHIBITION © HANS JØRGEN FRUENSGAARD

"The hybrid scheme proposes intense environments of cross fertilization, which mixes known genotypes and creates genetic allies to improve living conditions and revitalize their surrounding environments." (Per, Mozas and Arpa 2011: 45)

Another of ADEPT's projects, KU:BE Culture Center in Frederiksberg, works with packed typologies and turns the traditional culture centre inside out in an urban garden, thus generously exceeding the competition requirements and inserting a new architectural intent in urban space. Both projects are created in cooperation with MVRDV.

The urban and contextual intentions, and thereby also the generosity in relation to the surroundings, are also evident in ADEPT's library in Dalarna, Sweden. The project is carried out in collaboration with Sou Fujimoto from Japan. It interprets the city and the landscape linking the principal idea of the building to the flow and mobility of the place in order to reflect the movement from landscape to city in the central atrium of the library.

> "Architectural projects when imagined as structures in the urban network can be thought of as smaller related fields, containing their own individual combination of factors and sub-systems indirectly related to the greater field." (Musiatowicz 2005:7)

In the H+ project in Helsingborg, ADEPT shows that they do not only master the close encounter between city and building. In this mega-project, the blue and green qualities of the city are joined in the central urban development area of Helsingborg, which, in terms of scale, is very similar to Ørestaden. Here the entire city is treated as a project with innumerable investigations into the potentials of the future city in studies of one model after the other.

"When ADEPT works with architecture, it is, in our view, from a perception of the city in the building", says Martin Krogh, ADEPT,"…and in our planning it is the building in the city securing a more profound urban intention in every building scheme", Martin Laursen, ADEPT, adds. (Author's notes, interview 2011)

It is obvious that the partners at ADEPT have gathered inspiration from far and wide; from international companies such as MVRDV, Diller Scofidio + Renfro and WORK AC. They thus display a faceted understanding of the city, which transgresses scale. ADEPT's strength is that they constantly pursue an experimental approach to the city and to architecture in which they keep investigating the properties of urban design, architecture and large scale planning through endless physical model studies, just as the students are taught in the Abstraktistan workshops.

Space-Shapers versus Urban Life(style)

As stated earlier in this article, urban designers have to work with form finding and the constitution of space. Jacob van Rijs argues that urban designers are 'Space Shapers' just as architects are.

The four days of intense workshops at the fourth semester at Architecture and Design at Aalborg University and the We Love the City Exhibition at the Utzon Center is a contribution to this discussion of how the approach to urban design can be discussed, practiced and taught. The intention is not to state that an approach to urban life is bad for urban design. Rather it is to start a discussion regarding the reinstatement

of a balance between urban life and urban form when thinking, practicing and teaching urban design.

Perhaps a more correct title of urban design in this article would be Urban Architecture, as a way to stress that without an urban architecture there is no urban life or urban activities. Of course, this is a polemic statement and urban life certainly is important to cities. However, if the focus on activities, urban life, lifestyle, etc. becomes too strong the qualities of the built environment become secondary. Therefore we need to tip the balance towards the design of 'positive and negative space', but without losing track of the good urban life(styles).

References

ADEPT (2012) www.adeptarchitects.com

Bro, P., Laursen, L.L.H. and Andersson, L. (2010)´Civilingeniøruddannelsen i Arkitektur og Design – Urban Design – Spørgeskemaundersøgelse af de studerendes præferencer´. Working paper. Aalborg: Department for Architecture and Media Technology, Aalborg University.

Brorman Jensen, B. (2009) 'Mod en kritisk pragmatisme'. In: Arkitektur DK, 6.

Clemmensen, T. and Dahl, H. (2011) ´Modul 2.0, Bymorfologi´. Aarhus: the Aarhus School of Architecture.

Gehl, J. (2011) Life Between Buildings, using public space. Island Press.

Jacobs, J. (1961) The Death and Life of Great American Cities. New York: Vintage books.

Koolhaas, R. and Mau, B. (1995) S,M,L,XL. New York: The Monacelli Press.

Lund, N. (2008) Nordisk Arkitektur. Arkitektens Forlag.

Per, A. F., Mozas, J. and Arpa, J. (2011) This is Hybrid, An analysis of mixed-use buildings, a+t ediciones.

Mass, W. van Rijs, J. and de Vriess, N. (1998) Farmax – excursions on density. Rotterdam: 010 Publishers.

Meiss, P. (1991) Elements of Architecture: From Form to Place. New York: Spon Press.

Mumford, E. (2000) The CIAM Discourse on Urbanism, 1928-1960. Boston: The MIT Press.

Musiatowicz, M. (2005) ´Operating in an 'Expanding Field'´. In: Mozas, J. and Per, A. F. (2005) In Common, collective spaces. a+t ediciones.

Sørensen Brunsvig, A. (2006) The Aarhus protocols - The Michael Sorkin Workshop at Arkitektskolen Aarhus, 2005, October 3rd-8th. The Architectural Press B.

Vindum, K. & Weiss, K.L. (2012) The New Wave in Danish Architecture. Copenhagen: Danish Architectural Press.

WORK AC (2010) 49 Cities. WORKac, Storefront for Art and Architecture, NY

Websites

www.adeptarchitects.com
www.welovethecity.dk

Biographies

Ann Sofie Christensen
Currently studying Urban Design at Aalborg University. The nearest future involves travelling and internships in Japan and Denmark. Especially interested in concept and strategy development in a larger urban scale.

Daniel Bejtrup
Immediately after graduating, Daniel Bejtrup was employed at Schønherr A/S working with the planning and design of major master plan projects. He's interested in the interaction between people, architecture, space, art and programs in the city.

Anne J Andersen
Urban planner from the Architectural School of Aarhus. Currently employed at Aalborg Municipality as a business PhD fellow after 15 years as a project manager. Interested in discourses of urban regeneration and developing strategies with a strong consideration of place.

Dina Brændstrup
Employed at 1:1 landskab in Copenhagen, designing city landscapes and spaces. Her main interest lies in creating city spaces that give heightened experience and that initiate people to interact.

Anne L Jørgensen
Currently working as an urban designer at LÉVA urban design a/s in Norway doing urban analysis and designing public spaces. She is interested in strategic urban development and transformation.

Ditte B Lanng
PhD. Fellow urban design AAU. Currently exploring (trivial?) infrastructural spaces in search of insight into suburban mobilities and mobility designs. Likes leaps of the imagination and to question assumptions; What is a suburban road?

Anne-Marie S Knudsen
PhD student, human geographer and urban planner with a keen in interest in maps, technology, people and peripheral places! Holds degrees from Lund University, Sweden and University College London.

Esben Poulsen
Studied Digital Design at Aalborg University. He is currently engaged in the project Effect Light, which presents studies of adaptive and responsive urban environment. The studies are part of his phd project: Socially Informed environments.

Gitte Marling
Architect PhD, professor at the Department of Architecture and Media Technology, Aalborg University. Her research areas are urban design, urban architecture, urban spaces and urban life. Gitte Marling is research leader of the project 'Experience City – hybrid cultural projects and performative urban spaces'.

Henrik Harder
Studied at the Schools of Architecture in Copenhagen and Aarhus. Ph.D. from Aalborg University where he is now an Associate Professor. Main research: cross-disciplinary approaches that prompt discussions regarding relations and dynamics between humans, spaces, and flows.

Hans J Andersen
Hans Jørgen Andersen is an Associate Professor at the Department for Architecture, Design, and Media Technology. His research interests lie within media technology and human machine interaction.

Ida S G Lange
Graduate of Urban Design at Aalborg University, 2012.
Has worked as an intern at metopos by- og landskabsdesign. Currently working as a research assistant in the Urban Design Department, AAU. Main focus within concept development and context specific design solutions.

Hans Kiib
Architect PhD, Professor in Urban Design at the Department of Architecture and Media Technology, Aalborg University. His research areas are urban design, urban transformation, cultural planning and performance design. Hans Kiib is Head of Studies of the education in 'Art & Technology'.

Jacob B Mikkelsen
Studied Urban Design at Aalborg University and completed that with a Masters thesis on the oil industry. Currently a Research Assistant there. Has "negotiated" between cars and bikes through design and research in American cities. In general moved by urban movement.

Helena Kaae
Completed a Masters in Urban Design at Aalborg University. Main interest is designing the urban spaces of complex city structures and enhancing their special atmosphere.

Jakob C Nielsen
Studied Urban Design at Aalborg University. Interested in longterm urban strategies and temporary use of development areas - where social- and cultural conditions are implemented in order to rediscover new potentials.

Biographies

Jens Christian Overgaard Madsen
M. Sc., Ph.D., Senior Consultant at Ramboll Denmark. Jens Chr. works as traffic planner and consultant and has primarily done research within traffic safety and evaluation studies.

Line M Nielsen
Studied Urban Design at Aalborg University. Currently employed as an Urban Planner at the Danish Ministry of the Environment engaged in dialogue with various municipalities in order to ensure a municipal planning match with national planning interests.

Kristian Overby
After having done an internship at COWI where he worked, among other things, on the detailing of the Eternit Site of Aalborg, he returned in the Spring to successfully complete his Masters thesis.

Lisa Gedsø
Graduated from University of Aalborg, Urban Design in January 2009. Currently employed at Bascon, Aarhus in the Client Consulting Department as a strategic planner. Main interests are project and concept development, planning processes and the production of graphic material.

Lasse Andersson
Lasse (Vegas) Andersson, believes in teamwork, action research and fun as a shortcut to best results. Architect, Ph.D., Co-Founder and Co-head of Platform4. Owner of LasseVegas Kontoret awarded joint first prizes in architectural competitions e.g., Thomas B. Thriges Gade and Gellerup.

Lucile Hamoignon
French urban designer. Currently working as a landscape architect. Has created, in Lille, an organization working with the interaction between people, performing arts, technology and public spaces. Interested in integrating inhabitants in designing city spaces.

Lea L H Laursen
PhD, M. Sc.eng. urban design. Associate Professor at Aalborg University. Her research is placed within the field of differentiated urban development and spatial restructuring. It emphasizes an action-oriented perspective investigating the role and potentials of landscape and the potentials of using tourism strategies.

Mads Brath Jensen
Mads Brath is co-owner of the design firm Electrotexture Lab. and Research Assistant at the institute of Architecture, Design & Media Technology, AAU, where he works in the field of adaptive and responsive computational architecture.

Maria V Jensen
Educated as an urban designer from Aalborg University. Currently employed as a consultant in Business and Urban Development, Aarhus Municipality, dealing with infrastructure and urban development as well as architecture and design clusters.

Nicolai H Hansen
Studying Architecture & Urban design at Aalborg University. Interested in mobile and temporary urban spaces, and the fusion of landscape, buildings and urban spaces into a parametric design solution.

Marion H Jensen
Studied Urban Design at Aalborg University, graduated January 2012. Currently employed at LÉVA Urban Design AS. Designing for experiences and emotions with a focus on making site-specific design.

Ole B Jensen
B.Sc. Political Science, M.Sc. Sociology, PhD Planning. Professor of Urban Theory, AAU. Board member at 'Centre for Mobility and Urban Studies' (C-MUS), http://www.c-mus.aau.dk/. Research interest: Urban Design and Mobility.

Martin F Petersen
Studying urban design at Aalborg University, starting Masters Thesis in 2013. Currently in an intership at ADEPT. Especially interested in projects involving both urbanism and architecture. Main focus is concept development and the design of the urban typologies.

Peter Bro
Studied urban and traffic planning at Aalborg University. Currently employed at Rambøll. Strong interest in everyday mobility and the interaction between transportation and urban development.

Mikkel Stensgaard
Cand. Polyt. Architecture at Aalborg University. Focused on simplifying the architectural design process into a more visual, virtual and spaceous experience. Partner in Arkibot working with project visualizations and graphical communication.

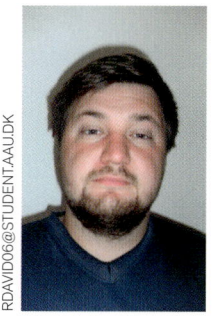

Rasmus Davidsen
An analytical and methodical urban designer used to working with problem-oriented projects and finding holistic solutions. With a great interest in creating cities and spaces with stories, but also working with the contrast between the built and the rural.

Biographies

Rikke S Brink
A former Urban Design student from Architecture and Design, AAU - recently graduated. Main objective is to create better living environments for people both in Denmark and in a broader context. Research and project work includes transformation of post industrial sites to city landscapes.

Sille C Linnet
Urban designer from Aalborg University, who is currently employed in the Department for Urban and Rural development in Skive Municipality. Tasks and interests are user involved strategy-making and designing according to development plans in different scales.

Sebastian Andersen
Studied at Aalborg University in urban design. Did an internship at SEA Architects in Copenhagen. Especially interested in mobility and concept development in a larger urban scale.

Simon Wind
Graduated 2009 Urban Design AAU. Working on understanding the human need for everyday mobility in Copenhagen – why and how do we move. Ask yourself how do you cope with your daily mobility?

Senad Gvozden
Currently taking a MSc in the interdisciplinary field of architecture and urbanism - interested in concept development, with a focus on how architectural and urban typologies, programmes and strategies can be developed through holistic methods, to meet aesthetic, cultural, social and political needs of the 21st century.

Siri Laursen
After achieving a bachelor in Urban Design at Aalborg University, moved on to new challenges at LIFE, KU, with the ambition of improving planning skills - Planning is my thing. Currently doing an internship at LÉVA in Stavanger.

Shelley Smith
BAAID, Architect, PhD. With a background as a designer (Canada), architect (Denmark) and a maker of films, now an Associate Professor in Urban Design, at AAU. Research interests are beyond big – more precisely how we as urban beings affect and are affected by our time and space.

Stine E Jakobsen
Studied Urban Design at Aalborg University. Interested in developing eventful and sensuous urban environments shaped with inspiration in the big curves and lively atmosphere of the landscape.

Stine Sonne
Studied urban design at Aalborg University. Currently she is a consultant at Via Trafik designing streetscapes and public spaces. She is interested in creating livable spaces and integrating environmentally sustainable elements in city design.

Sofie Brincker
After a 6-month student exchange in Sydney, completed a Bachelor degree in Urban Design at Aalborg University. Following this, studies continue in Landscape Architecture within the field of Urban Design at Copenhagen University. Photography and painting are spare time interests.

Thomas Oxvig
Have taken an internship in Japan spring 2012, an internship in Copenhagen fall 2012, and finalising education in spring 2013 with a Masters thesis. Especially interested in concept development.

Victor Andrade
Architect, PhD, Associate Professor at Aalborg University. Andrade's research interests focus upon urban design, urban life and mobility. He has developed projects in scales that range from houses to urban renewal. Andrade has been head of the Urban Design Research Group at Aalborg University.